BEING AN

9781376328486

BEING AND HAVING

An Existentialist Diary

by

GABRIEL MARCEL

HARPER TORCHBOOKS—The Cathedral Library
HARPER & ROW, PUBLISHERS, NEW YORK

BEING AND HAVING

Printed in the United States of America.
This book was originally published in 1949 by
Dacre Press, Westminster. It is here reprinted
by arrangement.
Introduction copyright © 1965 by James Collins
All rights in this book are reserved.
For information address
Harper & Row, Publishers, Incorporated
49 East 33rd Street, New York, New York 10016.
First HARPER TORCHBOOK *edition published 1965 by*
Harper & Row, Publishers, Incorporated
New York and Evanston.

CONTENTS

Introduction to the Torchbook edition
by James Collins   *page* vi.

PART ONE: BEING AND HAVING

I. A Metaphysical Diary   *page* 9

II. Outlines of a Phenomenology of Having   *page* 154

PART TWO: FAITH AND REALITY

I. Some Remarks on the Irreligion of Today   *page* 176

II. Some Thoughts on Faith   *page* 199

III. Peter Wust on the Nature of Piety   *page* 213

INTRODUCTION TO THE TORCHBOOK EDITION

by James Collins

The open countenance and welcoming presence of Gabriel Marcel encourage us to make his closer acquaintance. In doing so, it soon becomes clear that his is a complex and somewhat elusive mind. He defies easy classification by the breadth of his interests and the several mediums in which he works. What makes it difficult to reach a sharp focus is not any secretiveness on his part or any refusal to make himself available. Rather, the difficulty is an existential expression of his own teaching that the human spirit is not a piece of goods that can easily be dissected, tagged with a public label, and thus reduced to the category of some particular thing.

It is customary to count Marcel among the Big Four of contemporary existentialism, ranging him along with Sartre, Heidegger, and Jaspers. In general this is a sound judgment, since he does share many problems and methods in common with these other philosophers. They all agree that the really crucial questions today concern the human individual and the meanings he freely proposes for his relationship with nature, society, and any transcendent values. They view man as a center of freedom which realizes itself in definite acts of interpretation or assignments of meaning. And to examine these acts within their natural and social matrix, the existentialists have to devise some new methods of inquiry. Demonstration in the manner of the Aristotelian demonstrative argument does not suit their determining which kind respects the moral initiative of the human agent. Out of this basic disagreement between Marcel and Sartre over human freedom stemmed some other conflicts concerning the relation between humanism and God, the moral law and social planning, and the precise import of the movement toward transcendence. The personalist theism worked out by Marcel on all these matters clearly cannot be regarded as a variant of the atheism and naturalism advanced by Sartre.

There are some points of close kinship between Marcel and Karl Jaspers. They agree in affirming the actuality of God, the orientation of the human person toward Him, and the precarious state of human values in technological society. It is true that Jaspers treats all statements about God as being highly ambiguous, whereas Marcel finds the intimate presence of God in our personal acts. Yet both men continue the Kierkegaardian tradition of a moral criticism of our social institutions, insofar as the latter tend to prize the faceless and interchangeable cogs above the unique personal existents. This critique is not motivated by any foolish repudiation of social processes but by the aim of making them serve eventually for the individual exister rather than the mass entity. In recent years, Marcel has also noted some common convictions with Heidegger, in the degree that he becomes less remote and philological. They share a sensitivity to the poetic witness and the need for renovating the naming words with which we speak about being. Another joint matter is their effort to analyze our emotional attitudes, not for the sake of stirring up an emotional brew but to discover perhaps some responses bearing upon our common situation in being.

These comparisons are enough to show the presence of a common texture of existential thinking, but not enough to purpose, which is to criticize and reconstitute the basic judgments and concepts of Western man. They are as heavily dependent upon a description of the structures in human experience as are the empiricists and naturalists, but they also try to adapt their analyses to the personal mode of being which is proper to man.

On all these issues, Marcel is in broad agreement with the other existentialists. Yet it is also a fact that, upon occasion, he has repudiated the name "existentialist" and called himself rather a "Christian Socratic." This move is intended primarily to differentiate his standpoint from Sartre's, but it also helps to set him off from the other existentialists.

Just after the Second World War, Marcel found himself in the truly paradoxical position of being interpreted according to the canon laid down by Jean-Paul Sartre. This was a doubly inacceptable situation to him, first because the two men were diametrically opposed on many substantial questions, and next because Marcel's own views had been formulated and published while Sartre was still a schoolboy. The real divergence between these thinkers began at the fine point of the human soul, that is, at the significance of human freedom. Making his own reading of Descartes and Kant, Sartre postulated that we are either radically free and in no way dependent upon God or else dependent upon Him and thus robbed of the ground for moral creativity. During a full generation of wrestling with this alternative under various forms, however, Marcel had already come to the conclusion that it was an arbitrary dilemma which should not regulate our thinking about man. For it assumed that moral freedom is incompatible with any sort of dependence upon another being.

Much of Marcel's early research aimed at distinguishing the various kinds of dependency of man upon other beings, and justify a reduction of the existentialists to a uniform mold. In what sense does Gabriel Marcel, the Christian Socratic, remain a distinctive mind? His new Socratism manifests itself negatively in a refusal to harness his ideas too closely to a systematic framework, and positively in a persistent activity of self-interrogation and search after the meanings imbedded in our ordinary situations.

Marcel himself underwent a rigorous academic training in philosophy, disciplined himself to write for the great philosophical journals, and occasionally did a stint of philosophical teaching at the *lycée*. He mastered the great systems of the idealists, acknowledging a special debt to Schelling and F. H. Bradley. Moreover, he was one of the first Europeans to assimilate the subtle dialectic of the American idealist, Josiah Royce, whose notions of the self and the beloved community made a deep imprint upon his mind. Thus Marcel's wariness about using the systematic mode of conceptual construction did not spring from an irrationalist bias or from sheer inability to appreciate the virtues of consistency and rigorous development in philosophy. Rather, he believed that these values were being threatened by the impersonal demands of the system and that there was a corresponding need for a free and personal sort of philosophizing. Even in his most sustained exposition, the Gifford Lectures on *The Mystery of Being,* therefore, Marcel hugged close to the context of the story and the way of personal reflection.

This modern Socrates forges a close link between self-interrogation and his capital distinction between problem and mystery. Philosophical awareness is not yet fully acquired at the problematic level. We treat ourselves as problems in the degree that we submit to the methods governing the analysis and control of impersonal things. There is a real sense in which human existence can be studied problematically as being part of the natural terrain, the political crisis, and the statistical report on the economy. But the philosopher persists in his questioning until he discerns within the public domain of problems those aspects which lead him to the human person and his responsibility for meanings. In Marcel's graphic phrase, a mystery is nothing more than a problem which invades the very being of the inquirer and exposes its precarious condition. Behind the vital statistics is the mystery of my attitude toward my own death, just as behind the dialectical talk about immortality lies the troubling consideration of whether I will survive in any personal way.

Naturalistic thinkers advise us to avoid any fuzzy references to the mystery of being. Contrariwise, Marcel's argument is that the region of personal mystery is unavoidable when questions are pushed far enough, and that we can develop the type of philosophical reflection which will remove the fuzziness and attain the appropriate determinate significance of questions involving my own self. Problem and mystery are not antithetic opposites, only one of which can engage our attention, but rather the problematic standpoint eventually concerns itself with human freedom and thus prolongs itself into the region of mystery or recognition of the distinctively personal aspects of our existence. All reflection does not then come to a halt, but we do have to adapt our inquiry to the new conditions and employ the means of reflective analysis suited to the irreducibly personal order.

Marcel describes his quest for self-understanding as a religious and Christian sort of Socratism. He suggests that the time has come when we have to reconsider the separatism of religion and philosophy. Granting their difference in method and purpose, they nevertheless draw common nourishment from our awareness of participating in being and show a common concern for our use of freedom in regard to our fellow men and God. Marcel does not advocate any identification between the philosophical act of reflection and the religious act of worship. But he does feel the need to explore more fully their points of relationship.

Alone among the existentialists, Marcel also accepts the Christian faith and regards it as a spur rather than a deterrent to his philosophical work. It makes him more sensitive, rather than less, to the great human problems of evil, social responsibility, and the abyss of freedom. It also makes him skeptical about the inference that, since we are living in a post-Christian civilization, we can conduct our inquiries as though the Christian experience never occurred in our history. On the contrary, Marcel holds that a realistic appraisal of our language, modes of thinking, and prevailing imagery reveals the depth and persistence of Christian faith and its institutions. We cannot pretend to discuss the meaning of marriage, the value of hope, the import of death, and the religious search for God as though these topics can be divested of their Christian context through a simple stroke of methodology.

Two more facets of Marcel's Christian philosophy deserve our notice. First, his work furnishes a good illustration of the fact that there is no massive uniformity about Christian philosophies. His approach is a non-Scholastic and non-Thomistic one, and remains deliberately such. Like Newman in the nineteenth century, Marcel embodies a way of philosophizing which stands much closer to the Patristic tradition than to the pattern of the medieval and modern Scholastic thinkers. His is the path of concrete description rather than formal argumentation, of personal invocation rather than impersonal demonstration. In the second place, Marcel distinguishes sharply between the relevance of Christianity for philosophy and the confusion of Christianity with philosophy. Religious faith can make the philosopher aware of many strands of meaning that might otherwise escape him, but it cannot thereby release him from the necessity of painstaking analysis of the data and supplying philosophically tested grounds of assent. Our philosophical assent must be regulated by the evidence turned up reflectively in the course of investigation.

For this reason, there is nothing sectarian and separatist about Marcel's way of philosophizing. He addresses himself to every man of good will and attentive mind, not just the Christian believer. Even when he is examining situations originally presented with a religious context, his intent is to uncover those common human structures which we can all recognize. All that Marcel requires of us is the readiness to look for ourselves and to determine our philosophical judgment by what we can discern. Expressed in another way, the sole requirement for drawing profit from his studies is to remain fundamentally open to whatever relations and participating acts constitute the reality of man.

In his latest writings, Marcel relents sufficiently to permit himself to be regarded as an existential thinker. However, this now requires us to introduce a further qualification. He is not exclusively a philosopher but a man of two careers. Together with working in philosophy, Marcel has been active for many years as a playwright. One of his plays, *Ariadne,* is included in Barry Ulanov's recent collection of makers of the modern theater. There is a quiet intensity in his plays, many of which unfold the human agencies at work in the family situation. They reflect his love of music in the mode of the fugue and the improvisation, his concern with vows and stations in life, the consequent struggle between social function and personal realization, and the basis of fidelity toward the living and the dead. These themes are also present in his philosophy, and Marcel has always kept open the roads of communication between his philosophical and his dramatic works. He often finds himself expressing on the stage in a vivid, exploratory way the same situations and leading ideas which later engage his philosophical analysis. Marcel's theater serves his philosophical purposes in a way similar to the role of arresting metaphors in the books of one of his masters, Henri Bergson.

Bearing in mind that Marcel is both a literary craftsman and a philosopher, we can appreciate the unusual form of the present work, *Being and Having.* It is not organized like a conventional philosophical treatise, but combines a metaphysical diary with a group of essays originally delivered as papers before definite audiences. The diary and the reflective conference are, indeed, the chief creative instruments used by Marcel in his philosophical investigations. Ever since the First World War, he had kept a record of his reflections on philosophical questions. Like Emerson and Kierkegaard, he has discovered certain advantages in this medium. It is unpretentious enough to undermine the grandiose facades of impersonal systems. In true existential fashion, the journal calls attention to the personal mode of philosophizing, replete with its false starts and fragmentary insights. Yet there is enough continuity here to permit a theme to be developed through symphonic recurrence to the central motif. The metaphysical diary shows us, in the concrete, what it means to be a Socratic mind and to engage in constant self-questioning and dialogue.

The year 1927 marked the publication not only of Heidegger's *Being and Time* but also of Marcel's *Metaphysical Journal,* the first book which brought him before the philosophical world. Here he recorded his long struggle with idealism, his arrival at the basic notions of communicative being and my body, and his personal efforts to establish a personal relation of I-and-Thou with God. Now in the first section of *Being and Having,* Marcel allows us to share his personal thoughts for the crucial years 1928–1933. In somewhat indirect fashion, he tells the story of his conversion to Catholicism in the wake of a disturbing question contained in a letter to him from François Mauriac: "But after all, why aren't you one of us?" This diary also develops Marcel's characteristic questions on fidelity, suffering, and communion with others. American readers will be interested in the entry for March 8, 1929, where he attacks the spectator attitude as vigorously as does John Dewey, but where Marcel goes on to deny that the practical emphasis is sufficient to liberate us from the condition of the unengaged spectator. The practical orientation does not fully engage us as persons, and hence it retains a secret alliance with the illusion of the spectator of the universe.

In this journal, Marcel develops many aspects of his view that "there must be a *hold* on the real at the root of intelligence." His existentialism does not accept an irrationalist split between being and knowing, but requires that the latter act transpire at the heart of being. Marcel is disturbed by the inadequacy of the concept to express existential reality, but he also gropes toward some intellectual grasp upon the real which will respect the latter in its proper actuality. Man is a reflecting exister, whose hold on the real is also his token of participating in being and having the capacity to enter freely into communion with God. These entries also show that, long before Sartre came on the scene, Marcel was analyzing the view that social life is hell and tracing it to the refusal to make oneself personally available to others. We have to move beyond the Kantian alternative of autonomy versus heteronomy, since it breaks down in the case of man or the being who is both free and dependent. Marcel is the kind of personalist philosopher who also acknowledges the values springing from man's relatedness with the natural world, fellow men, and God.

Under the somewhat forbidding title "Outlines of a phenomenology of Having," Marcel next directs our attention to his key distinction between being and having. He terms his approach a phenomenological one, both because it moves descriptively and concretely and also because it studies the relations between acts and their real objects (rather than confines itself to a psychological treatment of mental states). One way to describe our human reality is to call it a unique complexus of having and being. We are not pure instruments or possessions "had" by another, since we exist and act in our own right. And yet we are not pure being, in the sense of existing without any real dependence upon other actualities. Man is a personal existent who needs and appropriates things in this world: he combines being and having intimately in his own reality.

For this reason, our selfhood is that of an incarnate awareness. Marcel shows the significant difference between this or that body, which is distinct from me even though I may own it, and my own body. It is in my own body that the domains of being and having, personal act and instrumentality, are found in visible union. Unlike other bodily things, my own body is not a possession or sheer instance of having, for it belongs to my very being and helps to constitute what I am as distinct from what I

xiv

have. And yet I do put my body to use and thus bring out its instrumental character and status of having.

Although all the existentialists treat the theme of my own body, Marcel does so in closest reference to our common experiences and ordinary language. He stresses that my own body is the point of involvement and also of exposure for the human self. Through my body I find myself already engaged in the world of having, and thus I become a man of possessions and functions. At the same time, my body makes me vulnerable to the contingencies and needs of life, as well as specifies my peculiar way of confronting the grand test of death. Pascal said that we are already embarked, and Marcel adds that the point of embarkation for each person is his own bodily existence. This is not only a matter of peril but also of encouragement. For my body is the visible pledge of the hold which reality has upon my most private reflections; it is the first step taken in the direction of making myself available to others; and it opens up the possibility of my participation in the interpersonal and incarnate community of men and God.

The three essays in the second part of *Being and Having* are more restricted in scope and circumstance. But the spiritual and intellectual climate of France in the nineteen-thirties which they reflect presents some factors still among us in other guises. For instance, the shibboleth of transparent sincerity to which André Gide then appealed is brought up to date in the norm of perfect lucidity celebrated by Sartre and Simone de Beauvoir. Marcel's pointed comment also still applies. Sincerity is a weapon which attains moral significance from its user's intention, and which should not be permitted to render all moral differences unimportant. Another question which has grown more acute in the intervening years is the relation between a life organized around the mastery of objects and the full development of the human person. We now have even more evidence than was available to Marcel for concluding that a society directed primarily toward the control and distribution of objects will generate severe tensions, which are an index of a failure to subserve our personal existence and interpersonal community.

Finally, it may be well to ask whether Marcel's manner of philosophizing has had any reciprocal influence upon the quality of his religious faith. In *Being and Having*, there are three passages indicative of an incisive influence in this direction. In one place, he remarks that "it is on the ground of Truth that we should fight our first battle for religion; on this field only can it be won or lost." The intellectual quality of his existential philosophy carries over into his treatment of religious questions. It is not the undergoing of an experience that is decisive for him, but the ability of human reflection to interpret that experience and establish whether or not it has a religious import. A second clue is provided by a quite characteristic entry in Marcel's diary. "My deepest and most unshakable conviction— and if it is heretical, so much that the worse for orthodoxy—is, that whatever all the thinkers and doctors have said, it is not God's will at all to be loved by us *against* the Creation, but rather glorified *through* the Creation and with the Creation as our starting point." This is spoken with the voice of a realist and a humanist who wants to assure that his religious position will respect the significance of the created world. As Marcel has continued to pursue his religious studies, he has found much more support than he originally expected in the religious tradition for taking our start with the visible world and retaining its permanent function in the approach to God.

There is one more revealing remark to underline. Marcel applies to religious existence his conviction that man is not accidentally but essentially a wayfarer and pilgrim. "For I believe that no man, however enlightened and holy he is, can ever arrive until the others, *all* the others, have started out to follow him. . . . We never climb alone, though we often seem to do so." The solidarity of all men is ineradicable, and their spiritual destinies are intertwined. What Marcel writes about in *Being and Having* is set down not only as an intellectual and spiritual log book but also as a personal call to the rest of us. He wants to share with us some of the fruits of his climb.

St. Louis University
St. Louis, Missouri
April, 1965

PART ONE

BEING AND HAVING

I

A METAPHYSICAL DIARY

(1928-1933)

November 10th 1928

I have today made a firm resolve to continue my metaphysical diary, perhaps in the form of a series of consecutive reflections.

I caught sight of an idea just now which might be important. Returning to my fundamental views on *existence*, I was wondering whether it is possible to say in any sense that an idea exists; and this is how I see it. The idea, so far as it is represented—on the pattern of an object (I was thinking the other day of what we mean by the aspects of an idea)—shares with the object as such the characteristic of *non-existence*, the object only existing in so far as it shares in the nature of *my body*, i.e. in so far as it is not thought of as object. In the same way, must we not say that an idea can and does have existence, but only and exactly in so far as it is irreducible to the pseudo-objective representations which we form of it? The materialist interpretation, however absurd in itself, does at least imply a confused notion of what I am trying to get at here. We might say that an idea exists proportionately to its being more or less *adherent*. I should like to find some concrete examples for illustration, but this is of course very difficult to do. The starting point of my reflections the other day was the idea of an event (X's operation) which I had many reasons to be anxious about. One might have said that I revolved the idea, or that it revolved of itself, and showed me its different aspects in turn; i.e. I thought of it by analogy with a three-dimensional object, a die for instance.

November 22nd

An interesting point. Is responsibility, or rather the need to attribute responsibility—the need to have something or someone to fix it on—at the root of all 'causal explanation'? I feel that this might take us a long way. It seems to me very near to Nietzchean psychology.

NOTES FOR A PAPER TO THE PHILOSOPHICAL SOCIETY
Undated, written in 1927 or 1928[1]

When I affirm that something exists, I always mean that I consider this something as connected with my body, as able to be put in contact with it, however (indirect) this contact may be. But note must be taken that the priority I thus ascribe to my body depends on the fact that my body is given to me in a way that is not exclusively objective, i.e. on the fact that it is *my* body. This character, at once mysterious and intimate, of the bond between me and my body (I purposely avoid the word *relation*) does in fact colour all existential judgments.

What it comes to is this. We cannot really separate:—

1. Existence
2. Consciousness of self as existing
3. Consciousness of self as bound to a body, as incarnate.

From this several important conclusions would seem to follow:

(1) In the first place, the existential point of view about reality cannot, it seems, be other than that of an incarnate personality. In so far as we can imagine a pure understanding, there is, for such an understanding, no possibility of considering things as existent or non-existent.

(2) On the one hand, the problem of the existence of the external world is now changed and perhaps even loses its meaning; I cannot in fact without contradiction think of my body as non-existent, since it is in connection with it (in so far as it is *my* body) that every existing thing is defined and placed. On the other hand, we

―――――――――
[1] This paper was never delivered.

a rationalizer could be construed by

ought to ask whether there are valid reasons for giving my body a privileged metaphysical status in comparison with other things.

(3) If this is so, it is permissible to ask whether the union of the soul and body is, in essence, really different from the union between the soul and other existing things. In other words, does not a certain experience of the self, as tied up with the universe, underlie all affirmation of existence?

(4) Inquire whether such an interpretation of the existential leads towards subjectivism.

(5) Shew how idealism tends inevitably to eliminate all existential considerations in view of the fundamental unintelligibility of existence. Idealism *versus* metaphysics. Values detached from existence: too real to exist.

Existential and personalist interests closely linked. The problem of the immortality of the soul is the pivot of metaphysic.

Every existent is thought of like an obstacle by which we take our bearings—like something we could collide with in certain circumstances—resistant, impenetrable. We *think* of this impenetrability, no doubt, but we think of it as not completely thinkable.[1] Just as my body is thought of in so far as it is *a* body, but my thought collides with the fact that it is *my* body.

To say that something exists is not only to say that it belongs to the same system as my body (that it is bound to it by certain connections which reason can define), it is also to say that it is in some way united to me as my body is.

Incarnation—the central 'given' of metaphysic. Incarnation is the situation of a being who appears to himself to be, as it were, *bound* to a body. This 'given' is opaque to itself: opposition to the

---

[1] It is thought of, but it is never resolved. The opacity of the world is in a certain sense insoluble. The link between opacity and *Meinheit*. My idea is opaque to *me* personally in so far as it is mine. We think of it as an adherence. (Note written Feb. 24th, 1929.)

cogito. Of this body, I can neither say that it is I, nor that it is not I, nor that it is *for* me (object). The opposition of subject and object is found to be transcended from the start. Inversely, if I start from the opposition, treating it as fundamental, I shall find no trick of logical sleight of hand which lets me get back to the original experience, which will inevitably be either eluded or (which comes to the same thing) refused. We are not to object that this experience shews a contingent character: in point of fact, all metaphysical enquiry requires a starting-point of this kind. It can only start from a situation which is mirrored but cannot be understood.

Inquire if incarnation is a fact; it does not seem so to me, it is the 'given' starting from which a fact is possible (which is not true of the *cogito*).

A fundamental predicament which cannot be in a strict sense mastered or analysed. It is exactly this impossibility which is being stated when I declare, confusedly, that I *am* my body; i.e. I cannot quite treat myself as a term distinct from my body, a term which would be in a definable connection with it. As I have said elsewhere, the moment I treat my body as an object of scientific knowledge, I banish myself to infinity.

This is the reason why I cannot think of *my death*, but only of the standstill of *that* machine (*illam*, not *hanc*). It would perhaps be more accurate to say that I cannot anticipate my death, that is, I cannot ask myself what will become of *me* when the machine is no longer working.[1]

[1] 'To be involved.' *(idée d'un engagement)* Try to shew in what sense this implies the impossibility (or absolute non-validity) of my representing my death. In trying to think of my death I break the rules of the game. But it is radically illegitimate to convert this impossibility into a dogmatic negation. (Note written Feb. 24th, 1929.)

It is evident that this whole train of thought is at the root of *le Gouvernail*: the first notes on the theme of *le Gouvernail* were composed a few days after these. (Note written April 13th, 1934.)

Have detected, perhaps, an important fallacy involved in the idea (cf. my previous notes on incarnation) that opacity must be bound up with otherness. But surely the contrary is really the case. Surely opacity really arises from the fact that the 'I' interposes between the self and the other, and intervenes as a third party?

The obscurity of the external world is a function of my own obscurity to myself; the world has no intrinsic obscurity. Should we say that it comes to the same thing in the end? We must ask up to what point this interior opacity is a result; is it not very largely the consequence of an act? and is not this act simply sin?

My ideas are hardest for me to grasp where they are most completely *my* ideas; that is where they are impenetrable to me.[1] The problem I am setting myself is to find out whether this applies to the whole of reality. Is not reality impenetrable to me just in proportion as I am involved in it?[2]

Of course all this is horribly difficult to think out clearly. In a different terminology (that of the *Journal Métaphysique*) I could easily say that in so far as my body is an absolute mediator, I so far cease to have communication with it (in the sense that I have communication with any objective sector of the Real). Let us say again that my body is not and cannot be given to me. For everything 'given' attracts to itself a process of indefinite objectification, and that is what I understand by the word 'penetrable'.[3] The im-

---

[1] And where they become a principle of interior darkening; to this extent, in fact, they dominate me and make me into a sort of slave-tyrant. Light is thrown on all this by *le Phénoménologie de l'Avoir* outlined in 1933. (Note written April 13th, 1934.)

[2] I was here anticipating what I wrote later on 'Mystery'. But this passage surely implies a confusion between opacity and mystery (*id.*).

[3] Here, too, there appears to me to be a confusion: the object as such is by definition accessible to me, but not penetrable. It is the Other, or more exactly the Thou, which is penetrable (*id.*).

penetrability, then, of my body belongs to it in virtue of its quality of absolute mediator. But it is obvious that my body, in that sense, is myself; for I cannot distinguish myself from it unless I am willing to reduce it to an object, i.e. unless I cease to treat it as an absolute mediator.

We must, therefore, break away once and for all from the metaphors which depict consciousness as a luminous circle round which there is nothing, to its own eyes, but darkness. On the contrary, the shadow is at the centre.

When I try to make clear to myself the nature of my bond with my body, it appears to me chiefly as something of which I have the use (as one has the use of a piano, a saw, or a razor); but all these uses are extensions of the initial use, which is simply the use of the body. I have real priority to my body when it is a question of active use, but none whatever when it is a question of knowledge. The use is only possible on the basis of a certain felt community. But the community is indivisible; I cannot validly say 'I and my body'. The difficulty arises from the fact that I think of my relation with my body on the analogy of my relation with my instruments—whereas in fact the latter presupposes the former.

February 28th, 1929

I was thinking this afternoon (with regard to the meeting to take place on the 9th at the *rue Visconti*) that the only possible victory over time must have fidelity as one of its factors. (Cf. Nietzche's remark—so profound—'man is the only being who makes promises'.) There is no privileged state which allows us to transcend time; and this was where Proust made his great mistake. A state such as he describes has only the value of a foretaste. This notion of a foretaste is, I feel, likely to play a more and more central part in my thinking. But one point must be noticed (and here I think I part company with Fernandez): the fidelity, unless it is to be fruitless or, worse, reduced to mere persistency, must spring from something that is 'absolutely given' to me. (I feel this is especially true in my relation to the people I love best.) From the very beginning there must be a sense of stewardship: something has been entrusted to us, so that we are not only responsible towards ourselves, but towards an active and superior principle—and how it goes against my inclinations to use such a disgustingly abstract word!

As I was writing to M—, I at once fear and long to commit myself. But here again I feel that at the very beginning there was something else beyond myself—a commitment that I *accepted* after an offer had been made to the most hidden depths of my being. The question is, how can I deserve it? It is strange—and yet so clear—that I shall only continue to believe if I continue to deserve my faith. Amazing interdependence between believing and desert!

March 5th

I have no more doubts. This morning's happiness is miraculous. For the first time I have clearly experienced *grace*. A terrible thing to say, but so it is.

I am hemmed in at last by Christianity—in, fathoms deep. Happy to be so! But I will write no more.

And yet, I feel a kind of need to write. Feel I am stammering childishly . . . this is indeed a birth. Everything is different.

Now, too, I can see my way through my improvisations. A new metaphor, the inverse of the other—a world which was there, entirely present, and at last I can touch it.

March 6th

Notes on time; I feel they must be important. So far as the subject is thought of as pure receptivity, the problem of the relations between time and the timeless is comparatively simple: I can, in fact, conceive of myself as apprehending successively something which is, in a certain sense, given all at once (a metaphor from reading). But this is merely an abstraction. The subject is not pure receptivity; or, more accurately, apprehension is itself an event (an indefinite series of events—it is carried by a series of events inseparable from the story it discloses). In other words, the subject is involved *qua* agent (and he has the character of receptivity only on condition of being at the same time an agent) in the content which he was supposed merely to decipher. An extraordinarily complicated situation which I must manage to *think* about. I am sure I am on the right lines, but shall I manage to work them out?

Put it formally. Given the intelligible total, the *totum simul* which I will call L, I will make λ stand for the reading of it, the total of operations by which I gradually gain consciousness of its elements. The reading splits itself up into λ_1, λ_2, λ_3, but these steps in consciousness are obviously related to acts a_1, a_2, a_3. These acts, however, appear on reflection to be completely exterior, indifferent to L (and to the steps by which it appears that this L has been built up, steps which, we must clearly see, belong to the past). Notice that the fact of these steps belonging to the past is closely connected with another fact, viz. that L represents itself to me as an object (book, picture of which I successively discern the parts, etc.).

We can now imagine a more complex case. Suppose I am present at an improvisation (I). I am conscious, successively, of the phases of this improvisation. It may happen that these phases appear disconnected to me. But it is also possible that I may *recognise* the unity of the improvisation, although it cannot be given to me, properly speaking, as object, since it is after all an improvisation. (This is the counterpart of what I was saying just now about the connection between Fact A, that the steps in building up the whole belong to the past, and Fact B, that the *totum simul* is object, is 'given' to me.) The *recognition* which occurs in the case of the improvisation is already really a kind of participation; that is, it can only take place if I am in some way 'on the inside'.

But we can go a step further. It is not inconceivable that the participation contributes in some way to the improvisation itself. The more effective this participation is, the more actively shall I be involved in the improvisation (i.e. I shall be in a relation towards it of less pure receptivity), and so it will be more difficult for me, in a certain sense, to treat it as a *totum simul*. But this difficulty, this quasi-impossibility, will be connected much less with the actual structure of the whole, than with the way in which I am actively and personally involved in it. My situation in the whole is not, to tell the truth, of such a kind that I cannot detach myself in some sense from the function there assigned to me: but I must still find out what attitude I am to take up towards the detachment itself, and this seems to me of the utmost importance.

(*A*) It may happen that I decide to disregard my detachment, and turn myself into a pure spectator. But this change of front carries with it the risk that the whole may also tend to appear to me as a pure spectacle, perhaps even a spectacle lacking in sense. For the intelligible force informing the improvisation could perhaps only be grasped by me in so far as I was actively associated with it. A kind of rift then appears, either between me and the total, or, still more serious, between me and myself. (This will be the case if I somehow dissociate myself, the pure spectator, from the immanent actions by which my participation was expressed: but these actions, thus isolated and robbed of their meaning, lose all significance; and their intrinsic nothingness may even be passed on, like a contagious disease, to the improvisation itself.)

(*B*) It may appear, on the contrary, that I really think of my detachment as an interiorised mode of participation. If this is so, I continue to be part of the system; my place has changed, and that is all.

March 7th

It is a serious error, if I am not mistaken, to treat time as a mode of apprehension. For one is then forced to consider it also as the order according to which the subject apprehends himself, and he can only do this by breaking away from himself, as it were, and mentally severing the fundamental engagement which makes him what he is. (I take the word 'engagement' here to represent both 'involvement' and 'committal'.)

This is the point of what I was trying to say yesterday afternoon, when I reflected that time is the very form of experimental activity. And from this point of view, to take up once more the metaphor of the absolute improvisation (a metaphor which seems to me inexhaustible) one finds oneself thinking like this. To transcend time is not to raise ourselves, as we can do at any moment, to the actually empty idea of a *totum simul*—empty because it remains outside us and thereby becomes in some way devitalised. By no means. It is rather to participate more and more actively in the creative intention that quickens the whole: in other words, to raise ourselves to levels from which the succession seems less and less *given*, levels from which a 'cinematographic' representation of events looks more and more inadequate, and ceases in the long run to be even possible.

I think this is of the utmost importance. There, and perhaps only there, is the way open from creative evolution to a religious philosophy, but this way can only be taken through a concrete dialectic of participation.[1]

I believe also, though I cannot yet establish it, that we have here the basis for a Theory of Evil, which would maintain its reality without denying its contingency.

The more we treat the world as a spectacle, the more unintelligible

[1] This remark, made in 1929, holds good for me even since the publication of M. Bergson's work, *Les Deux Sources de la Morale et de la Religion* (April, 1934.)

must it necessarily seem from a metaphysical point of view, because the relation then established between us and the world is an intrinsically absurd one. Perhaps this is relevant to what I was writing the other day about interior opacity.

My yesterday's notes have, I think, an important bearing on the problem of the genesis of the universe, or the finitude of the world in time. In proportion as I treat the universe as object (detachment in the *A*-sense), I cannot help asking myself how this object was formed, how this 'set-up' started: and this implies the mental reconstruction of a series of operations which has unfolded successively. The two facts of (*a*) being thought of or treated as object and (*b*) possessing a past that can be reconstructed, are essentially connected. The simplest and clearest example is that of a person empirically given.

But this, I repeat once more, presupposes the initial action by which I separate myself from the world, as I separate myself from the object which I consider in its different aspects. Now this act, while entirely legitimate or even necessary each time I consider a particular thing, becomes illicit and even absurd as soon as I begin to consider the universe. I cannot really stand aside from the universe, even in thought. Only by a meaningless pretence can I place myself at some vague point outside it, and from thence reproduce on a small scale the successive stages of its genesis. Nor can I place myself outside myself (a revealing parallel) and question myself upon my own genesis, I mean of course the genesis of my non-empirical, or metaphysical reality. The problem of the genesis of the I and of the genesis of the universe are just one and the same problem, or, more exactly, one and the same *insoluble*, the insolubility being bound up with my very position, my existence, and the radical metaphysical fact of that existence. And here, I believe, we can attain to an absolutely positive notion of eternity. The universe as such, not being thought of or able to be thought of as object, has strictly speaking no past: it entirely transcends what I called a 'cinematographic' representation. And the same is true of myself: on a certain level I cannot fail to appear to myself as contemporary with the universe (*coaevus universo*), that is, as eternal. Only, of what order is this apprehension of one's-self as eternal? That is no doubt the most difficult point. And here, I think, we get back to what I was writing this morning.

At bottom, the method is always the same; it is plumbing the depths of a given fundamental metaphysical situation of which it is inadequate to say 'it is mine', since it consists essentially in *being me*.

I cannot help recording that this illumination of my thought is for me only the extension of the Other, the only Light. I have never known such happiness.

I have been playing Brahms for a long time, piano sonatas that were new to me. They will always remind me of this unforgettable time. How can I keep this feeling of being entered, of being absolutely safe—and also of being enfolded?

March 8th

I am more and more struck by the difference between the two modes of detachment: the one is that of the spectator, the other of the saint. The detachment of the saint springs, as one might say, from the very core of reality; it completely excludes curiosity about the universe. This detachment is the highest form of participation. The detachment of the spectator is just the opposite, it is desertion, not only in thought but in act. Herein, I think, lies the kind of fatality which seems to weigh on all ancient philosophy—it is essentially the philosophy of the spectator.

But one thing must be noted: the belief that one can escape pure spectatorship by devotion to a practical science, which modifies the Real by its applications, is founded on a misconception. Here I vaguely see a very important line of thought, but confess that I cannot quite clearly formulate it as yet. I should express it by saying that the modifications which such a science imposes on reality have no other result (metaphysically of course) than of making that science in some sense a stranger to reality. The word 'alienation' exactly expresses what I mean. 'I am not watching a show'—I will repeat these words to myself every day. A fundamental spiritual fact.

The interdependence of spiritual destinies, the plan of salvation; for me, that is the sublime and unique feature of Catholicism.

I was just thinking a moment ago that the spectator-attitude corresponds to a form of lust; and more than that, it corresponds to the act by which the subject appropriates the world for himself. And I now perceive the deep truth of Bérulle's theocentrism. We are here to serve; yes, the idea of service, in every sense, must be thoroughly examined.

Also perceived this morning, but still in a confused way, that there is profane knowledge and sacred knowledge (whereas previously I have wrongly tended to assert that all knowledge was profane. It isn't true, *profane* is a supremely informative word). Inquire on what conditions knowledge ceases to be profane.

Incredible how thronged these days are spiritually! My life is being illuminated right into the depths of the past, and not *my* life only.

Every time we give way to ourselves we may unawares be laying an additional limitation on ourselves, forging our own chain. That is the metaphysical justification for asceticism. I never understood that till now.

Reality as mystery, intelligible solely as mystery. This also applies to myself.

March 9th

An important observation has just occurrred to my mind. I can no longer accept the idea, in any sense, of something beyond truth:

as a matter of fact the idea has made me uncomfortable for some time now. This gap between Truth and Being fills up, in a manner, *of itself*, the moment we really experience the presence of God. It is the half-truths which cease to deserve the name to the eye of faith.

Faith, the force of invisible truths. I say this illuminating sentence over and over to myself—but it only illuminates *after the event*.

Also, I become conscious more and more of the part played in faith by the will. The thing is, to keep myself in a certain state analogous, on the human level, to the state of grace. In this sense, faith is essentially fidelity, and in the highest possible form. I realised this at once, with shattering clarity, on February 25th, and have known it ever since.

March 11th

A wholesome thought has come to me: let me write it down. Deep down beneath the critical attitude to the Gospel stories, is the implicit assertion 'It oughtn't to have happened like that'. In other words, we inwardly sketch the idea—with really paralysing presumption and folly—of what revelation *ought to have been like*. And I have a very strong suspicion that in this criticism there is always the idea 'this can't be true', so that of course one must be able to pick holes, find contradictions, etc. It seems to me that this laying down of law by the individual consciousness ought to be rejected in principle. The Gospel words, in fact: 'become as little children.' Glorious words, but quite unintelligible to anyone who believes that there is an intrinsic value in maturity. I must go into all this and subject it to an infinitely more careful scrutiny.

It is quite certain that from the moment that miracles are said to be impossible *a priori*, the arguments of a negative exegesis not only lose all their value, but become in essence suspect.

I was thinking, too, that the credibility of miracles is positively demonstrated by such facts as the conversion of Claudel or Maritain. That these events can be believed in, is absolutely undeniable. Now nobody can think that these men believed without adequate facts to go upon. So taking their belief as a base, we must ask on what conditions it is possible, we must rise from the fact to the conditions on which it depends. This is the best and only way for genuine religious reflection to take.

March 12th

I have been feeling rather poorly this morning, and have made heavy weather of the pages on baptism in the catechism of the Council of Trent. This is all still very difficult for me to accept, but at the same time I have a strange feeling that a work is being done in me—a feeling that each resistance I put up is being disintegrated or burnt away. Is this an illusion? I have seen it from outside for much too long. I must now get used to quite a different way of looking at it. It is not easy. I have a constant feeling of inward cauterisation.

March 21st

I have just passed through a painful, dark time; a passage full of obstacles that were difficult to anticipate. The worst day, I think, was Sunday. On Monday evening, the long talk with M—— did me an enormous amount of good, and also my last meeting with the Abbé A——. The real trouble was the teaching of the catechism, which I have literally had difficulty in assimilating, especially at a time when the vital link with God was, if not broken, at least stretched beyond description. Today I feel I am recovering in the full sense of the word. The thing that most helps me is the desire not to be on the side of those who betrayed Christ, nor just with the blind men. It is that part of the Gospel which is the spring of inspiration in my present state.

23

March 23rd

I was baptised this morning. My inward state was more than I had dared to hope for: no transports, but peaceful, balanced, and full of hope and faith.

An idea came to me in the Luxembourg, and I will put it down at once. At bottom, space and time are in a way the forms of temptation. Pride and false humility combine in the act of recognising our insignificance when compared with the infinity of space and time, for we are then claiming to put ourselves in imagination on the same plane as this pair of infinites, realised as objects of knowledge. *Our heads are turned by such an approximation to God!* Return to the *here* and *now*, which recover an unparalled dignity and worth. This for later examination. Too tired tonight to write any more.

April 12th

I suspect that we have a mass of ideas here, and they will be hard to sort out; a tangled skein.

I want to make a new and more thorough examination of the nature of the prejudice expressed by the words 'we have reached a point when we can no longer believe that . . .' etc. It contains a certain *a priori* notion of experience and growth (experience in the sense of growth, or growth in the sense of experience) which first needs to be drawn out. I was reflecting yesterday on the basic ambiguity of the idea of age when applied to mankind. Is the thing that has happened last the oldest of all things or the youngest? We vary, I think, or (more accurately) *swing* between the two views. At this present hour I see the Christian miracle, without qualification, as the absolute point at which youth is renewed. And perhaps the eternal and irremovable fountain of all the renewal of youth there can be.

May 10th

Have begun to philosophise again this afternoon, perhaps as a consequence of the wonderful Office for yesterday morning at the church in the *Rue Monsieur,* and also after my conversation with C——, who came and talked to me about my letter in which I had poured out to him all the misery I feel when I am confronted by the Thomist claims. My thoughts turn on the ideas of salvation and perdition, in connection with an important passage in the *Journal Metaphysique.* Here are my main points.

Only what is alive is capable of salvation or damnation—what has a share in life, or is treated as having such a share. But above all, that which incorporates in itself existence and value. We must, however, go beyond these categories, and there perhaps we approximate to Aristotelian theories. That which is saved is obviously that which keeps its form—and is consequently, in a sense, withdrawn, if not from life, at least from becoming. And yet—here is the difficulty—only that which could be damned is capable of being saved: and this cannot therefore be either the worth, or the form itself. The form is eternally safe, it cannot even be *threatened.* The essential word is 'threatened': the idea of the 'threat' must be explored, and on all levels. On the biological level (or if we consider, for instance, a work of art, a picture or statue, from a purely material point of view) the idea of *threat* is comparatively clear. The gigantic ethical and metaphysical mistake of the present day is the refusal to recognise that the soul can also be threatened; or rather, this refusal comes down to the pure and simple *denial of a soul.* It may be noticed that in the realm of mind, or more accurately, of intelligence, we readily agree that the notion of a threat continues to mean something to us. Thus, we would all agree that certain mass-prejudices (national, social, etc.) can threaten the integrity of our judgment. But many people would be reluctant to extend the notion of integrity to cover *personality* unless they understood the word 'personality' in a purely biological sense, i.e. really just considering the working of a sort of machine. It is perfectly clear that, for a Christian, there could never be any question of considering the soul in this light, and perhaps it is here that the idea of normal function, or even health, ceases to be applicable.

May 11th

It is clear that salvation cannot be thought of otherwise than as directly or indirectly connected with a certain desire (which may, indeed, not be the desire of the person to be saved; as in the case of a child or of the soul treated as a child). It is an important question whether it is not the same with regard to damnation.

We are apt to think that, in the realm of life, loss or perdition just implies a sort of passivity: the only positive thing would be to put up an effective resistance against the forces of disintegration; but they, for their part, work mechanically. But is this the case? An essential problem, if we want to define the nature of evil. A sort of fundamental paradox seems to be written on the very heart of things, since death may be regarded either as the pure triumph of mechanical process, working automatically—or, on the contrary, as the expression of a destructive will. This paradox appears once more in the realm of spirit, but there we are able to clear it up. In this realm, it is certainly possible to discover a will to destroy one's-self (or to destroy another, which comes in a sense to the same thing). Our problem will be to see how far we may consider the order of nature itself in the light of this evil will unveiled in the heart of man.

June 12th

The question of the priority of essence in relation to existence has always interested me. I think we can really regard it as a pure illusion, which arises because we oppose something merely conceived

26

(which we think justifies us in treating it as non-existent) to something actualised. But in fact we have there simply two distinct modalities of being. Thought cannot go beyond existence; it can only in some degree abstract from it, and it is of the first importance that it should not be deceived by this act of abstraction. The jump to existence is something quite impossible to *think* of, and which does not even make sense. What we *call* 'the jump to existence' is really a kind of intra-existential transformation. That is the only way we can avoid idealism. We must say, then, that thought is *inside* existence, that it is a mode of existence which is privileged in being able to make abstraction from itself *qua* existence, and this for strictly limited purposes. It would not be untrue to say that thought involves in this sense a sort of lie, or rather a sort of fundamental blindness; but the blindness disappears in proportion as it is accompanied by knowledge, which I take to mean the return to being. But such a return can only be made intelligible if the initial blindness has been explicitly recognised. In this regard certain kinds of Cartesianism, and above all some sorts of Fichteanism, seem to me the most serious errors of which any metaphysic has been guilty. It is impossible to exaggerate how much better the formula *es denkt in mir* is than *cogito ergo sum*, which lets us in for pure subjectivism. The 'I think' is not the spring of inspiration. Far from it, it actually dams the flow.[1]

June 26th

I feel that I am today rid of whatever traces of idealism remained in my philosophy. I feel exorcised (by the influence of Father Garrigou-Lagrange's book on God, though it is very far from satisfying me completely).

[1] I would not today unhesitatingly subscribe to these sweeping assertions. But I thought it right to record them, as they bear on that stage of my philosophical journey when I made my greatest effort to break with every form of idealism, whatever it might be. (April, 1934.)

The order of the problems seems to me to be as follows. Does our knowledge of particular things come to bear on the things themselves or on their Ideas? Impossible not to adopt the realist solution. Hence we pass to the problem of Being in itself. A blindfold knowledge of Being in general is implied in all particular knowledge. But here, take care in what sense we use the words 'Being in general'. Obviously there is no question of Being emptied of its individual characteristics. I should express myself better if I said that since all knowledge concerns the thing and not the Idea of the thing—the Idea not being an object in itself and being incapable of conversion into an object except by a subsequent thought-process of doubtful validity—it implies that we are related to Being. The sense of these last words must be thoroughly explored.

June 28th

The fact that I cannot possibly deny the principle of identity, except *in verbis*, at once prevents me from denying Being and also from holding an aloof attitude tantamount to admitting that 'there may be Being, or again there may not'. And, what is more, Being cannot by definition be put into the category of mere possibles. On the one hand, it is out of the question to think it contains a logical impossibility; on the other, we cannot treat it as an empirical possibility. Either there is not and cannot be experience of Being, or else this experience is in fact vouchsafed to us. But we cannot even conceive of a more privileged position than our own, in which we could *affirm* what our experience, as it now exists, does not let us affirm at present. Such a situation would be, at best, that of a being who *saw*, but was *ipso facto* beyond affirmation. The last refuge now possible for the opponent of ontology is to deny that an unconditional affirmation of Being is possible; in short, to take up his quarters in a relativist pluralism which asserts beings or lists of realities, but does not pronounce on their unity. But still, either words have no sense, or he is none the less implicitly asserting a unity which enwraps them. He will then have to take refuge in pure nominalism; that, I think, is the only cover left to him. He will have to deny that there is even an idea, much less a reality, corresponding to the word 'Being'. From this point of view, the principle of identity will be treated just as a 'rule of the game of thought', and thought itself will be left radically separated from reality. From pure nominalism we slide into pure idealism. It is a dangerously slippery path, for idealism cannot reduce an idea to a symbol; it must see in it at least an act of the mind. And that introduces a new series of difficulties.

July 17th

After reading Fr. Garrigou-Lagrange, I should like to make my position clear on the legitimacy of the classic proofs of the existence of God. I must honestly admit that under the persistent influence of idealism, I have been continually evading the ontological problem, properly so called. I have always, I admit, had the deepest reluctance to think according to the category of being: can I justify this reluctance to myself? I have really grave doubts of this. Pure agnosticism, i.e. a completely open mind about the affirmation of being, today appears to me untenable. On the other hand, I cannot take refuge in the notion that the category of being is in itself lacking in validity. Thought is betraying itself, and ignoring its own demands if it claims to substitute the order of value for the order of being, and at the same time is condemning itself to a state of most suspicious ambiguity in face of the given, even where it is its real business to grasp and define this given. On the other hand, can I maintain that the affirmation *'Being is'*, is despite appearances the mere formal enunciation of a 'rule of the game' which thought must observe in order merely to work? To put it another way, is it a mere hypothetical inference equivalent to saying that if I assert a certain content, this assertion implies itself and consequently excludes those assertions which do not agree with it?

When I affirm that *A* is *A*, this means in idealist language that my thought, in asserting *A*, commits itself in a certain manner to an *A*-position; but this version does not really represent what I, in fact, think when I assume the identity of *A* with itself. This identity, for me, is really the condition of all possible structure (logical or real—this is not the place to take account of the distinction). We could not, in fact, deny the principle of identity without denying that thought can have a bearing on anything. We should be holding that, in proportion as I think anything, I cease to think because my thought becomes the slave of a content which inhibits or even annuls it. We could imagine a Heracleitanism or a hyper-Bergsonism which would go as far as that. Only the question would then be, whether this thought, which was not the thought *of* something, would still *be* a thought, or whether it would be lost in a sort of dream of itself. For my own part, I am convinced that the second alternative is the true one; and accordingly we may wonder whether I myself can think of myself (as thinking) without converting this 'me' thought of, into something which is nothing, and which is thus a mere contradiction. But here I join forces with Thomism or at least with what I understand to be Thomism. Thought, far from being a relation with itself, is on the contrary essentially a self-transcendence. So the possibility of the realist definition of truth is implied in the very nature of thought. Thought turns towards the Other, it is the pursuit of the Other. The whole riddle is to discover whether this Other is Being. I must here note that it may be important to refrain from the use of the term 'content', because of its idealist overtones. It is abundantly clear to me that access to objectivity, in the sense in which it is a stumbling-block to a certain type of mind, must either be posited from the beginning or remain for ever unattainable.

July 18th

Have been reflecting much on the difference between thinking (a thought) and thinking *of* (an object). Thinking is recognising (or building, or isolating) a structure: thinking *of* is something quite different. German helps here: *denken, an etwas denken, andenken, Andacht.* One thinks *of* a *being* or even an *event*, past or to come. I am not sure if one can think *of* God in the same sense that we can think *of* the incarnate Christ—in any case one can only do so on condition that one does not treat God as structure.

It would be risky, or at least premature, to deny all ontological value to this order or structure—and there I may have been very rash. All this must be thought out far more deeply. It is obvious that I may treat even an individual person as an object of thought (I make this transposition when I move from the Thou to the He).

Find out if God as structure is implied in all particular structures.

July 19th

In brief, *thinking* does not come to bear on anything but essences. Note that depersonalisation, while perfectly allowable in this case, is impossible in the order of thinking *of.* Only a *certain* person can think *of* a certain being or a certain thing. This is very important.

Note, on the other hand, that the more we fill in the context, the more we slide from just *thinking* to thinking *of.* This is important in order to understand in what sense the infinite is involved in the fact of thinking (or conceiving) the individual as essence.

Another point: we must try to understand how it is that to pray to God is without any question the only way to think of God, or more accurately, a sort of equivalent raised to a higher power of the action which would, on a lower plane, be thinking of someone. When I think of a finite being, I restore, in a manner, between him and myself, a community, an intimacy, a *with* (to put it crudely) which might seem to have been broken (I noticed this these last few

31

days in thinking of school friends I had *lost* sight of). To ask myself how I can think of God is to enquire in what sense I can be with Him. Quite obviously there is no question of such co-existence as that which may bind me to a fellow-creature. And yet, do not let us forget that there is already, in the fact of *thinking of someone*, an active denying of space, that is, of the most material and also most illusory character of the 'with'. *Denying of space—denying of death—* death being in a sense the triumph, and the deepest expression, of such separation as can be realised in space. What is a dead man? A man who is no longer even elsewhere, no longer anywhere. But thought about him is the active denial of his extinction (consider the metaphysical value of memory, or even, in a sense, of history). We might here examine the strange idea, commonly held, that the absent or dead friend is 'no longer anywhere', but just 'in me'; at bottom a belief in a sort of photograph which outlives the original, a photograph which is undeveloped, fleeting, fading—but a photograph none the less. ('He has gone away, but I have his photograph.') But here again, we are aware of the complete evasion of the spontaneous assertions of consciousness. When I think of him, it is himself I am thinking of, and the 'photograph' is just a sort of mediating element, a *point d'appui* (which varies, moreover, according to the powers of memory in different individuals). I might express this by saying that *Andenken* is deeply magical; that it reaches Being itself *past* those intermediaries we call psychological (whose ontological nature remains, anyhow, impenetrable for us). The idealist, Proustian notion, that this Being is a pure construction, should be treated as it deserves. No account can be given of it if it is reduced to a mere imaginative synthesis. But at the same time this metaphysical act which puts me in touch with a being—with Being—will always show an aspect corresponding to the activity of thought taken as construction or as recognition.

Result of a morning's thought: Given a certain structure, whether spatial, temporal, or spatio-temporal (it is surely very important to get to the bottom of the notion of temporal structure, which Bergson seems to me to have scamped or evaded: a *certain* tune, a *certain* life)—given this structure, it is obvious that by the very fact that it is *such* a structure, it is 'a certain' structure and not 'a certain other one'. Here the principle of identity takes on its full significance. But should we not deduce from this that in proportion as the structure loses its clear outlines, and more nearly approaches the ἄπειρον, the principle will correspondingly lose its significance? But in that case immensely important problems arise. Can I say with the Thomists that the principle of identity forces me to assert Being? I cannot do so unless I am sure that Being is distinguishable from the ἄπειρον; in other words, in order not to be forced to admit that the principle of identity is only valid in the realm of the finite, I must be able to distinguish the ἄπειρον from the infinite, which ancient philosophy did not do and even expressly refused to do. Otherwise, all I can say will be that the principle of identity is inapplicable to the ἄπειρον for the simple reason that the ἄπειρον is not thinkable: to put it differently, the principle of identity only ceases to apply at the point where thought itself can no longer work. So there is a series of possibilities to be distinguished:

(*A*) We can make the principle of identity the principle of the finite world (finite being equated with determinate), and we can admit the possibility (to be considered more closely) of a transcendent thought which would overleap the finite world and not be subject to the principle of identity.

(*B*) We could, again, deny the above possibility; this would be tantamount to admitting that there is no thought except in the finite order (relativism under all its shapes). This denial would imply the postulate that the indeterminate and the infinite were one.

(C) Finally, we could refuse to accept such a hypothesis, and so could separate the infinite and the indeterminate; in other words, conceive or even affirm the existence of an absolute structure which would be at the same time an absolute life, that is, an *ens realissimum*. This would be equivalent to saying that the principle of identity accompanies the exercise of thought throughout, but that thought can, without leaving the determinate, rise to the notion of a positive infinite. The affirmation '*Being is*' can only be rejected under hypothesis *B*, i.e. if Being, considered as ἄπειρον, as essentially 'not such-and-such', is found by this very definition to be outside the operation of a principle which is only valid in the realm of the 'such-and-such', the realm of the qualified. In the realm of what I call particular structures, I am always in the sphere of the hypothetical. *Supposing S* is given me in certain conditions, which, however, remain to be fixed (we must not forget that *appearances* are also given to me, and yet do not exist), I may then affirm that 'it is'; or again 'if it is, it is'. A formula which is far from clear and far from satisfactory. I can no longer see and shall have to stop.

July 31st

Can we treat Being as an element of structure, as a determination belonging or not to a certain type of structure? It seems quite obvious to me that we cannot; this was the sense in which Kant was right to deny that Being was a predicate. But then, must we say that Being is a subject—must we identify *Seyn* and the *Seyende*?

I can get no further along those lines today, I don't know why.

We must rid ourselves once and for all of the notion, or pseudo-notion, of a refraction of the real in passing through a certain medium, the appearance being this refracted reality. Whatever is the proper way of conceiving the ideal (in the sense of *mere* ideal), we cannot picture it to ourselves as a refracting medium, if only for the reason that the 'ontological status' of such a medium is impossible to fix, it remains, indeed, hanging between being and not-being. It is here that the principle of the excluded middle takes on its full meaning, when it is supplemented by the idea of degrees or spheres of reality. We are involved in Being, and it is not in our power to leave it: more simply, *we are*, and our whole inquiry is just how to place ourselves in relation to plenary Reality.

I think I noticed something of importance yesterday. Pure phenomenalism being contradictory and even meaningless, the denial of ontology must come back to alternative *B*, according to which Being is the ἄπειρον—I will not press the point that to express it thus is still to use the language of definition. The opponent of ontology will say that he does not allow himself to leave the realm of the 'such-and-such'. And that is the point on which we must manage to take a definite line. I see it something like this: fragmentation of the Real ('this exists, that exists', etc.), if it is not to lead to the unthinkable, that is to say to a sort of transposed atomism, implies as a balancing factor the idealist assertion of the unity of thought, and we shall have to look more deeply into the nature of that unity. I think, though I cannot prove it yet, that if we admit that thought is essentially access to Being, *transitus*, we can no longer be content with a piecemeal realism. Return to this later.

To say '*A is, B is*, etc., but I cannot assert that Being *is*' seems to me equivalent to saying '*A* participates in Being, *B* participates in Being, etc., but this Being in which they participate is not, perhaps, anything of which we can say that it *is*'. It is obvious that such a hypothesis is in contradiction to the principle of identity, since it is equivalent to the admission that perhaps (but the perhaps makes no difference) Being does not exist. But is not this treating Being in the way we treat a quality such as colour, hardness, etc.? This surface is coloured, so is this, but I cannot therefore conclude that colour exists. But notice that the colour appears essentially as an element of a μῖξις, or if you like, in my terms, of a structure. But this is obviously inconceivable for Being; we cannot suppose for a second that a sort of mixture can be made of Being and something else. It really looks as if we should have to be more Eleatic than Plato, and say that strictly speaking non-being does not and cannot exist. Perhaps this is the same as saying that the Aristotelian-Thomist distinction between category and transcendental is rightly grounded, and this is important. But then we must also recognise that the very term 'participation' is ambiguous, and so even dangerous, for its use carries an inevitable risk of starting a confusion between Being and predicates or attributes.[1]

The sort of mistrust aroused by ontology would, then, be due to the fact that the ontologist seems to treat as a quality, and, I would add, hypostatise something which seems to us to be the supremely unqualified. It seems to follow that he is condemned to swing between a truism (that which is, exists) and a paralogism which would consist in attributing Being to the ἄπειρον (cf. my yesterday's notes). Does not the solution lie in positing the omnipresence of Being, and what I might (perhaps improperly) call the immanence of thought in Being, that is to say, *eo ipso* the transcendence of Being over thought?

August 5th

I have not yet quite managed to clear up the puzzle I sketched at the end of my notes for the 31st. To assert the immanence of thought in Being is to recognise with the realists that thought, as soon as it is there, refers to something which transcends it and which it cannot claim to reabsorb into itself without betraying its true nature. This reference is indeed implied in the phenomenologist idea of *Meinen* or *Bedeuten*. For someone whose formative training has been idealist, this will certainly come as a great shock. He will ask how this forbidden reabsorption can be avoided, how I can

[1] This seems to me today somewhat questionable. (April, 1934.)

36

help making the act of synthesis which contains in itself, and is at the same time more than, the idea and the ideatum. But I will ask in my turn whether this act of synthesis, supposing it is possible, does not overstep the very bounds of discursive thought. There is a whole bag of tricks here, and we cannot be too wary of them.

I should like to see how far these remarks allow me to clear up the notion of participation in Being.

The uneasiness I feel on these subjects is partly due to my old difficulty in seeing the relation between being and existing. It seems obvious to me that existing is a certain way of being; we shall have to see whether it is the only one. Perhaps something could *be* without existing.[1] But I regard it as axiomatic to say that the inverse is not possible, except by an indefensible juggling with words. On these assumptions, I shall be able to study, with a few precautions, the problem of participation in Being seen in an existential example. What I said about the impossibility of a μῖξις obviously applies here; I cannot possibly say that a certain object or a certain being, so far as it exists, participates in the quality of existence, and ceases to participate in it when it ceases to exist.[2]

Perhaps the real origin of the mistake is this. (See my notes of July 17th, 18th, and 19th.) I confuse 'thinking' and 'thinking of'— a confusion which works in favour of the first mode. Thence I proceed to treat existence, which comes under the second mode, as if it were a *quality*; if it were, it would fall under the jurisdiction of the first mode. This is not yet quite clear in my mind. I think *of* a thing, *of* a person, and existence is here tied to this act of thinking *of* it or him; I think of them as existents, even in cases where I am denying

---

[1] The simplest example of this which occurs to me is that of the past, which no longer exists, and yet I cannot say purely and simply that it *is not.*

[2] We must ask ourselves whether no-longer-being is not, to a certain type of popular thought, being-lost-sight-of, and so returning to the ἄπειρον. This is worth looking into.

that they exist. But if I isolate existence from them, I think *it*, that is, I treat it as an essence or rather, to be more exact, as a pseudo-essence. Does not this come to the same thing as saying that there is no *idea* of existence in the strict sense of the term? and this because existence is the limit, or, if you will, the axis of reference for thought itself?

But the difficulty is unchanged: is it not after all because I think existence in a certain manner, and so because I form a certain idea of it, that I can deny that this idea is possible? *Antinomy.*

August 9th

I do really assert that thought is made for being as the eye is made for light (a Thomist formula). But this is a dangerous way of talking, as it forces us to ask whether thought itself *is*. Here an act of thought reflecting on itself may help us. I think, therefore, being is, since my thought demands being; it does not contain it analytically, but refers to it. It is very difficult to get past this stage. There is a sense in which I only think in so far as I am *not* (Valéry?), that is, there is a kind of space between me and being. But it is difficult to see just what this means. In any case, I do notice a close kinship between thought and desire.[1] Clearly in the two cases 'good' and 'being' play equivalent parts. All thought transcends the immediate. The pure immediate excludes thought, as it also excludes desire. But this transcendence implies a magnetisation, and even a teleology.

No date

The growing consciousness of our need for ontology is surely one of the most striking features of present-day thought; not only

[1] I wonder if this should not be corrected in the light of remarks offered later on the opposition between desire on the one hand and will and hope on the other. An analysis of thought might well make possible the discovery of an opposition or a hierarchy in it which would be completely analogous with this.

in its technically metaphysical expressions, but also on levels where the idea is only grasped through a whole world of images, which it conjures up but cannot ever assimilate or master. No doubt we can, strictly speaking, see in this just a simple fact which lies in the province of purely empirical explanations, and is perhaps the business of a psycho-analysis tinged with sociology. It is extremely easy and perhaps tempting for a certain type of mind to say that this need to affirm Being springs from a vital instinct, scarcely sublimated, reacting in its characteristic way to post-war pessimism. There we have a theme, I will not say for meditation, but for rhetorical elaboration, the fertility of which is only equalled by its essential insignificance. The question is really just this—and most of our contemporaries do not even think of asking it—up to what point does explanation actually possess the power to eliminate the thing explained, or at the very least to guarantee its harmlessness? for all belief, perhaps even all affirmation as such, has in the eye of the pure rationalist a peculiarly toxic character. I may be wrong, but it seems to me that this way of conceiving explanation, i.e. treating it quite literally as exorcism, starts from an unhealthy condition of the human mind, a condition contracted at a comparatively recent date under the sway of the influence exerted by positive science. To return to the example which was the starting-point of these remarks; is it not quite evident that the judgment of value, or, more precisely, the metaphysical appreciation which is called for by the ontological demand itself, cannot possibly depend in any way on the empirical conditions in which our experience, analysed more or less carefully, allows us to recognise the insistence and nature of this demand? It is perfectly possible that what we call the normal state (a term, by the way, quite void of meaning) of a human being —a state certainly implying some minimum of comfort and security—is by no means the most favourable for the inward alertness which a really profound metaphysical investigation both arouses and requires. Whatever the possible results of an enquiry into what might be called the empirical diet of speculative thought, the barest consideration gives the lie to the belittling claims of psycho-pathology, whose pretensions rest almost entirely on a mistaken assumption about the content of knowledge, and about the nature of the facts which enable our consciousness to apprehend it. The excellent criticism to which such a man as Chesterton has subjected the notion of mental health, with all the adulterated neo-paganism that goes with it, strikes here with its full weight. So we must not hesitate for a second to recognise that the present-day rebirth of ontology is, beyond doubt, dictated by a singularly strong and even obsessive sense of the threat which weighs on mankind—a threat, alas! of which it is all too easy to observe and record concrete examples. But this observation is altogether lacking in really fertile inspiration.[1]

No date

My life and I.

Can I 'think' my life? When I come to grips with the sense of these two words 'my life', it seems that all meaning has deserted them. There is my past: there is also the feeling of a pulsating Now. But is all this really my life? My past, in so far as I consider it, ceases to be *my* past.

---

[1] Or rather, it does not yield us an argument for the belittling of the ontological hunger itself. Still, we ought to ask whether a sharp awareness of the universal threat is not really a *normal* thing? and by no means just something corresponding to the accidental disturbance of an order which is in principle stable or stabilised (as some have thought). It would then follow that the ontological need is emphasised, or sharpened, whenever a man's circumstances show up more clearly that state of danger which is an integral part of his being. This would no doubt agree with the line of thought running from Kierkegaard to Heidegger. (April, 1934.)

Being as the place of fidelity.

How is it that this formula arising in my mind, at a given moment of time, has for me the inexhaustible inspiration of a musical theme?

Access to ontology.

Betrayal as evil in itself.

November 6th

How can I promise—commit my future? A metaphysical problem. All committal is partly unconditional, that is to say, it is of its essence to imply that we shall disregard some variable elements of the situation which is the basis of our entering the committal. For instance, I promise to go and see N—— tomorrow. At the basis of this committal, there may be present (*a*) my desire at the moment to give him pleasure; (*b*) the fact that nothing else is attracting me at the moment. But it is quite possible that *tomorrow*, i.e. at the time when I fulfil my commitment, I shall no longer have the desire, and shall instead be attracted by this interest or that, which I never dreamed of when I committed myself. I can by no means commit myself to the continued experience of the desire, or not to be attracted if the rival opportunity arises. In fact, there would be a tincture of deceit in extending my commitment to cover my own feelings on the subject. That would be an affirmation, a claim, to which reality (viz. my reality) might be found to give the lie. There is a supremely important distinction to be made between the committal in itself and an affirmation not implied by it which is concerned with the future; we must even say that it could not imply it without at the same time becoming invalid. For it would then become conditional: 'Suppose I still feel a desire tomorrow to come and see you, you may depend on me.' One sees at once where the commitment is partly unconditional: 'whatever my state of mind, whatever my temper (up to a point I cannot foresee them), I will come and see you tomorrow.' A kind of division takes place in me: on the one side, a ἡγεμονικόν which asserts its identity across time and plays the role of the guaranteeing power; on the other side, a conglomerate of elements of myself which the ἡγεμονικόν, with which I identify myself, makes it its business to control.

There is naturally an outer circle which is properly that of τῶν οὐκ ἐπ᾽ ἐμοί. For instance, if my state of health prevents me from going out, I shall not come. Clearly a careful analysis here would show that there was a sort of shading-off from what depends on me to what does not depend on me. But I must be permitted to harden the lines to some extent. No act of committal, then, is possible except for a being who can be distinguished from his own momentary situation and who *recognises* this difference between himself and his situation and consequently treats himself as somehow transcending his own life-process, and answers for himself. It is further evident that in the exercise of this faculty of answering for one's behaviour, the less twisted and inwardly discordant the life-process which we have to discount, the easier will our task be. Add to this that if I know myself, I shall less easily commit myself in a case where I am conscious of my own instability. But be that as it may, a consistent phenomenalism, supposing we could think it, asserting that the ego coincided with its immediate present, ought to exclude even the possibility of a commitment; for indeed, how could I bind a someone else, a someone whom, by definition, I cannot know because he does not yet exist?

The problem of commitment logically comes before that of fidelity; for in a sense I cannot be faithful except to my own commitment, that is, it would seem, to myself. Must we then say that all fidelity is fidelity to one's-self? and what should we understand that to mean? Surely it would be possible to distinguish a hierarchy of commitments, in order to elucidate this problem? Are not some commitments in a way essentially conditional, so that I cannot *unconditionalise* them except by making a presumption which is in itself impermissible? e.g. a commitment which depends on an opinion (literary, political, etc.). It is clear on the one hand that I cannot guarantee that my opinion (on Victor Hugo, socialism, etc.) will remain unchanged; and on the other hand it would be quite ridiculous to commit myself to a future course of action in conformity with an opinion which may cease to be mine. Obviously my human aesthetic experience in such realms may undergo almost unpredictable changes. We must see, then, whether there exist commitments which can be recognised as transcending whatever experience may add to us. To pass on to the problem of fidelity pledged to a person: it is clear that experience may influence not only the opinion I form of that person, but also my knowledge of him and the feelings I have about him. Here we are not merely talking about a desire which can cease to exist, but also of a sympathy which can be thrown off for antipathy or hostility.

But then, in what sense can I sanely pledge myself to be faithful to him? Is it not just as ridiculous as pledging myself to vote for the Conservative candidate if I become a Socialist before polling-day? If there is a difference, where does it lie? A fundamental problem. We have seen at the beginning of our analysis that there can be no act of commitment unless some identity has been posited, even if it is only posited implicitly. But we must not take our stand upon abstractions. The identity in question cannot be simply abstract; it is the identity of a certain direction of will. The more abstract this will is, the more I become the prisoner of a form, and build a wall up between myself and life. It is quite different when there is, at the root of the commitment, a fundamental apprehension; but surely it is clear that this must be of a religious kind. This is what I must consider. In any case, this apprehension must be directed towards Being or towards a human being.

43

There is certainly a very serious problem here. Can I commit myself to feeling tomorrow what I feel today? Surely not. Can I commit myself to behaving tomorrow in accordance with my feelings of today, which will not be my feelings of tomorrow? Again, surely not. But then must we admit that in swearing fidelity to a person, I am going beyond the bounds of all legitimate commitment, i.e. commitment which corresponds to my nature? There is, of course, one solution: to say that in any case I must honour my word and that I consequently create the motive for fulfilment by the very act of making the commitment. Is that an answer I can be content with? Cannot I reply that if today I have the desire to keep my word, tomorrow that desire may be found infinitely weaker, and that for a score of reasons? By what right is it asserted as a constant? I cannot so assert it, in any case, unless I treat the desire as more than a simple state. So I should have to distinguish the fact of my feeling from the act of recognising obligation; and admit that this recognition is independent of the feelings which may or may not accompany it. Tomorrow, perhaps, I shall not feel inclined to keep my word, but I shall know I am bound to do so. But here again we must beware of formalism and of the dangers of mere abstraction. Might not somebody point out that I am simplifying the problem by giving the impression of thinking that nothing binds me but myself? There is the other party too, and the fear of the other party's reactions to my not keeping my word. I think, however, that we are within our rights in discounting this element. There may be cases where my failure to keep my word is only known to myself. The problem may be restated: what is the nature of this bond (implied in the action of swearing I will, etc.)? To recognise one's obligation is to establish a fact, if you like, but what fact? I have put my signature to this; I am obliged to honour it—I establish that it is indeed my signature. Must we say that I am

44

translating into a purely personal realm something which makes no real sense except in the social order?

I think we must leave entirely aside such pseudo-explanations: they have no power except to confuse the issue. But then why do I consider that I am bound to honour my signature? Mainly, it is clear, so that the worth of this signature may be safeguarded. It is rendered worthless by the very act of repudiating it in a particular instance, (whatever my desire to let this particular case stand as an exception). But after all, surely there is an illusion here, which I have every interest in exposing. Socially, no doubt, I lay myself open to painful sanctions if I fail my commitments. But surely it is only to my interest to keep them strictly to the extent I am forced to do so. So why not reduce the part played in my life by *religio* to a minimum? See what this implies (in any case it reduces the part of the unconditional practically to disappearing point).

Examine how far I have the right to bind myself: this touches on the question approached yesterday. A certain 'philosophy of becoming' refuses me this right. This is the most serious problem.

I have no right to enter upon a commitment which it will be materially impossible for me to keep (or rather which I should know to be so if I were perfectly sincere). *Frivolity.*

But is there a single commitment which cannot be regarded as frivolously entered upon? Compare the cheque. I know what my realisable assets are; my commitments are only legitimate or valid in so far as they refer to sums which are, at the most, equal to these assets. Only here we are in a realm where this comparison does not apply: I made that clear at the start when I spoke of the unconditional element.

I see it like this. In the end there must be an absolute commitment, entered upon by the whole of myself, or at least by something real in myself which could not be repudiated without repudiating the whole—and which would be addressed to the whole of Being and

45

would be made in the presence of that whole. That is faith. Obviously, repudiation is still a possibility here, but cannot be justified by a change in the subject or object; it can only be explained by a *fall*. An idea to work out.

Another thing that I notice is this. There is no commitment purely from my own side; it always implies that the other being has a hold over me. All commitment is a response. A one-sided commitment would not only be rash but could be blamed as pride.

The notion of pride, indeed, plays a part of paramount importance in this discussion. It seems to me that it is essential to show that pride cannot be the principle upon which fidelity rests. As I see it, and despite appearances to the contrary, fidelity is never fidelity to one's-self, but is referred to what I called the hold the other being has over us. But I am putting these points in a topsy-turvy way. I must get some order and clarity into my scattered ideas. Perhaps examples would help. The key-point is that we must take account, when we are considering if a committal is valid, of the state of mind of the person who is entering upon it (e.g. the promise of a drunkard). The mind must be *compos sui* and declare itself to be such in its own judgment (without reserving to itself the possibility of afterwards alleging that it was wrong). Here then we have a judgment of the deepest importance, lying at the root of the commitment. But it does not at all discount the hold which a reality exercises over us; on the contrary, this *hold* is at the base of the judgment itself; the judgment simply prolongs and sanctions an *apprehension*.

November 8th

The love—or respect—for truth reduced to fidelity. A mistake, which consists in treating it as the will for self-consistency (cf. the connection between pride and fidelity which is only pledged to itself). In other words, beware of defining intelligence by a sort of

46

formal identity. There must be a *hold* on the real at the root of intelligence. Am enormously struck by this correlation.[1]

Perhaps we should also show how far fidelity is linked up with a fundamental ignorance of the future. A way of transcending time in virtue of the very fact that it is absolutely real for us. In swearing fidelity to a person, I do not know what future awaits us or even, in a sense, what person he will be tomorrow; the very fact of my not knowing is what gives worth and weight to my promise. There is no question of response to something which is, absolutely speaking, *given*; and the essential of a being is just that—not being 'given' either to another or himself. There is something essential here, which defines spirituality (as opposed to the relation contained in desire, a relation which, if not physical, is at least actual. But we cannot reduce ourselves to things of the moment, or at least we are no more than function if we are momentarily considered).

No date

I promised C—— the other day that I would come back to the nursing home where he has been dying for weeks, and see him again. This promise seemed to me, when I made it, to spring from the inmost depths of my being. A promise moved by a wave of pity: he is doomed, he knows it, he knows I know it. Several days have gone by since my visit. The circumstances which dictated my promise are unchanged; I have no room for self-deception about that. I should be able to say—yes, I even dare assert—that he still inspires the same compassion in me. How could I justify a change in the state of my feelings, since nothing has happened since which could have the power to alter them? And yet I must in honesty admit that the pity I *felt* the other day, is today no more than a theoretical pity. I still judge that he is unhappy and that it is right

[1] Think what it would be like to live by penny numbers! It would be dreaming one's life away. It would be life without reality.

to be sorry for him, but this is a judgment I should not have dreamed of formulating the other day. There was no need. My whole being was concentrated into an irresistible impulse towards him, a wild longing to help him, to show him that I was on his side, that his sufferings were mine. I have to recognise that this impulse no longer exists, and it is no longer in my power to do more than imitate it by a pretence which some part of me refuses to swallow. All that I can do is to observe that C—— is unhappy and alone and that I cannot let him down; also, I have promised to come back; my signature is at the foot of the bond and the bond is in his possession.

The silence I feel within me is strangely different from that other cry of pity from the heart; yet it does not seem to me altogether mysterious. I can find a good enough explanation for it in myself and the rhythm of my moods. But what is the good? Proust was right: we are not at our own disposal. There is a part of our being to which strange, perhaps not altogether conceivable, conditions give us sudden access; the key is in our hands for a second; and a few minutes later the door is shut again and the key disappears. I must accept this fact with shame and sorrow.

But this commitment that I took upon myself the other day— surely it rested upon my ignoring, and wrongly ignoring, these fluctuations and interruptions in my states? Surely it was rather presumptuous of me to assert that, on such-and-such a day in the future, I should still feel the same compassion which pierced me to the heart when I stood by the sick bed? Or did I really make no such claim at the time, did I really mean that a certain material fact—my visit—would take place after a certain interval? What shall I answer? I must not accept this alternative. I did not *ask* myself whether the feeling that impelled me towards him was going to die down like a fountain or the shape of a melody. *A fortiori* I could not commit myself to feeling tomorrow as I did yesterday.

But suppose I leave aside whatever I was conscious of at that fleeting moment, and suppose I try to discover what my promise means in so far as it was an act. Then I am bound to recognise that it contains a decree so daring that it surprises me now. Allowing for the possibility of exterior conditions which may put it out of my power to keep my promise, I have admitted, however implicitly, that the state of my feelings was capable of alteration, but I decided at the same time that this eventual alteration was something of which I should not take account. Between the being who dares to say 'I' and who has attributed to himself the power to bind *himself* (*I bind myself*)—between him and the endless world of causes and effects which simultaneously escape from my own jurisdiction and from all rational prevision, there is an intermediate realm, where events take place which are not in accordance with my desires or even with my expectation; yet I reserve to myself the right and the power to abstract from these events in my actions. This power of real abstraction is at the very core of my promise: this is what gives it its peculiar weight and worth. I will make an effort to fix my attention on this central datum, and not yield to the vertigo which threatens to overwhelm me when I see the gulf opening at my feet: in fact, what is this body of which I am at once master and slave? Can I, without folly or insincerity, relegate it to the huge foreign empire which eludes my grasp? But I cannot completely include it, either, in that subject realm where my own decree gives me the power to discount any of its contents. It seems to me equally true to say that I am and am not responsible for these bodily fluctuations; both assertions seem accurate to me, and both ridiculous. I will question myself no further on this point; enough to have recognised that in binding myself by a promise I have acknowledged the presence of an inner hierarchy, consisting of a ruling principle, and a life whose details remain unpredictable, but which the principle subjects to itself, or, still more accurately, which it pledges itself to keep under its yoke.

I cannot help seeing that here I am repeating one of the common-places most often explored by the wisdom of antiquity; but perspective plays us strange tricks: what seemed self-evident long ago takes on, in my eyes today, a paradoxical aspect. And what is more, I cannot help wondering if this decree will not be called a shocking act of violence by the supporters of that ethic of transparent honesty which I hear most commonly professed around me. Is not the very language of 'abstracting' or 'discounting' (which I have had to use several times) enough to breed considerable disquiet? How can I justify this dictatorship which I claim to exercise over my future actions, in the name of some present state? Where does this authority come from, and what lays claim to it? Am I not over-simplifying, when I distinguish from my present a subject which claims to go beyond it in a mental dimension which is not be to confused with duration, and which I can hardly figure out, even in idea? To look more closely, is not my present itself making an arbitrary claim to a sort of eternity of right? But in that case false-hood is established at the very heart of my life. For this pretended 'eternity of right' no corresponding continuity of fact can be found; and it seems that I am brought up against the following dis-concerting alternatives. At the moment of my commitment, I either (1) arbitrarily assume a constancy in my feelings which it is not really in my power to establish, or (2) I accept in advance that I shall have to carry out, at a given moment, an action which will in no way reflect my state of mind when I do carry it out. In the first case I am lying to myself, in the second I consent in advance to lie to someone else.

Shall I seek reassurance by telling myself that these are just a cloud of subtleties concealing a really very simple problem, which life will make it its own business to solve?

I cannot be content with such a lazy answer; the less so, since I can imagine at this moment a dozen cases where the problem is still the same, but where its terms are of a kind which proclaim its seriousness even to the most careless thinker. To swear fidelity to a creature, to a group, to an idea, even to God—in every case, is not this to expose ourselves to the same disastrous dilemma? Is not any promise whatever rooted in a state of mind which is entirely of the moment, and whose permanence nothing can guarantee?

When I look at it like this, the very nature of fidelity seems to me suddenly covered by a thick veil; I can no longer understand what meaning the term 'commitment' has ever had for me. And now I call to mind once more the memory of all the disappointments, all the hatreds of myself and others which were the ordinary results of too hasty promises. Were they mere accidents? or must we see them, on the contrary, as the natural effects of a most inexcusable presumption? At what price are they to be avoided? If we are to remain tied by our inward bond, must we not learn to shut our eyes to the contorted but fateful life-process which only a feeble sight will fail to discern beneath the accumulations of habit? To swear fidelity—whatever the object to which the vow is taken— what is it really but committing myself to ignore the deepest part of my being, to learn the art of duping myself constantly with tricks that I play upon myself, for my own deception? Indeed, can a commitment exist that is not a betrayal?

But there is no betrayal which is not a repudiation of fidelity. Is there, then, such a thing as a basic fidelity, a primal bond, which I break every time I make a vow which in the least degree concerns what I vaguely call my soul? (Obviously there is no question here of vows about mere matters of the most outward and socialised activity, where I am as it were using a tool ready to my hand.) This primal bond can only be what some people have taught me to call fidelity to myself. Myself, they will say, is what I betray when I so bind myself. Myself: not my being but my becoming; not what I am today but what I shall perhaps be tomorrow. Here the mystery thickens. How can I be faithful, or again how can I be unfaithful, to the Me whom today cannot know, and only the future will reveal? Surely they mean me to understand just this; that I must keep myself at the disposal of the unknown Me, so that one day he can come into my place without meeting any resistance from the Me that I still am, but shall in that second have ceased to be? They are just asking me to lend myself to the game, and not in the least to stiffen my muscles and resist. The word fidelity has certainly undergone a change here! It now sketches no more than a lazy acquiescence, a graceful passivity. Well, but who prescribes it for me? this unknown whose prestige is entirely due to the fact that he does not yet exist? Amazing privilege for the unborn! But at least the privilege must be recognised, and once more I am in the dark. For the act by which this privilege of my future being is so consecrated is in fact part of my present: so we admit a value in the future in so far as it is a future which is attached to my present state, but which is nevertheless distinct from it, since it somehow has control of its successor.

Shall I yield to the temptations of dialectic? Shall I admit that it is really my present state which is denied and claims to be transcended? Surely we cannot help regarding this as a manipulation to be mistrusted, since it implies, suppose I allow it, some sort of truth which transcends the life-process and is capable of serving as its foundation. But if this is so, there is no further question of my lending myself unresistingly to the current of my moods of the moment. Something which forms no part of them rules their caprices, perhaps a law. And it is my business to remain faithful to this law or unity. Terminology, however, threatens once more to lead me into error. This unity is just me; it is a single unvarying principle—whether form or reality—which insists upon its own continuity. The fidelity is no longer to a life-process, a 'becoming', for this is meaningless, but to a *being* which I can see no possibility of distinguishing from myself. And so I escape from the mirage of a tomorrow which loses its colour as it sharpens its outlines.

Have I at last found the way out? Have I escaped from the horns of the dilemma which seemed to forbid me to be sincere and faithful at once? The solution which occurs to me is not just a logical invention; a very simple word describes the hidden spring of the action by which I bind myself. To make it a point of honour to fulfil a commitment—what else is this but putting an accent on the supra-temporal identity of the subject who contracts it and carries it out? And so I am brought to think that this identity has a validity in itself, whatever the content of my promise may be. This identity is the one important thing to maintain, however absurd the particular commitment may appear, to the eyes of a spectator, through my rashness or weakness in undertaking it. However overwhelmingly men of sense object, however often my friends remonstrate, I shall take no notice; I have promised and will keep my word. Perhaps my persistence will even be proportionally strengthened as the carrying out of the promise looks to myself and others more and more like the fulfilment of a wager.

But if this is so, the particular object, were it God himself, to which fidelity binds its votaries, must remain a pure accident, a sort of pretext. It cannot enter the closed circle in which the will returns upon herself in her effort after the demonstration of her own power.

But I cannot really confuse this attachment of the soul to its own glory—the most arid, strained, and irritable of all the forms of self-love—with that which I have all my life called Fidelity. It cannot be pure chance that fidelity shows itself in its most unmistakable garb among those who have, on the contrary, the least concern to cut a figure in their own eyes. The face of a servant or a farm-labourer is its place of revelation for me. What can be the ground of so ruinous a confusion of two spiritual states, when the most superficial judgment will assure me that they are forever incompatible? How can we help seeing that a fidelity to another of which I was myself the ground, the spring, and the centre—that such a fidelity as this would expose yet again, by the furtive act of substitution it reveals, the lie at the heart of that existence which it shapes?

How to get out of this deadlock? I must again tackle the precise problem, the dilemma, which I stated at the beginning; especially the problem of fidelity vowed to a person. I must refuse the choice of alternatives (continuity of the inner disposition or insincerity of action). I cannot base my argument on the effort of my own will. I must admit, then, that something unalterable is implied in the relation itself. Must see further into the nature of this unalterable: where do I start if I am to get hold of it? Need to start from Being itself—from commitment to God.

It is an act of transcendence having its ontological counterpart in the hold God has over me. This hold is the term in relation to which even my freedom is ordered and defined.

The mysterious relation between grace and faith exists wherever there is fidelity; and wherever a relation of this sort fails to appear, there is room for no more than a shadow of fidelity, a mere constraint imposed upon the soul, although it may be both culpable and full of lies.

A philosophy which refuses me the possibility of grasping anything but what it calls my 'states of consciousness' is seen to be manifestly false when we confront it with the spontaneous and irresistible assertion which forms, as it were, the ground-bass of human knowledge. In the same way, the contention that fidelity, despite appearances, is never more than a mode of pride and self-regard, unquestionably robs of their distinctive character the loftiest experiences that men think they have known. The correlation which unites these two 'ventures' cannot be over-stressed. I believe I see a centre of light here; I feel I must try to get nearer to it. And I

54

believe that if a refution can be attempted in the one case, it should also be possible in the other, and along the same line of thought.

When I say that I am unable to grasp any knowledge which transcends my states of consciousness, am I not lazily opposing this knowledge (a knowledge disappointing and even deceptive, since it contains a claim it cannot make good) to a knowledge which is not actually given, but which is at the very least ideally conceived, and, unlike the first, touches a reality independent of the mind which construes it? Without this axis of reference, however imaginary I may consider it, it is clear that the expression 'my states of consciousness' is emptied of its meaning, since that meaning is only definite if it remains restrictive. The important question to ask is: how can I conceive of a knowledge thus irreducible to that which according to this hypothesis I really enjoy? or even, a deeper question, do I actually conceive of it? If I admit that perhaps I do not conceive of it, that is enough to make the insecure doctrine which I claimed to preach fall to the ground at once. But it is scarcely in my power to understand how the idea of a real knowledge, i.e. a reference to Being, could come to birth inside a world of pure states of consciousness. And so I begin to find a secret way of escape in the outer bailey of that tall keep in which I pretended to immure myself. Shall I not be forced to recognise from now onwards that this very idea is, as it were, the indelible mark which another order has left upon me?

The same is true of fidelity. Across the attachments which the I vows to itself lies the shadow of another fidelity, and only the fact that I have first conceived it enables me to deny its existence myself. But if it has been given me to conceive it at all, surely this is because I have dimly experienced it, whether in myself or in others? Surely it is no accident that I use those things which I affect no longer to believe in, as the models for my tentative picture of personal reality, even while I allege that the distinctive character of this reality is the continually renewed effort of coherence and balance between its two aspects?

Am I not, moreover, justified in mistrusting the actual nature of the step by which I claim to gather up into myself the roots or links of all fidelity? How can I help seeing that such a dogged and determined contempt of evidence cannot have its origin in experience, however central and however hidden you suppose it to be: it can only originate in prejudice, in the act of fundamental negation by which I banish the Real to infinity, and then dare to usurp its place and dress myself up in its stolen attributes—degrading them, it is true, in the process.

Can we only rescue fidelity at this price? I think it would be a thousand times better if I resolved to see in it nothing but a survival, a lingering shadow which melts right away under the light of thought. Better that than to set up such idolatry at the centre of my life.

Although I would not venture to assert that the connection can be observed in every case, yet I cannot fail to notice that where Fidelity is at her most unmistakable, where her face shines with clearest light, she goes hand in hand with a character as opposed to Pride as anything we can imagine. Patience and Humility gaze from the depths of her eyes. Patience and Humility; virtues whose very names today are forgotten, and whose true nature is further darkened to our sight with every step forward in man's technical and impersonal equipment, his logical and dialectical equipment with the rest.

The alliance of these three virtues into a unity—the unity of a being whose ever-changing structure psychology has no power to fathom—could not exist, could not even be thought of, in a purely personal system: where the self, and only the self, was the centre for those roots and links with reality, which uphold the commitments which Life may inspire us to undertake.

Consider non-representative musical expression. It is a sphere where the thing stated cannot be distinguished from the manner of stating it. In this sense and in this sense only, music has, strictly speaking, no meaning, but perhaps just because it *is* meaning. Explore this.

The fact is that we introduce a relation into the heart of the music, a relation between the content expressed (?) and the expression, which is of the same type as that which joins the expression to the execution. But this is an illegitimate transference. From this point of view the idea of objective music takes on a meaning, but it is a negative meaning.

But is the term 'expression' really one that can still be used with regard to music? Could there really still be expression when we can no longer speak of content expressed—a content distinct from the expression itself? I think the notion of essence, anyhow so difficult to define, might be introduced here. There is an *essence* of Schubert, of the later Beethoven, of the later Fauré, etc. The expression would then be the opening-up of the essence to itself. I believe this is the idea to be explored. Combine the idea of essence with the idea of universe. The essence regarded as the highest point of a certain universe. It is almost impossible here to make abstraction from the metaphor of 'the summit', and this is the metaphor whose roots could usefully be laid bare. The idea of 'the summit' could perhaps be replaced by that of 'the *centre*'. In both cases there is a periphery, or to put it more accurately, precincts (zones of encroachment).

NOTES ON JULIEN BENDA'S 'LE DISCOURS COHÉRENT'

I propose to examine only the principles expounded in the first parts of the *Discours Cohérent*, for the principles alone concern us here.

M. Benda, on his own admission, has tried to construct a

thorough-going philosophy of the Infinite, or rather a sort of hyper-Eleaticism in which the principles of Parmenides are for the first time pressed to their final conclusions. In theory, I think, we may consider an attempt of this sort in the light of an interesting intellectual experiment, perhaps a stimulating one too, at any rate in so far as it provokes reactions and forces the critic to make his own position clear in his turn.

M. Benda is really working up to a kind of confrontation; not a confrontation of two ideas but rather of two aspects of one and the same constant and central idea, that is, the idea of the world. 'Sometimes I think of it as identical with itself, or in the mode of the phenomenal, and sometimes I think of it as contradictory to itself, or in the mode of the divine, but in the second case as in the first, it is still the world that I am thinking of.' An Eleatic—if indeed there are any Eleatics—who read this sentence, would certainly think at first that here was a typographical error of the worst kind; an inversion which turns the sense of the sentence topsy-turvy; since for him, obviously, to think of the world according to the phenomenal mode is to think of it in a contradictory way. All the same, the Eleatic would be wrong, and M. Benda is here saying exactly what he means.

His contention in the first part of the *Discours* is in fact that to think of Being as infinite is really to think of it as contradictory. Let us see exactly what he understands by that. The demonstration he gives us refers to temporal being, but he hints that this demonstration can and should be extended to other modes of being.

'In so far as the duration which I assign to the world from today right back to its beginning, is represented in my mind by a finite number, however large, this duration will admit of another still larger one. If,' adds M. Benda, 'I want to conceive of a quantity of being, whose duration from the present moment right back to its beginning will *not* admit of a larger than itself, i.e. which will be infinite, I am obliged to conceive of a duration whose measure will be a number which escapes from this inherent slavery to finite number, i.e. a number n such that, if I add a unit to it, I obtain the number $n+1$, which is in no way different from n: a number n such that I have:

$$n = n + p$$

p being some finite number.

From this point of view it may be said that my time is the same as Julius Caesar's.'

But we must not be taken in by the paradoxical look of the formula: in reality it is a complete truism. I have no right to say 'my time is the same as Julius Caesar's', unless I just mean 'Given that there was no beginning of the world, I am no further away from this non-existent beginning than Julius Caesar was'. As a matter of fact, M. Benda avoids this explicit way of speaking, so that he leaves the reader with a confused notion that this beginning, placed in infinity, does nevertheless exist.

To say 'I am no further away from the beginning of the world than Julius Caesar was, since this beginning does not exist', is equivalent to saying that an event can only be placed by its relation to another event, and since there is no event which can be called 'the beginning of the world', no absolute temporal fixing of any event is possible.

No absolute fixing of an event in time is possible if one does not admit that the world did really begin. But M. Benda declares that to think of the world as infinite in respect of time is to think of it in such a way that its distinctions in time no longer exist, that is, to think of it in such a way that the differences it contains do not differ. I think there is a rather serious confusion here. So long as we are moving on the level where the distinction of times, or chronology, holds good, it is quite impossible for us to consider this distinction to be removed or liable to be removed.

All one has the right to say is, that the meaning of these temporal distinctions is not ultimate, but only superficial, though within a certain register they retain their full validity. I may here use a simile to illustrate my meaning. A book is something which admits of a perfectly fixed pagination, and the person who has to arrange the sheets is bound to respect this single and irreversible order. But it is perfectly clear, on the other hand, that this book admits of types of unity which are far deeper than the unity expressed by the order of the pages. And yet this does not mean in the least that the order of the pages is 'illusory'. Now chronology is a sort of pagination of the world, and it would be quite absurd to speak of a beginning of this pagination which was placed at infinity. It would be a contradiction of terms, or rather it would be to think nothing at all, whereas it is not only permissible, but even inevitable, to rise to a point of view where this order of the pages appears as the superficial expression of something infinitely deeper which can certainly be apprehended from other aspects.

From this point of view the formula $n = n + p$ is pure nonsense. We only have the right to say this; that from a certain point of view the difference between n and $n + p$ ceases to tell us anything or mean anything to us. This is a completely different thing and implies no contradiction.

And so the definition according to which infinite Being is Being in so far as it is self-contradictory, rests on a paralogism and can be ruled out at once. This affirmation would only be legitimate if we could think of temporal distinctions as being at once *there* and, as it were, *not there*. And this is just what we cannot do. We could also show that the confusion extends still further. M. Benda seems to identify the indeterminate with the self-contradictory. But this is unjustifiable. The contradiction only arises where definitions incompatible with each other are attributed to the same subject; and in that case we should already have left the realm of the indeterminate. The indeterminate is in fact prior to this double attribution. We could go much further yet in our criticism, and show in particular that M. Benda has no grounds for considering Being as the totality of its relations, since from his point of view (which is that of indeterminate being) it is inconceivable that these relations could form a totality. It is only too clear that he here swings light-heartedly between two opposite ontological positions whose opposition he has never even noticed.

The remarks I have just offered nullify in advance all the developments following on the exposition of his principles. It is quite clear, especially in Chapter V,[1] that M. Benda is continually mixing up the indeterminate, which is only pure potentiality, and the supra-determinate of Being in its fulness, in whose depths all oppositions melt away. Are we to say that this supra-determinate, this fulness, is the place to which we clearly should turn our thoughts? All the indications are to the contrary—to begin with, the text of p. 621, where M. Benda speaks of logical solitude or the sterility of the Absolute. It can be clearly seen, throughout the whole of his dialectic, that the more a being differentiates itself, the more it is guaranteed against the return to God defined as initial indeterminacy. And here one fact (and I will return to it) is already clearly apparent, namely that the metaphysician—the metaphysician in spite of himself!—to whom M. Benda is most nearly akin, is not Parmenides or Spinoza, but the Spencer of the First Principles, a Spencer who has read and made notes on Schopenhauer.

I must now attack a different class of difficulties; this time we must consider the actual notion of God as it appears in the *Discours Cohérent*. God, he says in §59, is nothing but the world thought of in a certain way. M. Benda specifies still further by saying that what exists for him is not Divinity (noun) but the divine (adjective applied to the world). Here a preliminary question arises, which I

[1] These references are to the text published by N.R.F.

61

will not take up but which ought at least to have been asked, namely, is it legitimate to speak of existence with regard to something which is just an *adjective*? It is perfectly clear that what exists here is just the world: to say that the divine exists as such is nonsense. On the other hand I cannot take refuge in saying that 'the divine' is the world thought of as divine, for in that case I make it depend upon a subject which asserts itself to be such: but this dependence is radically excluded by M. Benda's position.

But we shall see yet another contradiction arising here. If God is just the world thought of by me (or by X) as the simple undefined, what can be the sense in asking what God knows? Yet we read in §58, 'God knows neither anxiety nor serenity; he knows freedom.' Should we object that the word 'know' cannot here be taken in its strict sense? As a matter of fact, M. Benda does explain in his development of the passage that the idea of God is bound up with the idea of freedom. But elsewhere, the term 'knowledge' is taken in its usual sense. In fact, M. Benda distinguishes two ways of thinking of the indeterminate. The first corresponds to the condition of the phenomenal world arriving at the point where it changes to thinking of itself in the divine mode. The second corresponds to the condition of the world thinking of itself in the divine mode without having known the phenomenal world. M. Benda then declares (§10, p. 481) that the first way is perhaps that in which indeterminate Being thinks of itself, knowing itself anew and never having known any other condition. This sentence is extraordinarily significant, and it is very clear that the 'perhaps', without altering its scope, only introduces an extra element of confusion. If we are to be allowed to speak of a 'way of thinking of itself' which belongs to indeterminate Being, of a knowledge which is peculiar to it, then it is quite obvious that it is once more being conceived as a noun. This is a formal contradiction of the declaration in §59.

I think that if we examined the latter part of his exposition, we should be met by a cloud of new and baffling difficulties. For instance, when M. Benda says that the idea of God and the idea of the phenomenal world, although irreducibles, are nevertheless correlatives (§13, p. 624), we cannot help wondering what unity embraces this correlation, if it is not the subject which I spoke of just now. We can see at least the ghost of a third sphere coming into sight at this point, a sphere which would by definition be neither that of the phenomenal, nor that of indeterminate Being; but a sphere whose metaphysical and ontological status M. Benda cannot, as far as we can see, have a hope of defining. The fact is that in this line of country Plato and Hegel really carry all before them. We cannot play a part in their dialectic; it is simply imposed upon us, and to resist it as M. Benda does is pure and simple suicide. And no doubt that is an attitude permissible for an irrationalist. The irrationalist is within his rights to refuse dialectic. But if he does refuse dialectic, he *a fortiori* refuses indeterminate Being which is itself nothing but the most tenuous product of this dialectic. And here M. Benda's thought looks to me like a shamefaced irrationalism which is afraid to show itself in its true colours, and routs out of Heaven knows what old cupboard the most drab and shapeless cloak of reason that it can possibly find. This brings us to what I think is the most interesting and elusive part of the problem set by the *Discours Cohérent*. The really important question, which M. Benda does not ask but which we must certainly ask, is how the metaphysical primacy which he gives to indeterminate Being can possibly be justified. I want to press this point a little further.

Actually this point is all the more important since M. Benda, unlike the metaphysicians of the past, absolutely refuses to identify the infinite with perfection. This is a point upon which he had already explained himself in his study on the idea of order and the idea of God. 'Perfection is an attribute entirely foreign to the nature of God. The idea of something perfect, that is, finished, accomplished, is essentially incompatible with the idea of infinite Being, but rather bound up of necessity with the idea of determinate Being.' In the *Essay on the Idea of Order and the Idea of God*, he made an explicit attack on the idea of supreme Being, absolutely refused to place God at the apex of a hierarchy, and even went so far as to say that this hierarchy was foreign to God. I note in passing that there does not seem to be complete agreement between the two texts, since M. Benda, in the Idea of Order, might seem disposed to attribute to God an infinite perfection, whereas later he flatly denies Him perfection. But I think that the second position is really his own, so this is the one to be examined.

The infinite God of M. Benda is a God certainly not imperfect, but not perfect either. But then we shall again be met by the difficulty I pointed out a minute ago; the easier it is to understand that the name God can be given to a being defined as perfect, the harder is the position when a reality is in question which is not existent and not perfect, because infinite. And I repeat my question; whence the primacy? M. Benda will no doubt try to exclude the very word primacy, alleging that it *ipso facto* re-establishes the hierarchy which he will not have at any price. But my answer is, that God is not a word which we have the right to use arbitrarily, for it embodies certain values, and certain feelings are crystallised round it (and here it is clear that the notions of perfection and supremacy reappear instantly). But we may well ask whether these values are compatible with the attributes of Being as M. Benda defines it. At the worst, no doubt, I should understand him if he refused to consider things from this angle and established himself in a sort of enclosed sanctuary where he remained alone with his own particular God, but unfortunately he does not do this, as witness p. 475. 'Not to speak of philosophers,' says he, 'it seems to me that simple people, those who only seek their theology in the needs of their hearts, have (among many other ideas which contradict them)'—I will return

64

to this parenthesis—'an idea of God remote from all notion of the particularity and limitation which at times causes suffering to them. This is what they seem to indicate, when they express the hope that in God all our pride will be melted away,' etc. . . . But surely it is these 'other' ideas, these 'contradictory ideas', and especially those of divine justice and charity, which constitute the conception of God fostered in the minds of the humble folk whom M. Benda is kind enough to remember here. But this just or charitable God, this God who is God only because of His infinite justice and charity, has clearly nothing to do with the indeterminate Being of M. Benda; he cannot hope to find a single ally among the simple folk. Then must he not recognise, if he wants to make his position in the least coherent, that his God has no *value*, in the usual or even in the technical sense of the word? But then, given that anyhow it is probable that He does not exist, it is difficult not to ask what prevents us from simply deleting Him. I think we must expect M. Benda, in spite of everything, to try to take his stand on the line of value: only I here repeat my question: What kind of value is it possible to impute to an indeterminate Being? It is on this question that I should personally be most anxious to see him explain himself, but as I said at the beginning, I very much doubt if he can do it. In fact I feel sure that the whole thing is really a mask—the mask huddled on by a will which is perfectly resolved not to be explicit with itself. Personally, I should have little hesitation in calling it the expression of a sterility somewhat after the Mallarmé pattern, a conscious sterility which cannot bear its own presence and so converts itself into a will for sterility, and deifies itself under that aspect. This self-deification is only too obviously at the heart of M. Benda's writings. I will even go so far as to say that it is doubly present there, and instantly self-destroyed; for the curious theogony which is pictured for us, the double process whereby the world is divided from God in order to return to Him, all takes place in the consciousness of M. Benda, who seems to be somehow divided between his God and his universe. I may add in conclusion, that idealism, which I personally reject, regains all its force in the presence of such a doctrine as this; since in the final analysis, and taken on the whole, this is perhaps the poorest and most contradictory of all its expressions.

But suppose we admit, for the moment, that the previous objections can be met. Suppose—which I most expressly deny—that this idea of God can be regarded as tenable. Even so we have still to ask how the passage from God to the world can take place in M. Benda's system. Here we shall be witnesses of an extraordinary drama.

M. Benda thinks that he has established the irreducibility of the two fundamental ways of thinking of the world: the first a divine mode in the category of contradiction, the other a phenomenal mode in the category of identity. What does this mean? It means that there are here two ideas which do not touch at any point, so that we can no more pass from one idea to the other than, for instance, we can pass from blueness to triangularity. But the surprising thing is, that M. Benda passes quite unconsciously from the consideration of ideas to that of things; we read immediately afterwards that the phenomenal world cannot be conceived in relation to God except by a separation from God, and not by a continuous emanation from God to itself. But indeed there was no question of anything of the kind: and I deny that this separation, which is given as an act (obviously a non-temporal act) has the least connection with the irreducibility *of ideas* which M. Benda thought he had previously established. This word *separation*, already far too concrete, will not content him: immediately afterwards he will be speaking to us of *aversion*, no doubt speculating with a view to later elaborations on the emotional significance of that word. Three lines further on he speaks of *impiety*. But the simplest metaphysical reflection will be enough to show us how fundamentally unintelligible all this is—I would even say, *un-thought-out*. How can determinate Being separate itself from indeterminate Being? It is inconceivable except in a philosophy of the neo-Platonic type, in which the absolute principle is not indeterminate, but rather, if I may so express it, supra-determinate. In that case, determinacy seems to denote an impoverishment, but in these systems of philosophy the indeterminate, i.e. matter, is at the lowest point in the series. Besides, M. Benda cannot make room for such an idea in his system, since he will not so much as hear of hierarchy. It therefore seems clear to me that M. Benda is transposing what he believes to be a radical hiatus between determinate and indeterminate being, into a sphere where this hiatus cannot help altering its character. At the same time those very metaphysical categories, which he claimed to have eliminated, begin to multiply round this hiatus. And this is all due to the fact that he is really intent on constructing a system with a sort of Schopenhauerian modulation. An entirely unconscious dialectic which governs his most hidden will, compels him forthwith to bring into his premisses, in a way that changes and shatters them, just those dynamic elements which it was characteristic of his metaphysical position to exclude, but which he needs to justify his self-consciously priest-like attitude.

At the point we have now reached, there is one question which we should find it difficult not to ask; why do we not just get rid of this indeterminate or infinite Being, which looks sometimes like a mere non-being and sometimes like a sort of depository containing, all higgledy-piggledy, those elements which the phenomenal world has foolishly claimed to arrange in hierarchical order? Why not simply keep the third part of the *Discours Cohérent*, which gives us, in substance, a Spencerian picture of the universe, enriched (or complicated) by additions borrowed from Schopenhauer, Nietzsche, and M. Bergson? Could we not build up a philosophy of imperialism on a foundation of almost traditional notions, such as the will to live or the will to power? But in that case, what would become of the fourth part, that is, the return of the world towards God? Remark in passing that this fourth part is a kind of pendant to the fourth book of *The World as Will and Idea*. This is, for the moment, unimportant; as I was saying just now, M. Benda is forced to take his stand on the line of value. It *must* be damned, this world of the phenomenal, that is, of particularity, of individualisation and of imperialism, or at least it must be able to be thought of as damned. Why the 'must'? Why, just because M. Benda has written *La Trahison des Clercs*.[1] 'That is absurd,' you will say. 'It is the opposite which is true. M. Benda wrote *La Trahison des Clercs* to bring the world back to reason.' But I think I can uphold my assertion. The fact that there is a book called *La Trahison des Clercs* is a reason why the phenomenal world must be conceivable as being capable of damnation: but it cannot be unless it is thought of as having separated itself from something which is . . . which is what? We cannot say that it is either the Good, or absolute intelligence. We will just say that it is God. The existence of God hangs on the existence of *La Trahison des Clercs*. You return to the charge, and tell me 'If M. Benda wrote *La Trahison des Clercs*, he did so in the name of the metaphysic which is developed in *Le Discours Cohérent*'. I do not believe a word of it. *La Trahison des Clercs* is a book which seems to me based solely upon a psychology of temperament, a psychology, moreover, which is narrowly Jewish. But we are in a realm where every assertion aspires to justify itself; so *La Trahison des Clercs* has naturally enough brought up from the basement a whole system of protective screens which we have before our eyes today and which is naturally called upon to function in a certain quite definite sense. But it is just like human nature that the man who invented them should be the last man to realise where they came from or what their results will be.

[1] *The Betrayal of the Clerks.*

68

Charity thought of as presence, as absolute disposability; I have never before seen its link with poverty so clearly. To possess is almost inevitably to be possessed. Things possessed get in the way. All this needs much more thorough treatment.

At the heart of charity is presence in the sense of the absolute gift of one's-self, a gift which implies no impoverishment to the giver, far from it; and so we are here in a realm where the categories valid in the world of things entirely cease to be applicable. These categories, as we must see, are strictly bound up with the very idea of a thing. If I have four things and give two away, it is obvious that I only have two left, and that I am correspondingly *impoverished*. But this only makes sense if I suppose a certain close relationship between myself and the things, if I consider them consubstantial, so to say, with myself, if I am myself affected, in the strongest sense of the word, by their presence or absence.

Thresh out the notion of non-disposability. I think it corresponds to that which fundamentally constitutes the creature considered as such. From this point of view, I wonder if we could not define the whole spiritual life as the sum of activities by which we try to reduce in ourselves the part played by non-disposability. Note connection between the fact of being non-disposable and the fact of feeling or thinking we are indispensable. Show, in fact, that this non-disposability is inseparable from a kind of self-adherence, which is something more primitive and still more fundamental than self-love.

Death as the flat denial of non-disposability.

To my mind, we have here a mine of important considerations. For we see here the necessity for distinguishing between love of one's-self regarded as non-disposable, and love of one's-self regarded as disposable, that is, love of what God may make of me. This lawful self-love is illuminated by its opposite, namely, the hatred of self which may be contained in a certain kind of death-wish. The question also of the relative non-disposability of the self for itself. Some extremely interesting questions to work out here.

Analysis of the notion of non-disposability.

It seems to me that it always implies the notion of transference. Non-disposable capital is capital which is already partially transferred. This is perfectly clear in the case of material wealth. Now we must see how the notion can be extended in the way I pointed out this morning. A typical case comes into my mind. Some misfortune I hear about demands my pity, but I feel that I cannot give it. Theoretically I realise that what they are telling me is strangely worthy of pity, yet I feel nothing. If the wretchedness they describe were actually before my eyes, it would no doubt be otherwise. An immediate experience would unseal the springs of my compassion, would force the damned gates. A strange thing! I should like to feel the emotion which seems to me to 'impose itself' (I judge that it is normal to be touched in such cases), but I feel nothing; I am not at my own disposal. No doubt by putting myself through my mental paces I could flog myself into something resembling this emotion, but if I am sincere it cannot deceive me; I shall know quite well that it is a worthless imitation. There are two limiting cases, the child and the saint, where this pawning of one's liberty, so difficult to define strictly, does not take place: it is evidently bound up with what may be called the normal growth of experience. And here we return to what I wrote about a few years ago; life cannot be played without stakes; life is inseparable from some form of risk. As my life becomes more and more an established thing, a certain division tends to be made between what concerns me and what does not concern me, a division which appears rational enough in the making. Each one of us thus becomes the centre of a sort of mental space, arranged in concentric zones of decreasing interest and decreasing adherence, and to this decreasing adherence there corresponds an increasing non-disposability. This is something so natural that we forget to give it any thought or any representation at all. Some of us may have happened upon an encounter which in some fashion broke up the lines of this personal egocentric topography. I can understand, for I have experienced it, that from a stranger, casually met, may come a call too strong to be resisted: suddenly all our perspectives are turned inside-out; what seemed inseparably near is suddenly at an infinite distance, and the distant near. Such experiences are fleeting, breaches that are instantly closed, and yet I believe that these experiences—however disappointing, and they can be so disappointing that they leave us with a bitter sadness and sense of mockery at our very hearts—still have this inestimable benefit; they force us to become sharply aware of the accidental character of what I have called our mental space, and of the rigidities on which its possibility rests. Above all there is sanctity, realised in certain people, which is there to show us that what we call the normal state is assuredly, from one point of view, simply the perversion of a state diametrically opposed to it.

It is doubtless a metaphysical falsity to say 'I am my life'. The statement implies a confusion which thought will bring to light. The confusion is not only inevitable, but it even lies at the roots of the human drama and gives it a part of its meaning. The drama would lose its majesty if the man who laid down his life did not find himself so placed that the sacrifice could—or must, if faith is lacking—seem to him to be a total sacrifice.

We must see that in presuming to break fundamentally with what I called the normal state of secular experience, we should be guilty not only of rashness, but also of real error, unless we were responding to some clarion call. All that we can do is to admit, at least in thought, that these conditions imply an anomaly if we look at them from that transcendent point of view which something within us seems to demand that we should occupy.

Could we not maintain that what we call space, in the ordinary sense of the word, is really nothing but a kind of translation of the system of concentric zones which I described above? But, in this connection, we may ask whether the doing away with distance has not a twofold significance. It implies a change in our physical idea of space, but at the same time it deprives the distinction between the far and the near of its qualitative value. There is no parallel result, it seems, with regard to time: but this is just because the past escapes our grasp because it *is* the past, because it is essentially something before which we are powerless. Even here we should go still deeper: for if the materiality (!) of the past is immutable, it still takes on a different value and colour according to the aspect from which we consider it, and this aspect varies with our present, that is to say, it varies with the changes in our action. (I quote an example which happened to come into my mind. A man has lived a lightless life and worked himself to death, perhaps in despair. It obviously depends upon those who come after him to bring out the consequences of his life which are capable of giving it meaning and worth *a posteriori*. Yet even this is not enough. Something in us demands that those consequences should be known to the man who by his life, by his obscure sacrifice, made them possible. We must ask what this demand is worth: is it *de jure* valid? and up to what point should we say that real fact can ignore it? Difficult questions to put in an intelligible way.)

The connection of non-disposability—and consequently non-presence—with self-preoccupation. A kind of mystery there; I believe we could find a whole theory of the Thou within it. When I am with a non-disposable person, I am conscious of being with someone for whom I do not exist, and so I am thrown back upon myself.

Can I define God as absolute presence? This would embrace my idea of absolute succour.

Being non-disposable; being occupied with self. But this 'with self' needs consideration. We can see by analysis that there is no difference, from the point of view I am taking up, between being occupied with one's health, one's future, one's mistress, or one's temporal success. Surely the conclusion follows that to be occupied with one's-self is not to be occupied with a determinate object, but rather to be occupied in a certain way which remains to be defined. We might approach our definition by way of the idea of a spiritual opaqueness or blockage. When I look at my own deepest experience, it seems to me that in every such case, we are conscious of being fixed within a zone or determinate scale, in an anxiety which is itself essentially indeterminate. But, contrary to what a superficial inquiry would seem to show, this anxiety (even, this indeterminacy) remains present at the heart of the fixation; it gives a character of *exasperation* which causes it to remain compatible with the agitation constantly going on at the centre of this limited zone. This anxiety —here I join with Heidegger and perhaps Kierkegaard—this anxiety is surely the agony of a creature living in time, the agony of feeling one's-self at the mercy of time. (Not that it is necessary to bring in here the element of reflection properly so called.) The agony brings with it *unhope*—a word from one of Thomas Hardy's poems—and this *unhope* in relation to a determinate object changes to *despair*. In contrast to all this see what we mean by 'not caring'.

If all this is well-founded, *the metaphysical origins of pessimism are the same as the origins of non-disposability*. This should be related to what I have said about joy and hope.

We must return to my former observation, that the make-up of our universe admits of hope, and we must see its ontological significance.

We shall also have to ask whether the Thou, regarded as worth or reality, is not a function of what I have called my inward disposability. And we must study the place of hope in the theory of the Thou (what is *putting trust in?*—putting your trust in the universe?).

Anxiety, as I called it, seen as a radical deformity, as a datum (or at least possible datum) that is universal. The most concrete image I can form of it is drawn from the horrible feeling I have sometimes had in the dark, of feeling myself at its mercy, with nothing to hold on to.

I am wondering just now whether there are not grounds for showing that the various technical accomplishments are salutary weapons of defence against this state of powerlessness. They by no means imply in themselves that fixation of which I spoke. There is a healthful value in doing as such. But it is possible to pass on to the idolatry of technical ability, analysed elsewhere in this book.

It is so important to show that fear and desire are both on the same level, and inseparable, but that hope is placed in another zone, which is not that of Spinozan ethics and with which Spinoza himself was unacquainted. (Spinoza spoke of *spes* and *metus* correlatively; and our natural inclination is certainly to do the same.) The zone of hope is also that of prayer.

March 15th

On analysing the question closely, we find that the nature of hope is very hard to define. I will take two examples: to hope for the recovery from illness or for the conversion of a person dear to us, and to hope for the liberation of one's oppressed country. The hope here is for something which, according to the order of nature, does not depend upon us (it is absolutely outside the zone where stoicism can be practised). At the root of the hope is the consciousness of a state of things which invites us to despair (illness, damnation, etc.). To hope is to put one's trust in reality, to assert that it contains the means of triumphing over this danger; and here it can be seen that the correlative of hope is not fear, far from it, but the act of making

74

the worst of things, a sort of pessimistic fatalism which assumes the impotence of reality or which will not grant that it can take account of something even if it is not just *our* good, but rather, as we think, a good in the absolute sense of the word.

This evening I have apprehended the nature of hope more clearly than I have ever done before.

It always has to do with the restoration of a certain living order in its integrity.

But it also carries with it the affirmation of eternity and eternal goods.

It is therefore of her very essence that when Hope has been deceived in the realm of the visible, she should take refuge on a plane where she can be disappointed no more. This links up with my most time-honoured meditations on the unverifiable, which were a groping anticipation of what I see clearly today.

Even the integrity of the organism—when I hope for the recovery of an invalid—is, as it were, the prefiguring or symbolical expression of a supreme integrity.

In this sense I say that all hope is hope of salvation, and that it is quite impossible to treat of the one without treating of the other. But in someone like Spinoza, and also among the disciples of Stoicism, this idea of salvation is literally stripped of all meaning. There is no place for salvation except in a universe which *admits of real injuries*.

It should now be shown that the object of desire is never integrity as such, but that it is always a mode of enjoying, just as the object of fear is a mode of suffering. But salvation is undoubtedly above this opposition. Yet all this is still not quite clear to me.

I was thinking this morning that hope is only possible in a world where there is room for miracles; and this evening the sense of this reflection is becoming clearer to me. Here, too, I believe I join forces with Kierkegaard, or at least with some of his continuators.

If I have discerned rightly, there is a close bond of union between hope and a certain affirmation of eternity, that is, of a transcendent order.

On the other hand—as I say in *Remarks on the Irreligion of Today* —a world where techniques are paramount is a world given over to desire and fear; because every technique is there to serve some desire or some fear. It is perhaps characteristic of Hope to be unable either to make direct use of any technique or to call it to her aid. Hope is proper to the unarmed; it is the weapon of the unarmed, or (more exactly) it is the very opposite of a weapon and in that, mysteriously enough, its power lies. Present-day scepticism about hope is due to the essential inability to conceive that anything can be efficacious when it is no sort of a power in the ordinary sense of that word.

Here I am afraid we come up against one of the hardest of metaphysical problems, and one which seems almost a contradiction in terms. We cannot help asking ourselves how hope can be effective; but the very form of the question takes it for granted that we are unconsciously comparing hope to a technique which operates in a mysterious fashion, let us say magically.[1]

We must be perfectly clear that this real efficacy, which is the counterpart of a complete inefficacy on the phenomenal level, can only be conceived when the powerlessness is in fact absolute; where there is no pretence or evasion (such as we find in a consciousness which through sloth or cowardice falsely persuades itself that it can do nothing).

Could we not say that a certain activity—we should have to clarify the sense of the word later—finding its way barred in the empirical realm, that is, in the realm of action, changes its level and

[1] It is hardly necessary to point out that all this has a bearing on the metaphysical problem of prayer.

turns into hope, but for all that does not lose the efficacy with which it was in some manner endowed from its birth? There is a kind of parallel to this in what happens to a river when its course is dammed by an obstruction. I would say that the estuaries of Hope do not lie entirely within the bounds of the visible world.

Hence, perhaps, we can see why the prayers of a defenceless creature are endowed with a greater efficacy.

And yet I know quite well that here I am merely skirting the problem, and that I cannot escape from *stating* it, and from *asking myself* confusedly what sort of power can belong to *no-action* and to *no-technique*. We are here at the heart of the problems raised by the essential Christian data, especially non-resistance to evil.

I can just make out the following in a very disjointed way:

(1) We are no longer in the realm of causes or laws, the realm of the universal. Hope not being a cause, and not acting mechanically, it is quite obvious that we cannot say, 'Every time somebody practises the virtue of hope, such and such a thing will come to pass:' for this would in fact mean that we were making hope into a technique, that is to say, into its own opposite (incidentally, I notice what a strong temptation there is to regard it in this light).

(2) Is it not clear that the efficacy of hope, in some cases, lies in its *disarming* value? In the case of non-resistance at least, this is quite intelligible. If I oppose violence, that is, if I put myself on the same ground as violence, it is quite certain that I tend to keep it up and thereby even to reinforce it; in this sense it is true to say that all combat implies a sort of fundamental connivance between the two sides, a common will for the battle to go on; this state of affairs does not end until they reach the point where it becomes radically impossible to treat war as if it were a game, and the will to destroy takes its place; and this will lets loose an opposite (i.e. an identical) will on the other side. Could we not maintain that the will to destroy cannot be justified in its own eyes unless an identical will

can be presumed in the other, that is, the enemy? Can it conceive itself except as lawful defence? If it thenceforth meets with non-resistance, it is negated at once, is completely disarmed.

I hasten to add that I have the gravest hesitation in concluding from these reflections that unilateral disarmament is *de jure* justified. If we had to examine the question, we should begin by asking why the transition from the metaphysical to the empirical should raise such serious difficulties in this province.

It would seem, then, that Hope has the unusual virtue of some-how putting in a false predicament the powers over which it claims to triumph, not by fighting them, far from it, but by transcending them. Moreover, its efficacy seems all the surer when the weakness accompanying it is more real and less of a sham; in other words, when it is less liable to be considered as a hypocritical disguise of cowardice.

The spontaneous objections we feel against this way of thinking may seem almost irresistible. For instance, how can we explain a recovery from illness in that way?

But then it must be not forgotten that it is in the invisible world that Hope flows out to sea. Hope is nothing like a short cut for pedestrians, taken when the road is blocked and joining the road again on the other side of the obstacle.

No need to say that all these reflections go hand-in-hand with my remarks on non-disposability. The more non-disposable a man is, the less room there is in him for hope. And we should here mention the growing non-disposability of the whole modern world.

I wondered this afternoon whether the efficacy of hope might not be related to the very force of the grip on reality which it pre-supposed (this is the working-out of what I was writing yesterday evening about integrity). But this interpretation, though attractive, is a little dangerous. To tell the truth I still do not see my way clearly. The problem is infinitely complicated by the fact that hope obviously partakes of the nature of 'gift' or 'merit'. This must be sifted out methodically, but I do not yet know how to go about my task.

We ought to note, without delay, the point at which hope overflows the affirmation of a *sollen*. It is really a prophetic power. It has no bearing on what *should* be or even on what *must* be; it just says 'This will be'. Reflecting on hope is perhaps our most direct means of apprehending the meaning of the word 'transcendence', for hope is a spring, it is the leaping of a gulf.

It implies a kind of radical refusal to reckon possibilities, and this is enormously important. It is as though it carried with it as postulate the assertion that reality overflows all possible reckonings; as though it claimed, in virtue of some unknown secret affinity, to touch a principle hidden in the heart of things, or rather in the heart of events, which mocks such reckonings. Here I might quote excellent sayings from Péguy and perhaps Claudel, which touch the very depths of my own perceptions.

Hope, in this sense, is not only a protestation inspired by love, but a sort of call, too, a desperate appeal to an ally who is Himself also Love. The supernatural element which is the foundation of Hope is as clear here as its transcendent nature, for nature, unilluminated by hope, can only appear to us the scene of a sort of immense and inexorable book-keeping.[1]

Another point; I wonder if we do not see here some of the limitations of Bergsonian philosophy, for it seems to me that there is not the least room in it for what I call integrity. To a Bergsonian, salvation lies in pure freedom; to a metaphysic which is Christian in its

---

[1] We should ask ourselves what sort of science leads to despair, and how far a science of this sort damns itself. The problem of hope and science, still more fundamental than the problem of determinism and freedom. I shall have to take up the idea of perdition again, which has already attracted me at an earlier stage. See how hope, in its essence, dives into the invisible world. (Note written Dec. 8th, 1931.)

essence, freedom has an aim assigned to it, and that aim is salvation. I can only repeat once more, that the archetypal hope is the hope of salvation; but it seems that salvation can only be found in contemplation. I do not think we can reach beyond this.

The lines I wrote this afternoon on not-reckoning possibilities lead me to think that we ought to bring together hope and will (not, of course, the same thing as desire). Is not hope a will whose field of operation is in infinity? A formula to be worked out fully.

Just as there can be an evil will, so we should be able to conceive a diabolical hope, a hope which is perhaps the very essence of him whom we call the Devil.

Will, hope, prophetic vision: all this stands, all this is firmly fixed in a man, outside the range of a purely objective reason. I shall now have to develop the notion of disillusionment, the idea of a power of automatic refutation belonging to experience as such. The soul lives by hope alone; hope is perhaps the very stuff of which our souls are made. This, too, should be worked out. To despair of a man—is not this to deny him as a soul? To despair of one's-self—is it not anticipating suicide?

March 22nd, 1931 (a miserable Sunday)

Time is like a well whose shaft goes down to death—to my death—to my perdition.

The gulf of time: how I shudder to look down on time! My death is at its bottom and its dank breath mounts up and chills me.

March 25th

We must finish with the notion of divine prescience, which distorts everything and makes the problem absolutely insoluble: from the moment we assume that the divine vision is prior, in whatever sense, to the free action to which it refers, we cannot avoid pre-destination. And yet we must not fall into the opposite error of speaking of God's *observation*, as Father A—— was doing yesterday at Berdyaev's. God does not *observe* anything.

I think I see it something like this. First of all, this apprehension of my act by God cannot be posited as an objective datum (in the sense in which I might say, for instance, that someone is at this moment picking up my words by wireless). It cannot be conceived by me unless I am myself on a certain spiritual level. I still cannot see clearly what follows from this, but I feel it will be important.

March 27th

Substitute co-presence for prescience. But co-presence cannot be expressed in terms of co-existence. We must never forget that God is not 'someone who' etc.

I was led yesterday to consider more closely the distinction between thinking and understanding. Is there perhaps something rather fallacious about the idea of a thought which is *not* understanding? Surely thinking, in that case, is just believing that one thinks?

We only understand on the basis of what we are. It seems to me that co-presence can only be understood by a person placed in a certain spiritual position. Here again we come back to the metaphysic of the Thou and the notion of non-disposability. The more non-disposable I am, the more will God appear to me as 'someone who'.[1] And that is just a denial of co-presence. We should try to see how memory comes in here, memory considered as fidelity (to an act of comprehension remembered but not renewable at will).

[1] It seems to me that this lays bare the very roots of atheism. The God whom atheism denies is in fact a 'someone who' in his very essence.

Relate the notion of non-disposability with my earlier remarks on 'my body'.

I shall use the word 'corporeity' to mean that property which makes it impossible for me to picture a body as living except on condition of thinking of it as the 'body of . . .'.

Corporeity to be regarded as the frontier district between being and having. All having defines itself somehow in terms of *my body*, i.e. in terms of something which, being itself an absolute 'having' ceases in virtue of this very fact to be a 'possession' in any sense of the word. 'Having' is being able to dispose of, having a power over; it seems clear to me that this disposal or power always implies the interposal of the organism, i.e. of something about which, for that very reason, I cannot say that it is at my disposal. The metaphysical mystery of non-disposability may essentially consist in the impossibility, for me, of really being able to dispose of that which gives me the disposal of things. The objection may be made that I can nevertheless dispose of my body since I have the physical power of killing myself. But it is obvious that such a disposal of my body has as its immediate result the impossibility of disposing of it, and even coincides with this impossibility in the final analysis. My body is something of which I can only dispose, in the absolute sense of the term, by putting it into such a state that I shall no longer have any power to dispose of it. This absolute disposal is therefore in reality a putting out of use.

Shall we be tempted to object that I dispose of my body to the extent that, for instance, I change my position? But obviously, in another sense, and to an equal extent, I entrust myself to it and depend upon it.

In short, it is clear that I try with all my will to establish conditions such that I can *think* I dispose of my body. But it is no less clear that there is something in my very nature which blocks my power even really to make this relation between my body and me the same as my relation with other things, and this is because of the sort of irresistible encroachment of my body upon me which is at the basis of my state as man or creature.[1]

March 30th

Reflected this morning on 'having'. It seems evident to me that 'having' always implies an obscure notion of assimilation (I only have something which has been made mine, in some way, no matter what), and it therefore also implies reference to a past. On the one hand, we cannot help connecting having with the notion

[1] I think I have not made full enough use of these remarks. They seem to me to open perspectives, which are relatively new, upon a whole group of obscure problems centring round what may be called physical miracle, or more accurately upon the hidden connections which undoubtedly exist between the realisation of a certain degree of inner perfection (sanctity) and what appears to us as the exercise of supra-normal powers. Perhaps a man is really less of a slave to his body in proportion as he makes less of a claim to have it at his disposal. May it not be that this claim, which looks like a sign of power, is really a form of slavery? A throng of conclusions would follow. The problem of miraculous cures, in particular, should be considered from this point of view. It would not be out of place to ask whether the fact of self-surrender or self-abandonment might not have as a result (not, of course, a *necessary* result) a change in the union of the soul and body, as we so confusedly call it. It is conceivable that the rebellious invalid, who by definition clings to the claim to dispose of his body in his own sense, but who is actually forced to recognise at the same time that his claim is ignored by 'reality', finds himself *ipso facto* placed in a state of non-disposability which is even physical, and which is far more radical than that experienced by the other invalid who surrenders himself to a superior power, whatever his idea of that power may be. I will do no more than call attention to this. It would be rashness, even folly, to attempt a stricter treatment of the theme, and there could be no question of actually admitting that the invalid's act of putting himself in God's hand automatically causes his state to change for the better. If it were so, the act of surrender would lose its character; worse, it would, by becoming an expedient, actually change into its opposite. Surely this is an object-lesson of the workings of the mysterious link between liberty and grace. (Note written August, 1934.)

of containing; only we must clearly see that the container is not the haver. The haver is the subject in so far as it carries with it a container; it is almost impossible to put it precisely. At the root of 'having', then, there is an immediate term which causes 'something' to participate in its own immediacy. In fact it seems to me that corporeity (as I called it yesterday) is involved in having—just as corporeity implies what we may call historicity. A body is a history, or more accurately it is the outcome, the fixation of a history. I cannot therefore say that I have a body, at least not properly speaking, but the mysterious relation uniting me to my body is at the foundation of all my powers of having.

I have a feeling that much could be drawn from this in treating the far more concrete problems which have occupied my thoughts in these latter times, because of the connection between non-disposability and having. Having is a sort of signpost of possible non-disposability. The dead man is the man who no longer has anything (at least if we take the word 'have' in those senses which we can make precise). We are tempted to think that no longer having anything is the same as no longer being anything: and in fact the general trend of life on the natural level is to identify one's-self with what one has: and here the ontological category tends to be blotted out. But the reality of sacrifice is there somehow to prove to us in fact that being *can* assert its transcendency over having. There lies the deepest significance of martyrdom considered as witness: it *is* the witness.

The reflection which I have followed out this evening seems to me to be of the first importance: it gives us the most concrete possible way of understanding the ontological problem. But we must still take note that this negation of having, or rather of the correlation between having and being, cannot be separated from an affirmation on which it hangs. Here I will stop as I am seeing less clearly.

I am sure of this, anyhow: of the hidden identity of the way

84

which leads to holiness and the road which leads the metaphysician to the affirmation of Being; also that it is necessary above all, for a concrete philosophy, to realise that here is one and the same road. I would add that the significance of human trials, especially illness and death, and their ontological bearing, is here made plain. Only it is an essential character of such trials that they can be misunderstood. They are an appeal to a power of interpretation or assimilation which is identical with freedom itself.[1]

March 31st

Suffering: surely this is being touched in point of what we have, in so far as what we have has become an integral part of what we are? Physical suffering to be regarded as the prototype or root of all suffering.

Coming back from my walk I was wondering what we mean by 'having an idea'. I think there is a difficulty here. But even here I think that the process may be compared to a graft which is made upon a growing thing ('grafting upon' expresses my meaning much better than 'integration into'): that which grows tends, if not to think of itself *as* a vehicle, at least to seem to itself to be *endowed with* a vehicle.

But we might perhaps think that corporeity is not necessarily implied in the reality of this 'growing' or 'living' principle. Is our 'absolute having' of our bodies (which is, by the way, no 'having' at all) really a condition of a spiritual 'having' such as I referred to above? I cannot yet see the answer clearly, or rather I cannot manage to put the question in terms which seem fully intelligible even to myself. Yet it looks as if, here too, I have come back to the basic problem of attention, which has so much occupied my mind in the past.

[1] I think I should here point out the fundamental agreement between these views and those of Jaspers, which I did not know in 1931. (Note written August, 1934.)

This I do see: that the privilege or primacy which I ascribe to my mental equipment, and to what belongs to it, is conceived—or imagined—by analogy with the fundamental and unthinkable privilege which distinguishes my body in so far as it is mine. In this privilege my ideas, in so far as they are mine, have an indirect share.

Would it make sense to say that having and being are, as it were, essential concentrations of space and time? I am not sure.

April 7th

I shall not pursue this line of thought.

One thing is plain to me. Having is always the way in which I give suffering a hold upon me: but surely this is because having is in fact multiplicity? A being wholly simple, that is, entirely one, could not be subject to suffering.[1] But can this absolute simplicity

[1] None of the great metaphysicians of the past was ignorant of this truth: but it can disguise serious ambiguities. It is, for instance, quite clear that there is in fact a zone on the hither side of suffering. One can imagine, or rather conceive of, a being who is too rudimentary, too essentially undifferentiated, to be capable of suffering. But would it then still be a *being*? It is obvious (to me) that the condition, to which all the sages of all time and of every country urge us to raise ourselves, has nothing to do with such a unity as this. The difference is basically the same as the difference between the One and matter in Plotinus. But words are fundamentally unsuitable for stating this difference clearly, for the simple reason that they belong to the realm of discursive thought, and therefore we continually run the risk of falling into a confusion here which may have incalculable consequences; and if I am completely honest, I must recognise that I cannot avoid asking whether this confusion does not really spoil a certain type of asceticism, at least in some degree. We have here a group of questions to be boldly attacked after wiping all the traditional formulae right off the slate. We must never lose sight of the fact that salvation can only be found in plenitude, though of course we shall admit that a certain kind of richness, under whatever forms it appears, is so far from bringing us to salvation that it even withdraws us from it. But the problem in fact is how to pass through multiplicity so as to transcend it, and not at all how to escape it. (Note written August, 1934.)

be realised? It seems to me that there may be pseudo-mysticism here, a source of very serious difficulties.

April 8th

Metaphysics considered as a means of exorcising despair.

There is one philosophy which clearly claims to exorcise hope and despair at the same time; I mean that of Spinoza. I chiefly blame him for fundamentally ignoring the temporal structure of human existence. The Bergsonian position on this level seems to me impregnable.

I was thinking to myself this evening that I shall have to consider the need for an absolute evaluation, the need to be judged. (Cf. the conclusion of *Un Homme de Dieu*.)

April 10th

I see the clear necessity, this morning, of substituting the question 'Am I my life?' for 'Am I my body?' My body, if deprived of motion, is just my corpse. Now my corpse is essentially what I am *not*, and what I cannot be (and this is what we mean when we say of a dead man, 'he is no more'). But when I assert that I have a body, it is clear that I am really tending in fact to immobilise this body in some fashion and almost to devitalise it. I wonder now if having *qua* having does not always imply in some degree a devitalisation of this kind, in exact proportion as it corresponds to an incipient thraldom.

The difficulty is to understand how it can be metaphysically false to say 'I am my life' without its being legitimate to conclude from thence 'I have my life' or 'I have a life'. Here we return, I think, to my reflections of March 27th. I have only the absolute disposal of my life (we will no longer say, of my body) if I put myself in such a condition that I can never dispose of it again; here we meet the irrevocable. This is strikingly obvious in the case of suicide or the sacrifice of life, but it is really just as true of any act at all.

But the notion of irrevocability must be examined and expanded, otherwise the difference between suicide and sacrifice becomes unintelligible and even unthinkable. This difference entirely depends on hope. There is not, and there cannot be, any sacrifice without hope, and a sacrifice which excluded hope would be suicide. Here the question of disinterestedness arises. But we must make up our minds whether it is legitimate to identify disinterestedness and despair. It is true that the claim will certainly be made that where I hope *for myself* there can be no question of disinterestedness, but only where my hope is fixed on an order or a cause for whose good I give myself up. But it is our duty to ask if the meaning of the expression 'for myself' is as clear as it seems, or rather as clear as we are at first inclined to say. And here we shall in fact have to proceed in rather the same way as I did on March 15th: we shall first have to discover the nature of this hope *for one's-self*, and then (a deeper question) the nature of the *for one's-self* which remains at the heart of sacrifice.[1]

[1] The revolutionary who consents to die for the revolution, the party, etc., identifies himself with that for which he gives his life. And accordingly the party or the revolution becomes, for him, 'more myself than I am myself.' This is the adherence, this the identification which is at the heart of his act and gives it meaning. Someone will say: 'Yes, but he makes no claim to *see* the triumph of the cause for which he gives himself, no claim to enjoy it and so profit by it; and therefore he renounces all reward, all recompense. Whereas the Christian, for instance, fancies that he will himself be personally associated with the victory that he helps to prepare for, and so thinks that he will be in some way able to profit by it. You cannot therefore speak of disinterestedness in his case.'

The whole question depends on discovering what precise value we may attribute to the act by which, anticipating what I call my own annihilation, I nevertheless devote myself to preparing for a state of affairs subsequent to it, a state which I declare myself unable to enjoy. And here it seems that there are mistakes and illusions in plenty. 'I shall not enjoy it,'

I now take up once more my idea about the ontological hazard, life as implying a certain hazard which does not belong to the order of life. It is obvious that there is one type of experience which is by no means capable of confirming the notion. It is an essential element of this hazard that it can be denied; we might well ask what sense this denial would have.

This hazard I propose to call by the name of Soul. It is one of the essentials of the soul thus conceived that it may be saved or lost, precisely in so far as it is a hazard. This is worthy of notice, and

I say. And yet in a way I do enjoy it in advance; this enjoyment is at least as much the object of my anticipation as is my own destruction; what is more, it may be that this enjoyment is the only thing I do anticipate; for my destruction, as such, is just a void, and in so far as it is a void is not able to be anticipated. Still more, the idea that I shall no longer exist may increase my enjoyment, may clothe it in an element of pride or vanity which gives the enjoyment a sharper quality. But—and this is the crucial thing—this is just my *present state*, and not at all the question of whether I shall survive. My much-boasted disinterestedness seems to me, from this point of view, to contain an element of pride, or rather of defiance, which perhaps spoils it. How do I meet the hostile reality which is about to annihilate me? First I snap my fingers at it, then I claim to contribute in my own person to its shaping. Contrary to what we often think, there is no less humble attitude than this, nor any that implies a haughtier claim.

Our critics will no doubt return to the charge, saying that the revolutionary, for instance, who does not believe in his own immortality, does recognise *ipso facto* that he himself is unimportant, and that his personality is unimportant. But I think that is really just a displacement of what I will call his moral centre of gravity. The cause for which he devotes himself, as cause, is itself only an element of his own personality regarded as absolute.

They will say again, 'The sacrifice which is inspired by the hope of a recompense thereby ceases to be a sacrifice.' Obviously. But how false and how shallow is the psychology which represents the sacrifice of a believer as the result of calculation! Such sacrifice is carried on the stream, as it were, of hope and love. This does not detract from its value, far from it; and the contrary can only be maintained by those who cling to a clearly connected with the fact that the soul is not an object and can by no means be regarded as an object. For an object, the fact of being lost or retained ('saved' would be meaningless) remains accidental with regard to its own nature, which can be regarded as unaffected by the fact that the object is or is not lost (for instance a piece of jewellery).

This must be related with what I have written on 'having'.

On the one hand my soul seems to me that to which the relation (?) implied in the fact of 'having' seems least applicable; it is, of everything in the world, the least comparable to a possession.

hyper-Kantian moral formalism which would go so far as to eliminate the postulates of practical reason. And anyhow everything leads us to think that where neither the love of God nor the love of one's neighbour comes in, the real factor is the love of self; and that is a fundamental pretension to which we see no reason to grant an intrinsic value. I realise, of course, that some religious writers may have involuntarily helped to obscure the essential issues, by seeming to set up a scale of merits, which would have the effect of absolutely ruining the idea of sacrifice taken in its pure sense, that is to say, as consecration. I think we must begin with the idea of the *consecrated soul* if we are to dispose of these hoary misunderstandings. We then see that the soul which is consecrated is also indwelt with an unconquerable hope; she aspires to enter into an intimacy with her God, an intimacy ever greater, ever more complete. She has no reason to think that there can be any merit—quite the contrary —in her fighting against this aspiration. For this very reason, that she knows herself to be barren of intrinsic worth, that she knows that she derives from God whatever is positive within her—so that in disregarding herself she is disparaging God's gift, and incurring the shame of monstrous ingratitude. What worth could we see in the fact of a son's refusing to believe that his father loves him? This mistake begins from the moment when the creature begins to assign rights to himself and to treat himself as a creditor. It is more than an alteration, it is a radical perversion. But let us not forget that the unbeliever also often thinks of himself as the creditor of a God who will not pay, and this is serious in a different way.

We have here, I think, the elements of a criterion for judging whether the belief in immortality has any religious value in it or not: the whole question is whether it looks like an act of faith and love, or like an arrogation rooted in the concern for self. (Note written August, 1934.)

On the other hand, its possible loss is, as it were, the reverse side or disastrous counterpart of all possession.

But then it would seem that the soul is that which can least of all be lost.

This apparent contradiction allows us to unmask an ambiguity bound up in the very notion of loss. Could we not say that there is a loss on the level of Being[1] (it is in this sense and on this level that the soul can be lost) and also a loss on the level of having which is related to the actual nature of objects? But we should observe at the same time (this is of prime importance) that every loss in the order of having constitutes a threat to what I have called the

[1] Loss on the level of being is, properly speaking, perdition. Yet we must recognise that this distinction does not give a full account of the reality, which is curiously complex. For a clearer view, the reader should doubtless refer to indications already given on integrity with regard to hope. Hope (one cannot repeat too often) can only take root where perdition is a possibility, and it is the most instructive exercise imaginable to note that in this respect no distinction need be made between the order of life properly speaking, and the order of the soul. It is equally legitimate to hope for the recovery of a sick person and the return of the prodigal son. In both cases the hope is bent on the re-establishment of an order accidentally upset. We can go further; there is a sense in which even the recovery of something lost may admit of hope. But it can clearly be seen that there is here a sort of descending scale with hope at one end of it in its most fervent form, deeply rooted in God, and, at the other end, hope at its most selfish and superstitious; it would be extremely interesting somehow to follow the steps of this downward scale. Following this line, we should see clearly that the more the loss is related to possession, the more the protest it inspires looks like the assertion of a right; and the attitude of the man who makes this protest, who asserts this claim, proportionally ceases to be identified with hope in its pure state as defined above. Indeed, it may be that genuine hope always consists in awaiting a certain grace, the nature of whose power we may not clearly define to ourselves, but to whose bounty we think we can assign no end. Hope is centred in our consciousness of this beneficent power; whereas standing on one's rights is a thing which revolves, by definition, round the consciousness of self and its dues. (Note written August, 1934.)

soul and runs the risk of turning into a loss on the level of being: we return here to the problem of despair and what I wrote about death (*March 30th*).

My life. The fact that it can seem to me to be literally devoid of meaning is an integral part of its structure. It then appears to me as pure accident. But then, what is this 'I' which finds itself incomprehensibly dowered with this absurd existence, dowered with something which is the very reverse of a gift? It is irresistibly driven to self-negation: this life can have been given by nobody, it is in reality the life of—nobody. No doubt this thorough-going nihilism is just an extreme position, a position very difficult to hold and implying a kind of heroism. But here we are deep in contradictions, since this heroism, if it is experienced and recognised as such, immediately re-establishes the subject, and at the same time restores to existence the meaning that was denied to it; it does at least in fact exhibit one value; it serves as a springboard for the consciousness which denies it. And so, for the initial position to be maintained, it must not be made explicit, but instead be reduced to an auto-anaesthesia which, though it can take all sorts of different forms *in concreto*, yet remains in reality identical with itself as regards its essential characteristics.

Someone will object that the refusal to treat one's life as a hazard is not necessarily the same thing as abandonment to this state of anaesthesia and voluntary passivity. But just because life is being treated as an absolute (as something which does not exist in relation to anything else) it may at least be a recognition of the right to set one's-self free of it if certain conditions are not realised. Here the data become extremely complex. Life is really being identified with a kind of plenitude, a kind of expansiveness. When this plenitude or expansiveness is not forthcoming, such a life loses its intrinsic justification. I have grounds for saying that there is nothing to do but destroy myself. What is this 'I'? It is my life, which is this time ranged against itself and which has the amazing privilege of self-negation. It seems to follow from this that the thought of suicide dwells at the very heart of a life which is thought of and willed without a hazard (just as divorce is always kept within call when it arises from a union which implies no vow and has not been entered upon before anyone, and I think this parallel might be carried a long way).[1]

We cannot hope to find even there the clue for a purely logical refutation of the thesis upheld by the champions of suicide. Nothing will force us to conceive of the hazard; no objective reason can be found to stop us from killing ourselves. We are here at the common root of freedom and of faith.

December 9th, 1931

I return to the problem of hope. It seems to me that the conditions that make it possible to hope are strictly the same as those which make it possible to despair. Death considered as the springboard of an absolute hope. A world where death was missing would be a world where hope only existed in the larval stage.

December 10th, 1931

I was writing to L—— yesterday after reading his remarkable analysis of idealism: hope is to desire what patience is to passivity. This seems to me very important. Patience: I was thinking this

[1] I still think this parallel could be carried a long way, and that it is of a nature to throw greater light on the meaning of the Christian idea of the indissolubility of marriage. While thinking of this connection one might be led on to make this fact clear; that for a metaphysic of freedom and fidelity, the marriage tie has a substantial reality of its own, like what we call the union of the body and soul. To be quite honest, however, I must admit that this way of thinking makes me a little uneasy, and I find it hard to reconcile the lessons of experience (as I should be tempted to call them) with demands in the order of metaphysic and theology. (Note written August, 1934.)

morning of the patience of the scientist. But is not this rather like the huntsman's patience? We think of truth as a quarry, of a truth that is to be won. I wonder if at bottom the metaphysical problem of truth is not this, whether there is not something in truth which refuses to submit to the kind of subjection to which we try to reduce it.

A conversation with M—— infinitely profitable. He advises me to look at the book of Job and also proposes an unusual interpretation of Ecclesiastes (a philosophy providentially marked out as a possible frame of mind if . . .). He quoted to me this phrase from Cajetan: '*Spero Deum non propter me, sed mihi.*'

I said that hope, a purely Christian datum, enwrapped a notion of eternity quite different from that implied in the philosophy of '*nec spe nec metu*'. M—— also advises me to look at the notion of hope in St. John of the Cross; he does not, as I had feared, transcend hope. I told him of my concern to show how prophecy is only possible on a ground which is that of hope and not of knowledge: the common root of hope and of prophecy is—faith.

I was thinking just now on my way back of the coarser forms of hope: hope of winning the top prize. Importance of the idea of a lottery and the idea of assurance in the financial sense of the word. The claim to a guarantee against chance (treated in effect as an *element*, like heat or cold). We should also try to see how hope takes shape in prayer.

I was saying to M——, 'Looked at from outside, patience reduces to passivity, and hope reduces to desire.' Also: 'Hope may either be perverted, or emptied of its content, or impoverished of its ontological references.'

I have this moment noticed a problem. Could it not be objected that hope is a life-factor and bound up with life as such? The answer lies, I think, in showing that if this is so, it is in proportion as life itself is taken ontologically. This is all rather difficult, but it is a question that must be asked. The soul itself seems to me the intermediate term between life and hope.[1]

October 5th, 1932

Reread my remarks on the worth of life and the ontological problem, and on being as the place of fidelity. The centre of all my recent metaphysical development is here. The fundamental datum here is the fact that I can take a stand before life considered as a whole, that I can refuse it, that I can despair. And at this point I think we must entirely scout the interpretation that it is life itself which denies itself or refuses itself within me. A needless and perhaps nonsensical interpretation. Let us content ourselves, at least as a beginning, with facts as we know them. I put a value on my life It is in this province, and not in the province of knowledge, that the subject really confronts the object. I may add that here there is not really a separate action which may or may not be grafted on to life. To live, for man, is to accept life, to say 'Yes' to life; or else the opposite, to vow himself to a state of internal war, when in appearance he is acting as if he is accepting something, which, deep down, he refuses or believes he refuses. These remarks should be read in conjunction with what I have written elsewhere on the theme of existence.

The possibility of despair bound up with liberty. It is of the essence of liberty that it is able to be exerted in self-betrayal. Nothing which is outside ourselves can shut the door to despair. The way is

[1] For a commentary, see my note of April 12th, 1931. I think we cannot avoid placing life under a 'soul-sign' (a dreadful expression, but I cannot find a better) wherever we are speaking of a person treated or apprehended as 'thou'. If we separated the life from the soul, we should inevitably tend to turn it into essence, and this would be a subtle way of betraying it. (Cf. Antoine's remark in *Le Mort de Demain*, 'To love somebody is to say to him, "You will not die." ') (Note written August, 1934.)

open; one can even say that the world is so constructed that absolute despair appears possible in it. Things are constantly happening which counsel us, or so one would think, to drown ourselves in despair. This is of the first importance.

Fidelity considered as the recognition of something permanent. We are now beyond the opposition between understanding and feeling. The recognition of Ulysses by Eumaeus, of Christ on the road to Emmaus, etc., etc. The idea of an ontological permanence —the permanence of that which lasts, of that which implies history, as opposed to the permanence of an essence or a formal arrangement.

Witness considered as the beginning of things—the Church a perpetuated witness, an act of fidelity.

October 6th

It is an essential characteristic of the being to whom I give my fidelity to be not only liable to be betrayed, but also in some manner affected by my betrayal. Fidelity regarded as witness perpetuated; but it is of the essence of witness that it can be obliterated and wiped out. Must see how this obliteration can happen. Perhaps we think that witness is outworn, and no longer corresponds to reality.

Being is, as it were, attested. The senses are witnesses—this is important, and I think new: systematically ignored by idealism.

October 7th

The consideration arises: Is the object to which I have vowed myself worthy of my being consecrated to its service? The comparative values of causes.

Consider creative fidelity, a fidelity only safeguarded by being creative. Is its creative power in proportion to its ontological worth?

Fidelity can only be shown towards a person, never at all to a notion or an ideal. An absolute fidelity involves an absolute person.

96

Question: does not an absolute fidelity to a creature presuppose Him in whose sight I bind myself (as in the sacrament of marriage)?

It is not enough to say that we live in a world where betrayal is possible at every moment and in every form: betrayal of all by all and of each by himself. I repeat, this betrayal seems pressed upon us by the very shape of our world. The spectacle of death is a perpetual invitation to deny. The essence of our world is perhaps betrayal. But still, if we proclaim this betrayal, are not we becoming its accomplices?

Memory an ontological *sign*.[1] Inseparable from witness. Is it not the essence of man to be a being who can bear witness?

The problem of the metaphysical foundation of witness is obviously as central as any. Not elucidated. 'I was there, I assert that I was there.' The whole of history is the function of a witness which it prolongs: in this sense history is rooted in religion.

While I was walking about just now between the Pantheon and the Boulevard Raspail, a great many other things came into my head. My brain feels amazingly fertile.

I was thinking, too, of the Rite, as giving rhythm to fidelity, and of the betrayal which lurks in the very heart of religious practice under the form of habit. This is relevant to my notes this morning about creative fidelity. Surely this is, besides, the very definition of saintliness?

I also begin to realise the deeper meaning of piety towards the dead, taken as the refusal to betray a person who has existed by treating him just as no longer existing. It is an active protest against a kind of trick of appearances, a refusal to yield to it or to lend one's self wholeheartedly to the game. If you say 'they no longer exist', you are not only denying them, you are also denying yourself and perhaps making an absolute denial.

[1] Telepathy is surely in regard to space what memory is in regard to time. It is beside the point that telepathy only appears in flashes.

I believe that at last I have begun to see the possibility of examining the very idea of proving the existence of God, with regard to the Thomist proofs. It is a fact that they are not universally convincing. How can we explain their partial ineffectiveness? The arguments presuppose that we have already grounded ourselves on God, and what they are really doing is to bring to the level of discursive thought an act of a wholly different kind. These, I believe, are not ways, but blind ways, as one can have blind windows.

Thinking of all this, I began to wonder whether my instrument of thought is a reflexive intuition, whose nature should be defined more closely.

Perhaps we are living in a specially favourable period for religion, because that betrayal whose home is the world is now shown in its true light. The fundamental illusions of the nineteenth century are now dispelled.

October 8th

'Reflexive intuition' is certainly not a happy expression. But what I mean is this. It seems to me that I am bound to admit that I am—anyhow on one level of myself—face to face with Being. In a sense I see it. In another sense I cannot say that I see it since I cannot grasp myself in the act of seeing it. The intuition is not, and cannot be, directly reflected in consciousness. But in turning towards its object, it sheds light upon a whole world of thoughts which lie beneath it. Metaphysically speaking, I do not see how else we can account for faith. It seems to me that this all comes very near to being Alexandrine theology, but I must make sure of this. I think that an intuition of this sort lies at the root of all fidelity, but its reality is always open to question. I can always say 'Yes, I *thought* I saw this, but I was mistaken'.

Am very much absorbed by the question of witness. Is not the province of witness the province of experience at large? Today we tend to think too little of witness and just to see in it the more or less accurate report of an *Erlebnis*. But if witness is only that, it is nothing, it is impossible; for absolutely nothing can guarantee that the *Erlebnis* will be capable of survival or confirmation. Compare what I said yesterday—the world the home of betrayal (conscious or unconscious), and knowing itself to be so with an ever-increasing clarity.

October 9th

It is possible for pure reason to attack witness *in toto*, and to pretend that no valid witness can really be produced. It is of the essence of particular witness that it should be capable of being doubted. We are tempted to extend this suspicion to all possible witness, to witness in itself. Is this proceedure really justifiable? Surely only justifiable if we are capable of defining *a priori* those conditions which a witness *should* fulfil if it is to be recognised as valid—and of showing furthermore that such conditions are not realised or, at the very least, that they cannot be shown to be realised. But here, as in the case of doubting one's existence, the issue is nothing less than the question of a root-and-branch devaluation both of memory and of all translation into conceptual terms of this *Erlebnis*, which is in itself inexpressible.

Surely it is of the essence of anything ontological that it can be no more than *attested*?

But the attestation must be the thought of itself; it can only be justified in the heart of Being and in reference to Being. In a world where *Erlebnis* is everything, in a world of simple instants, the attestation disappears; but then how can it be attestation if attestation is appearance?

October 10th

Attestation is a personal thing; it brings the personality into play, but it is at the same time turned towards Being, and is characterised by this tension between the personal and the ontological factors.

And yet, in all this I find something unsatisfactory; and I still cannot manage to formulate it in my own mind. I do see clearly, however, that I am in complete opposition to such attitudes as Grisebach's; I see in memory one essential aspect of the ontological assertion. How much nearer I feel to Bergson in this regard, and also to St. Augustine! What is witness in Bergson? surely a consecration. But the very notion of consecration is an ambiguous one, and we must beware of interpreting it in a pragmatist sense.

Notice that attesting means not only witnessing but also calling to witness. There is an essential triad-relation here. This in the sense of the *Journal Métaphysique*.[1]

October 22nd

THE POSITION OF THE ONTOLOGICAL MYSTERY: ITS CONCRETE APPROACHES.

This is the proposed title for my paper to the Marseilles Philosophical Society. The phrase 'mystery of being, ontological mystery' as against 'problem of being, ontological problem' has suddenly come to me in these last few days. It has enlightened me.

Metaphysical thought—reflection trained on mystery.

But it is an essential part of a mystery that it should be acknowledged; metaphysical reflection presupposes this acknowledgment, which is outside its own sphere.

Distinguish between the Mysterious and the Problematic. A problem is something met with which bars my passage. It is before me in its entirety. A mystery, on the other hand, is something in which I find myself caught up, and whose essence is therefore not to be before me in its entirety. It is as though in this province the distinction between *in me* and *before me* loses its meaning.

[1] See *Journal Métaphysique*, p. 145. (Translator's note.)

The Natural. The province of the Natural is the same as the province of the Problematic. We are tempted to turn mystery into problem.

The Mysterious and Ontological are identical. There is a mystery of knowledge which belongs to the ontological order (as Maritain saw) but the epistemologist does not know this, makes a point of ignoring it, and turns it into a problem.

A typical example: the 'problem of evil'. I treat evil as an accident befalling a certain mechanism which is the universe itself, but before which I suppose myself placed. Thereby I treat myself, not only as immune to the disease or weakness, but also as someone standing outside the universe and claiming to put it together (at least in thought) in its entirety.

But what access can I have to ontology as such? The very notion of access here is obviously inapplicable. It only has meaning in a problematic enquiry. If a certain place has already been plotted out, the question is then, how can I gain access to it. Impossible to treat being in this way.

Presence and mystery equivalent—probe further into this.

Predisposition for revelation. Whereas in a world-picture constructed from a problematic point of view, revelation appears to be supererogatory.

It follows from my definition of metaphysical thought as reflection trained upon mystery, that progress in this sort of thinking is not really conceivable. There is only progress in problematic thought.

It is a proper character of problems, moreover, to be reduced to detail. Mystery, on the other hand, is something which cannot be reduced to detail.

October 29th

A first question of the phenomenological order: whence comes the almost insuperable suspicion aroused by all researches into being in most minds, even those most inclined to metaphysic? I doubt if the right answer is to cite the persistent influence of Kantianism upon intellectuals: it has in fact considerably diminished. To tell the truth, Bergsonianism has here acted in the same way as Kantianism. I think that we really find a feeling which as a rule we could not formulate, but which I will try to describe by saying that we become more and more convinced that, strictly speaking, there is no problem of Being and no problematic approach to it: I believe that if we examined the very idea 'problem' more closely, that would be enough to convince us. A considerable hindrance here is the fact that we have acquired the execrable habit of considering the problems in themselves, that is, in abstraction from the manner in which their appearance is woven into the very texture of life. A scientist is privileged in this respect. A scientific problem arises at a given point in his research, it is something the mind stumbles upon as the foot stumbles upon a stone. Any problem whatever implies the provisional breaking-off of a continuity which the mind has to re-establish.

October 31st

Consider Being as the principle of inexhaustibility. Joy is bound up with a feeling of something inexhaustible, as Nietzsche saw. Return to my former remark on Being, that it is resistance to critical dissolution. This links up with my remarks on despair. A knotty point. The place of despair is where we can make an inventory (where we can say 'I have made my reckoning, and I shall not have the means of doing', etc.). But Being is above all inventories. Despair is, so to speak, the shock felt by the mind when it meets with 'There is no more'. 'Whatever comes to an end is too short' (St. Augustine).

But this principle of inexhaustibility is itself neither a characteristic nor a series of characteristics: here we return to the opposition between mystery and problem which I described above.

November 1st

Space and time considered as manifestations of inexhaustibility.[1]

The universe as the dehiscence of Being? A notion worth trying.

Every individual being in so far as it is a closed-up thing (though infinite) is a symbol or expression of the ontological mystery.

November 7th

Start from the uneasiness felt before the problem of Being, when it is stated in theoretical terms, and also the impossibility for us of not stating it on this level.

The technical correlated to the problematic; every genuine problem is subject to its own technique, and every technique consists in resolving problems of a determinate type. Can we posit—hypothetically—a metaproblematic, metatechnical sphere?

November 8th

Deeper reflection on the idea of a problem leads us to ask if there is not a touch of contradiction in the very act of posing a problem of being.

Philosophy on its metacritical side is directed towards a metaproblematic inquiry.

The need to restore its ontological weight to human experience.

The metaproblematic—the peace that passeth all understanding —eternity.

November 9th

Must scrutinise the meaning of what I called the ontological weight of human experience; here Jaspers may be useful.

Analyse such a formula as:

[1] But elsewhere I define them as paired modes of absence. There is a whole dialectic to be drawn from this, and it lies at the heart of both travel and history. (Note written October 8th, 1934.)

'I am only what I am worth (but I am worth nothing),' a philosophy which has its issue in despair and can only be disguised by a carefully preserved illusion.

The fact that despair is possible is a central datum here. Man is capable of despair, capable of hugging death, of hugging his *own* death. A central datum for metaphysic, but such definitions of man as that proposed by Thomism cover it up and disguise it. The essential merit of Kierkegaard and his school, to my mind, is their having brought this datum into full view. And metaphysic ought to take up its position just there, face to face with despair. The ontological problem cannot be separated from that of despair. (But they are not problems.)

Must think about the problem of the reality of other selves. It seems to me that the problem can be stated in such a way as to exclude in advance any solution which can be accepted or even understood; that is, by centring my reality on my consciousness of myself. If we begin, like Descartes, by assuming that my essence is self-consciousness, there is no longer a way out.

November 11th

Not only do we have a right to assert that others exist, but I should be inclined to contend that existence can be attributed only to others, and in virtue of their otherness, and that I cannot think of myself as existing except in so far as I conceive of myself as not being the others: and so as other than them. I would go so far as to say that it is of the essence of the Other that he exists. I cannot think of him as other without thinking of him as existing. Doubt only arises when his otherness is, so to say, expunged from my mind.

I would go so far as to ask if the *cogito* (whose incurable ambiguity can never be too clearly exposed) does not really mean: 'when I think, I am standing back from myself, I am raising myself up before myself as other, and I therefore appear as existent.' Such a conception as this is radically opposed to the idealism which defines the self as self-consciousness. Would it be absurd to say that the self in so far as it is self-consciousness is only *subexistent*? It only exists in so far as it treats itself as being for another, with reference to another; and therefore in so far as it recognises that it eludes itself.

People will say: 'These assertions are as ambiguous in their real content as they are arbitrary in their form. What existence do you speak of? Empirical existence or metaphysical existence? Empirical existence is denied by none; but it has a phenomenal character, for nothing will stop *the others* from being *my thought of the others*. And then the problem has merely shifted its ground.' But I think that it is just this position with which we should refuse to have anything to do. If I admit that the others are only *my thought of the others*, my idea of the others, it becomes utterly impossible to break the circle one has begun by drawing round one's-self. If you posit the primacy of subject-object—the primacy of the category subject-object—or of the act by which the subject sets up objects somehow or other within itself, the existence of others becomes unthinkable. And so does any existence whatever; there is no doubt of that.

Self-consciousness and the He: the philosophy of self-consciousness. In this the others are truly outside a sort of circle which I form with myself. From this point of view, I have no power of making contact with them; the very idea of communication is impossible. I cannot help regarding this intra-subjective reality of the others as the emerging of an absolutely mysterious and for ever impalpable X. We have here, in a general form, the most abstract features of Proust's world, though one also finds hints in Proust which are not only different from these but even contradictory. These hints become more scattered as the book goes on, as the circle formed by the Me and itself becomes more marked and more enclosed. At Combray and in everything to do with Combray the circle still does not exist. There is a possible place for the Thou. But as the book develops, as the experience it describes is hardened, sharpened and elaborated, the Thou is banished from the story. This is decisively and terribly apparent in the passage about the death of the grand-mother. (I must say that I think we are here going far beyond the conscious knowledge which it was in Proust's power to arrive at about either his work or himself.)

People will say again, 'But this distinction between the Thou and the He only applies to mental attitudes: it is phenomenological in the most exclusive sense of the word. Do you claim to give a metaphysical basis to this distinction, or a metaphysical validity to the Thou?'

The sense of the question is the really difficult thing to explain and elucidate. Let us try to state it more clearly, like this, for example. When I treat another as a Thou and no longer as a He, does this difference of treatment qualify me alone and my attitude to this other, or can I say that by treating him as a Thou I pierce more deeply into him and apprehend his being or his essence more directly?

Here again we must be careful. If by 'piercing more deeply' or 'apprehending his essence more directly', we mean reaching a more exact knowledge, a knowledge that is in some sense more objective, then we must certainly reply 'No'. In this respect, if we cling to a mode of objective definition, it will always be in our power to say that the Thou is an illusion. But notice that the term *essence* is itself extremely ambiguous; by essence we can understand either a nature or a freedom. It is perhaps of my essence *qua* freedom to be able to conform myself *or not* to my essence *qua* nature. *It may be of my essence to be able not to be what I am*; in plain words, to be able to betray myself. Essence *qua* nature is not what I reach in the Thou. In fact if I treat the Thou as a He, I reduce the other to being only

106

nature; an animated object which works in some ways and not in others. If, on the contrary, I treat the other as Thou, I treat him and apprehend him *qua* freedom. I apprehend him *qua* freedom because he *is* also freedom, and is not only nature. What is more, I help him, in a sense, to be freed, I collaborate with his freedom. The formula sounds paradoxical and self-contradictory, but love is always proving it true. On the other hand, he is really other *qua* freedom; in fact *qua* nature he appears to me identical with what I am myself *qua* nature. On this side, no doubt, and only on this side, I can work on him by suggestion (there is an alarming and frequent confusion between the workings of love and the workings of suggestion).

And so light is thrown on this morning's formulae. The other, in so far as he is other, only exists for me in so far as I am open to him, in so far as he is a Thou. But I am only open to him in so far as I cease to form a circle with myself, inside which I somehow place the other, or rather his idea; for inside this circle the other becomes the idea of the other, and the idea of the other is no longer the other *qua* other, but the other *qua* related to me; and in this condition he is uprooted and taken to bits, or at least in process of being taken to bits.

November 14th

Everything that can be enunciated is thinkable—or, more accurately, there is nothing we can enunciate which some of us cannot also believe or think at a given moment. The resources of language can be compared at all points to an extremely efficient network of communications. But travelling round is in itself nothing. And discourse for the sake of discourse is less than nothing.

These observations were suggested by some sort of aesthetic pseudo-appreciations—I have forgotten now what they were. But alas! they are also applicable to a great deal of pseudo-metaphysics.

November 15th

Are there grounds which justify us in assuming the priority of the act by which the I builds up its own self-hood over the act by which it posits the reality of others? And if we are to accept this priority, how are we to understand it? It can be conceived either in an empirical or a transcendental sense. Empirically my province consists of the sum of my states of consciousness; this province has the distinctive characteristic of being felt, and of being *my* province in so far as it is felt. This seems clear enough, but it is not really at all clear; the appearance of clarity is entirely due, in my opinion, to a sort of materialist representation which underlies these formulae. Instead of concentrating on thinking of the felt *as* felt, we put in its place the idea of an organic event, something which 'goes on' in the allegedly perfectly distinct and limited sphere which I call my body. I believe that at the bottom of all empiricist notions of the primacy of self-consciousness, there really lies the rudimentary idea that everything that is for me must first pass through my body: there is this idea of my body as an absolute intermediary. The supporters of this theory do not dream of making an out-and-out effort to discover what order the body-self relationship belongs to, nor yet do they ask the meaning of the mental act by which I assert that this body is my body. It is possible—though I would not go so far as to assert it—that there is a vicious circle here, and that we cannot avoid passing from *feeling* to a certain representation of my body, in order that we may later explain, in terms of feeling, the privilege in virtue of which my body is my body. I am inclined to think that if one wants to keep to the empirical point of view, there can be no question of going beyond the assertion '*this* body', and that the expression '*my* body' only looks like a source of unintelligibility and radical irrationality.

It is quite different if we take what I called the transcendental point of view.

Notice that one kind of philosophy of Life constitutes an obstacle to meditation on Being. The meditation is in danger of appearing to develop beyond or below the philosophy. These first notes are essential and give us the key.

'The hiding' I wrote 'of my being from my consciousness by something which is not and cannot be given to me.' My life cannot be given to me; and in spite of appearances, my body cannot be given to me either, in so far as my life is incarnate in it. My body is not, and cannot be, an object in the sense that an apparatus exterior to myself is an object. There is a tendency to minimise as much as possible the difference between my body and an apparatus belonging to me (e.g. a watch). Americans have themselves 'checked up' in clinics. A revealing phrase. In practice you can go as far as you like in that direction, but there is always something that escapes the checking-up; there are accidents, etc.

As soon as distinction has been made between my life and my being, there is an almost irresistible temptation to set a problem about this being, and to wonder in what it consists: and every effort to picture it forces us to sketch this problem or pseudo-problem.

The question 'what am I?' seems to demand an answer that can be conceptualised; but at the same time, every answer that can be, seems in danger of being rejected or of falling short.

But is this a legitimate question? Here it becomes necessary to specify: the more I adhere to my actions, my social surroundings, etc., the *less* does this question really arise for me. I can always *formulate* it, but it does not ring true. The true question, the one which rings full and clear, so to say, the true question presupposes a certain detachment or separation of myself from what I do and from my manner of sharing in the common life of men.

Could it be objected that this detachment is an illegitimate abstraction? But it is an indisputable fact that my life, understood in this sense—i.e. as participation in this common world—may become for me an object of judgment, approval or condemnation. *My life is something I can evaluate.* An essential datum. But what am I, this I which evaluates it? Impossible to cling to the fiction of a transcendental I. The I that evaluates is the same as the I that is judged. It must be added that my life, just in so far as I lead it, is, as it were, shot through by an implicit evaluation (whether adhered to or disobeyed; for I may be leading a life which something within me is continually protesting against with a dull insistence). This is the state of things, complex and in some ways contradictory as it is, discovered by me when I ask the question 'What am I?' But it is a real situation, and just because it is real I can evade it and withdraw from it.

Our world (some day we must scrutinise the sense of that word) is so constituted that within it despair is a possibility. In this fact we see the crucial significance of death. Death at first sight looks like a permanent invitation to despair—indeed, one might almost say, to betrayal in all its shapes—at least in so far as it is seen in the perspective of *my* life and of the assertion that I make in declaring myself identical with my life. There is a collaboration (in the sense of betrayal) between this obsessive picture of death and the feeling that my life offers nothing to hold on to beyond the moment lived, and that therefore every bond, every commitment, every vow, rests on a lie, since it rests on the arbitrary prolongation into eternity of a mere passing moment. All fidelity being thus rejected or uprooted, the betrayal itself now becomes changed in character. Now it claims that it is itself the true fidelity; and what we call fidelity, it calls betrayal—betrayal of the instant, betrayal of the real Me experienced in the instant. But here we are in the realm of the unthinkable; for in setting up the principle of fidelity to the instant, we transcend the instant. This, however, is a merely dialectical refutation, which in my view is lacking in real effect. And anyhow, an effective refutation *ought* to be impossible here; despair *is* irrefutable. Here there is only room for us to *opt* on one side or the other; it is past the province of any dialectic.

I note in passing that absolute fidelity can only be given to us in the person of certain witnesses, above all the martyrs. And it must be given to something in us which itself belongs to the order of faith. Whereas experience of betrayal is everywhere; and first of all in ourselves.

November 18th

The transition from the problem of being to the question 'What am I'? What am I, I who ask questions about being? What am I like, that I should be led to ask these questions?

The transition from problem to mystery. There is an ascending scale here; a problem conceals a mystery in so far as it is capable of awakening ontological overtones (the problem of survival, for instance).

The problem of the relation of soul and body is more than a problem: that is the implicit conclusion of *Existence and Objectivity*.[1]

Something unrepresentable yet concrete—something which is more than an idea, and exceeds every idea we can form, something which is a presence. An object as such is not present.[2]

November 12th

I was talking to the abbé A—— yesterday about Theresa Neumann. This morning I was thinking with exasperation of the rationalist's attitude to such facts. They would refuse to give them a hearing. Reflecting next upon my own exasperation, I thought it

[1] Appendix of the *Journal Métaphysique*. (Ed. N.R.F.)
[2] A possible way towards a theory of eucharistic presence. (Note written October 10th, 1934.)

was surely to be traced to some residue of doubt in myself. If I were absolutely sure, I should only experience a feeling of pure charity and pity for doubters. I think this discovery is far-reaching. It seems to me that charity is bound up with being sure. This must be developed.[1]

November 28th

A sentence came to my lips as I looked at a dog lying down outside a shop. 'There is something called being alive, and something else called active existence. I have chosen the latter.'

December 5th

After the strains and stresses of the last few days (the putting of *Le Mort de Demain* on the stage) I reached the point this morning where one no longer understands one's own thought. I was tempted to say that the word *mystery* is stuck on like a label saying, 'Please do not touch.' In order to begin understanding again, we are always bound to refer back to the order of the problematic. Mystery is the metaproblematic.

We should also make use of the principle which I laid down last Saturday with regard to the reality of other selves: the possibility of denial and negation take on for us a greater consistency and (so to say) density, in proportion as we mount further up the hierarchy of realities.[2]

December 6th

I was thinking just now that our *condition*—I will not exactly define this term for the moment—implies or requires a kind of

[1] It contains an idea which must seem paradoxical; it comes down in fact to admitting that the quality at the root of fanaticism is not certainty at all—not even an unbalanced certainty—but a mistrust of one's-self, a fear which one does not admit to one's-self.

[2] This is why it is so much easier to deny God than to deny matter. (Note written October 10th, 1934.)

systematic sealing-off of mystery, both in ourselves and in our surroundings. The sealing is done by the almost indefinable idea—is it even an idea?—of the 'perfectly ordinary'. There is a close connection between the objective and the 'perfectly ordinary'. A grip on being is only possible for us when we suddenly break through the enclosing shell which we have grown round ourselves. 'Except ye become as little children . . .' Our condition can be transcended, but only by a heroic and necessarily intermittent effort. The metaphysical essence of the object as such is perhaps simply its power of sealing-off. We cannot specify it further than that. We cannot, in the presence of any object, question ourselves about the mystery hidden within it. Such a question would be no more than pseudo-problematic.[1]

December 11th

I have dwelt this morning on the subject of *recollection*.[2] This is a central datum upon which very little work seems to have been done. Not only I am in a position to impose silence upon the strident voices which usually fill my consciousness, but also, this silence has a positive quality. Within the silence, I can regain possession of myself. It is in itself a principle of recovery. I should be tempted to say that recollection and mystery are correlatives. There is, properly speaking, no such thing as recollection in face of a problem. On the contrary, the problem puts me in some ways into a state of mental tension. Whereas recollection is rather the banishment of tension. Notice, however, that these terms 'tension' and 'relaxation' are apt in some directions to mislead us.

[1] In this we see the metaphysical root of all genuine *poetry*, for the very essence of poetry lies in not questioning but asserting. There is a close link between the poetic and the prophetic. (Note written October 10th, 1934.)
[2] In the spiritual sense. (Translator's note.)

If we asked ourselves what could be the metaphysical make-up of a being capable of recollection, we should be a long way nearer to a concrete ontology.

December 13th

I must make one point clear at the beginning of my statement. The question I have in mind is: How to define the kind of metaphysical climate which seems to me the most favourable—perhaps the only favourable—for developing assertions about the supra-sensible order?

December 18th

After agonising hours of almost complete intellectual blindness, I suddenly came to a new and clearer comprehension while crossing the Monatgne Sainte-Géneviève.[1]

We must see that:

(1) The ontological need, in the effort to explain itself, is found not to be comparable with the search after a solution.

(2) The metaproblematic is a participation on which my *reality* as subject is built (WE DO NOT BELONG TO OURSELVES); and reflection will show us that such a participation, if it is genuine, cannot be a *solution*. If it were, it would cease to be a participation in transcendent reality, and would become, instead, an interpolation *into* transcendent reality, and would be degraded in the process.

We must therefore proceed to make two distinct inquiries. One of these prepares for the other, but does not condition it, and both, in a sense, lead towards each other. They are: (*a*) an investigation of the nature of the ontological need, and (*b*) an investigation of the conditions in which a participation assumed to be a participation in reality could become thinkable. We then discover that it is just this participation which passes beyond the order of the problematic,

[1] A district of Paris. (Translator's note.)

and beyond what can be stated as a problem. It must next be shown that in fact, as soon as there is *presence*, we have gone beyond the realm of problem. But at the same time we shall see that the motive power that activates all thought which proceeds by means of problems and solutions—that this motive power gives a provisional character to every judgment we make, so that every presence may always give rise to problems. But it can only do so in so far as it loses its worth as presence.

December 20th

Knowledge is within being, enfolded by it. The ontological mystery of knowledge. We can only arrive at it by a reflection at one remove, which depends upon an experience of presence.

December 22nd

Have seen clearly the connection between the problem of suffering (and no doubt of evil generally) and the problem of my body. The problem of the metaphysical justification of suffering contains a reference (which may be disguised) to *my* suffering, or to a suffering which I make mine by assuming it. If no account is taken of this reference, the problem becomes meaningless. Hence the curiously hollow note of Leibnitz's remarks on this subject (and even, in a way, of Spinoza's, by very reason of his heroism). But the difficulty we have noticed so often before arises here once more with its full force. The problem, it would seem, is stated with greater sharpness as the suffering invades my being more completely. Yet on the other hand, the more this is so, the less can I split it off from myself, as it were, and take up my position before it. It is embodied in me; it *is* me.

December 23rd

In this aspect, the problem of suffering, more deeply considered, tends to take on the same form as it does in the book of Job. But this problem, torn out of its theological context, means that the more nearly suffering touches me, the more arbitrary is the act by which I consider the suffering as outside myself and (as it were) accidentally endured: the act, that is, by which I assume a sort of underlying soundness in my being (this is particularly easy to see in cases of bereavement or illness). And yet I feel that I can still only see this through a veil. I hope it will not be long before the veil is torn away.

OUTLINE OF AN ESSAY READ TO THE SOCIETY
OF PHILOSOPHICAL STUDIES

at Marseilles, on January 21st, 1933, on the Position of the Ontological Mystery and the Concrete Approaches to it.

(A) If we consider the present position of philosophical thought, as expressed in the depths of a consciousness which is trying to fathom its own needs, we are led, I think, to make the following observations:

(1) The traditional terms in which some people are today still trying to state the problem of being, commonly arouse a mistrust which is hard to overcome. Its source lies not so much in the adherence, whether explicit or implicit, to Kantian or simply idealist theories, as in the fact that people's minds are soaked in the results of Bergsonian criticism. One sees this even in those minds which would not stand by Bergsonianiam in its metaphysical aspects.

(2) On the other hand, the complete withdrawal from the problem of being which characterises so many contemporary philosophical systems is in the last analysis an attitude which cannot be maintained. It can either be reduced to a kind of sitting on the fence, hardly defensible and generally due to laziness or timidity: or else—and this is what generally happens—it really comes down to a more or less explicit denial of Being, which disguises the refusal of a hearing to the essential needs of our being. Ours is a being

whose concrete essence is to be in every way *involved*, and therefore to find itself at grips with a fate which it must not only undergo, but must also make its own by somehow re-creating it from within. The denial of Being could not really be the empirical *demonstration* of an absence or lack. We can only make the denial because we choose to make it, and we can therefore just as well choose not to make it.

(B) It is also worth noticing that I who ask questions about Being do not in the first place know either *if* I am nor *a fortiori what* I am. I do not even clearly know the meaning of the question 'what am I?' though I am obsessed by it. *So we see the problem of Being here encroaching upon its own data*, and being studied actually inside the subject who states it. In the process, it is denied (or transcended) as problem, and becomes metamorphosed to mystery.

(C) In fact, it seems very likely that there is this essential difference between a problem and a mystery. A problem is something which I meet, which I find complete before me, but which I can therefore lay siege to and reduce. But a mystery is something in which I am myself involved, and it can therefore only be thought of as *a sphere where the distinction between what is in me and what is before me loses its meaning and its initial validity*. A genuine problem is subject to an appropriate technique by the exercise of which it is defined: whereas a mystery, by definition, transcends every conceivable technique. It is, no doubt, always possible (logically and psychologically) to degrade a mystery so as to turn it into a problem. But this is a fundamentally vicious proceeding, whose springs might perhaps be discovered in a kind of corruption of the intelligence. The problem of evil, as the philosophers have called it, supplies us with a particularly instructive example of this degradation.

(D) Just because it is of the essence of mystery to be recognised or capable of recognition, it may also be ignored and actively denied. It then becomes reduced to something I have 'heard talked about', but which I refuse as only being *for other people*; and that in virtue of an illusion which these 'others' are deceived by, but which I myself claim to have detected.

We must carefully avoid all confusion between the mysterious and the unknowable. The unknowable is in fact only the limiting case of the problematic, which cannot be actualised without contradiction. The recognition of mystery, on the contrary, is an essentially positive act of the mind, the supremely positive act in virtue of which all positivity may perhaps be strictly defined. In this sphere everything seems to go on as if I found myself acting on an intuition which I possess without immediately knowing myself to possess it —an intuition which cannot be, strictly speaking, self-conscious and which can grasp itself only through the modes of experience in which its image is reflected, and which it lights up by being thus reflected in them. The essential metaphysical step would then consist in a reflection upon this reflection (in a reflection 'squared'). By means of this, thought *stretches out* towards the recovery of an intuition which otherwise loses itself in proportion as it is exercised.

Recollection, the actual possibility of which may be regarded as the most revealing ontological index we possess, is the real place in whose centre this recovery can be made.

(E) The 'problem of being', then, will only be the translation into inadequate language of a mystery which cannot be given except to a creature capable of recollection—a creature whose central characteristic is perhaps that he is not simply identical with his own life. We can find the proof or confirmation of this nonidentity in the fact that I more or less explicitly evaluate my life. It is in my power not only to condemn it by an abstract verdict, but to set an effective term to it. If I cannot set an effective term to my life considered in its ultimate depths, which may escape from my grasp, I at least have power over the finite and material expression to which *I am at liberty to believe* that this life is reduced. The fact that suicide is possible is, in this sense, an essential point of reference for all genuine metaphysical thought. And not only suicide: despair *in all its forms*, betrayal *in all its aspects*, in so far as they appear to us as active denials of being, and in so far as the soul which despairs shuts itself up against the central and mysterious assurance in which we believe we have found the principle of all positivity.

(*F*) It is not enough to say that we live in a world where betrayal is possible *at every moment, in every degree,* and in every form. It seems that the very constitution of our world recommends us, if it does not force us, to betrayal. The spectacle of death as exhibited by the world can, from one point of view, be regarded as a perpetual provocation to denial and to absolute desertion. It could also be added that space and time, regarded as paired modes of absence, tend, by throwing us back upon ourselves, to drive us into the beggarly instantaneity of pleasure. But it seems that at the same time, and correlatively, it is of the essence of despair, of betrayal, and even of death itself, that they can be refused and denied. If the word transcendence has a meaning, it means just this denial; or more exactly, this overpassing. (*Uberwindung* rather than *Aufhebung*.) For the essence of the world is perhaps betrayal, or, more accurately, there is not a single thing in the world about which we can be certain that its spell could hold against the attacks of a fearless critical reflection.

(*G*) If this is so, the concrete approaches to the ontological mystery should not be sought in the scale of logical thought, the objective reference of which gives rise to a prior question. They should rather be sought in the elucidation of certain data which are spiritual in their own right, such as fidelity, hope and love, where we may see man at grips with the temptations of denial, introversion, and hard-heartedness. Here the pure metaphysician has no power to decide whether the principle of these temptations lies in man's very nature, in the intrinsic and invariable characteristics of that nature, or whether it lies rather in the corruption of that same nature as the result of a catastrophe which gave birth to history and was not merely an incident in history.

Perhaps on the ontological level it is fidelity which matters most. It is in fact the recognition—not a theoretical or verbal, but an actual recognition—of an ontological permanency; a permanency which endures and by reference to which we endure, a permanency which implies or demands a history, unlike the inert or formal permanency of a pure *validity*, a law for example. It is the perpetuation of a witness which could at any moment be wiped out or denied. It is an attestation which is creative as well as perpetual, and more creative in proportion as the ontological worth of what it attests is more outstanding.

(H) An ontology with this orientation is plainly open to a revelation, which, however, it could not of course either demand or presuppose or absorb, or even absolutely speaking understand, but the acceptance of which it can in some degree prepare for. To tell the truth, this ontology *may* only be capable of development *in fact* on a ground previously prepared by revelation. But on reflection we can see that there is nothing to surprise us, still less to scandalise us, in this. A metaphysic can only grow up within a certain situation which stimulates it. And in the situation which is ours, the existence of a Christian datum is an essential factor. It surely behoves us to renounce, once for all, the naively rationalist idea that you can have a system of affirmation valid for thought *in general*, or for *any consciousness whatsoever*. Such thought as this is the subject of scientific knowledge, a subject which is an idea but nothing else. Whereas the ontological order can only be recognised personally by the whole of a being, involved in a drama which is his own, though it overflows him infinitely in all directions—a being to whom the strange power has been imparted of asserting or denying himself. He asserts himself in so far as he asserts Being and opens himself to it: or he denies himself by denying Being and thereby closing himself to It. In this dilemma lies the very essence of his freedom.

EXPLANATIONS

(1) From this point of view, what becomes of the notion of proving the existence of God? We must obviously subject it to a careful revision. In my view, all proof refers to a certain datum, which is here the belief in God, whether in myself or in another. The proof can only consist in a secondary reflection of the type which I have defined; a reconstructive reflection grafted upon a critical reflection; a reflection which is a recovery, but only in so far as it remains the tributary of what I have called a blindfold intuition. It is clear that the apprehension of the ontological mystery as metaproblematic is the motive force of this recovery through reflection. But we must not fail to notice that it is a reflexive motion of the mind that is here in question, and not a heuristic process. The proof can only confirm for us what has really been given to us in another way.

(2) What becomes of the notion of Divine attribute?

This, on the level of philosophy, is much more obscure. At present I can only see ways of approach to the solution. And anyhow, there can only be a solution where there is a problem, and the phrase 'the problem of God' is certainly contradictory and even sacrilegious. The metaproblematic is above all 'the Peace which passeth all understanding', but this Peace is a living peace, and, as Mauriac wrote in *Le Noeud de Vipères*, a Peace which is somebody, a creative Peace. It seems to me that the infinity and the omnipotence of God, can also only be established in the reflexive way. It is possible for us to understand that we cannot deny these attributes without falling back into the sphere of the problematic. This is tantamount to saying that the theology which philosophy leads us to is an essentially negative theology.

(3) We must question ourselves about the sense of the copula in the light of the idea of the metaproblematic. For me, generally speaking, there is being in so far as there is rootedness in the ontological mystery, and I should say from this point of view that the abstract alone as such does not exist (all its life is in the pure problematic). We must attach the 'being' of the copula to 'being' simply. The latter irradiates the 'being' of the copula (for instance, the being of Peter irradiates the copula in *Peter is good*).

We must look more closely into my remarks on intuition; for it is not yet perfectly clear to me. I am really talking about an intuition which is, as it were, active and purely active—an intuition, in fact, of which I could not in any manner have the disposal. But its presence is expressed by the ontological unease which is at work in reflection. To explain this we should start with an example or illustration; perhaps the demand for purity or even for truth. This intuition is not *in me*. There is something to be discovered or invented here, if one does not wish to remain in a state of negation.

What really brings us to admit this intuition is the fact of reflecting on the following paradox, *I do not know myself what I believe*; (A paradox which has held my attention for a long time; it must be scrutinised and defined.) We instinctively assert the contrary. I can make a sort of inventory of my objects of belief or a kind of 'valuation' distinguishing between what *I believe* and what *I do not believe*. This implies that a difference is *given* me and can be *felt* by me between what I adhere to and what I do not adhere to.

Every specification (referring to a content in which I assert that I know myself to believe) presupposes at least the possibility of such an enumeration, such an inventory. But, on the other hand, it seems to me that the Being towards which the belief is directed is above every possible inventory. That is to say, it cannot be a thing *among others*, an object *among others*. (And conversely, 'among others' has no meaning except for 'things' or 'objects'.) Yet this is not absolutely clear, even to me.

(Of course we need not here take into account the articles of a positive Creed. In this case the inventory is not made by me. There is a whole which is given *as an indivisible whole*. Heresy consists precisely in making arbitrary deductions from the body of such a whole.)

I shall certainly be asked: 'of *what* belief do you speak? of *what* faith?'

This again is asking me to specify. If I refuse to do so, I shall be blamed for remaining in a state of such vagueness that all discussion, and all elucidation too, becomes impossible. Nevertheless this faith, solid, entire, and as it were prior to all possible elucidation, must be upheld. It implies adherence to a reality whose character is never to be given piecemeal or offered retail. Such adherence would be impossible if this reality were not present; perhaps we should say *if it did not invest me completely*.

Examine as thoroughly as possible the fact that *the most consecrated people are the most disposable*. A person who is consecrated has renounced himself. But is it the same for a person who has consecrated himself to a social cause?

January 15th, 1933

PHENOMENOLOGICAL ASPECTS OF DEATH

Death can appear as the extreme expression of our corruptibility (it is that in *Voyage au Bout de la Nuit*)—or, on the contrary, as 'pure emancipation'. (It can appear as the extreme of non-disposability or, on the contrary, as the elimination of non-disposability.) We can treat it as betrayal only from a different and more superficial point of view.

A person who has made himself more and more disposable

cannot but regard death as a release (I am thinking of what Mme. F was telling us in the car about Mme. B's death). It is impossible to allow the least validity to the opinion that that is just an 'illusion'. (The absurdity of 'you will see well enough that it isn't true—at least, you *would* see if . . .') In what degree does faith in this release render it actually possible? A problem to be stated with the greatest accuracy (what is in all other cases merely a 'hypothesis'[1] becoming here an unconquerable and insurmountable conviction). I note in passing that the Christian idea of mortification should be understood in the light of this 'releasing death'. It is the apprenticeship to a more than human freedom. I notice once more that there is a way of accepting one's death—how important one's last moments are!—whereby the soul is consecrated (and perhaps made disposable in the sense I have tried to define). Spinoza made a radical mistake when he denied that any meditation on death was worth while. Plato, on the other hand, may have foreshadowed it all. Consider suicide in the light of these remarks. (I am thinking of poor little N—— whose appalling death we heard of yesterday.) To dispose of one's-self in that way is the opposite of disposability considered as self-consecration.

January 16th

This is a most important question to examine. The being who is absolutely disposable for others does not allow himself the right to dispose freely of himself.

Link between suicide and non-disposability.

January 19th-20th

Reflection on the question 'What am I?' and upon its implications. When I reflect upon the implications of the question 'What am I?' taken as a single issue, I see that it means: 'What is there in

[1] The *perhaps* of the agnostic is fundamentally unacceptable to the dedicated soul.

me that can answer this question?' Consequently, every answer to this question *coming from me* must be mistrusted.

But could not someone else supply me with the answer? An objection immediately arises: the qualifications which the other may have which enable him to answer me, the eventual validity of what he says, are observed by me; but what qualifications have I for making this observation? I can, therefore, only refer myself without contradiction to a judgment which is absolute, but which is at the same time more within me than my own judgment. In fact, if I treat this judgment as in the least *exterior* to me, the question of what it is worth and how it is to be appreciated must inevitably be asked afresh. The question is then eliminated *qua* question and turns into an appeal. But perhaps in proportion as I take cognizance *of this appeal qua appeal*, I am led to recognise that the appeal is possible only because deep down in me there is something other than me, something further within me than I am myself —and at once the appeal changes its index.

Someone will object, 'This appeal may in the first sense be without a real object; it may, as it were, lose itself in the dark.' But what does this objection mean? That I have not perceived any answer to this 'question', i.e. that 'someone else has not answered it'. I remain here on the level of the observation or non-observation of facts; but by doing so I am taking up a position in the circle of the problematic (that is, of what is placed *before* me).

January 24th

While we were walking yesterday on the hills above Mentone, I thought once more about the mastery of our own mastery, which is obviously parallel to reflection in the second degree. It is clear that this second mastery is not of the technical order and can only be the perquisite of some people. In reality, thought in general is what 'one' thinks. The 'one' is the technical man, in the same way as he is the subject of epistemology, when that science is considering knowledge as a technic. This is, I think, the case with Kant. The subject of metaphysical reflection, on the contrary, is essentially opposed to 'one': this subject is essentially not *the man in the street*. Any epistemology which claims to be founded on thought-in-general is leading to the glorification of technics and of the man in the street (a democratisation of knowledge which *really ruins it*). Furthermore, it must not be forgotten that technics stand on a lower step than the creation which they presuppose—a creation which itself also transcends the level where the man in the street holds sway. The 'one' is also a step down; but by admitting him we create him. We live in a world where this man of straw begins to look more and more like a real figure.

February 2nd

I intend to return to the analysis of all this. We must say that mystery is a problem that encroaches upon the intrinsic conditions of its own possibility (and not upon its data). Freedom is the basic example.

How can something which cannot be reduced to a problem be actually thought? In so far as I treat the act of thinking as a way of looking, this question would admit of no solution. Something which cannot be reduced to a problem cannot be looked at or treated as an object, and that by definition. But this representation of thought is in fact inadequate: we must manage to make abstraction from it. We must recognise, however, that this is extremely difficult. As I see it, the act of thinking cannot be represented and must be grasped as such. And what is more, it must apprehend every representation of itself as essentially inadequate. The contradiction implied in the fact of thinking of a mystery falls to the ground of itself when we cease to cling to an objectified and misleading picture of thought.

I return to my remarks of last January 16th. Why does the being who is absolutely disposable for someone else refuse to allow himself the right of disposing freely of himself? Simply for the reason that in thus disposing of himself (by suicide), he renders himself non-disposable for others; or at least he acts like a man who does not give himself the least trouble to remain disposable for others. And so the whole thing hangs together. Suicide and martyrdom are strictly opposites. All this turns on the formula: the soul most essentially dedicated is *ipso facto* the most disposable. Such a soul wills itself to be an instrument; but suicide is the act of denying one's-self as an instrument.

My remarks of January 24th (at Mentone) still seem important to me. It is clear that 'one' is a fiction, but everything goes on as if that fiction were becoming reality. It is more and more openly treated as a reality. (Yet the technician is not a pure technician; his technics cannot be exercised except where certain minimal conditions of psycho-physiological balance are realised, and we should anyhow have grounds for asking whether a technic dealing with these conditions themselves is possible in the last analysis.)

Return to the notion of problematisation. It seems to me that every effort to problematise is conditioned by the ideal assumption of a certain continuity of experience which is to be safeguarded *against* appearances. In this connection, from any problematic point of view whatsoever, miracle equals nonsense. This cannot be too explicitly recognised. But cannot the very notion of this empirical continuum be criticised? We shall have to discover the exact connection between this way of asking the question and my definition of mystery. This will no doubt be best done by making use of a concrete problem (for instance, an encounter).

I should be inclined to say that the continuity implied in all problematisation is the continuity of a 'system for me'. Whereas in mystery it is quite different; I am carried *beyond* any 'system for me'. I am involved *in concreto* in an order which, by definition, can never become an object or a system for me, but only for a thought which over-reaches and comprehends me, and with which I cannot identify myself, even ideally. Here the word 'beyond' takes on its full and true significance.

All problematisation is relative to 'my system' and 'my system' is an extension of 'my body'.

The egocentricity will be contested, but the truth is that any scientific theory whatsoever remains in the last analysis tributary to the *percipio* and not at all to the plain *cogito*. The *percipio* remains the real centre of all problematisation whatever, however carefully it may be disguised.

From another side, I was thinking just now that our business here is to find a translation into speculative terms of the practical theocentricity which adopts as its centre, 'Thy will and not mine'. This seems to me essential. But it must be seen, on the other hand, that the theocentricity itself presupposes theoretical assertions to which it is extremely difficult to give a form. 'Thy will' is not absolutely given me in the sense that my will to live and my appetite is given me. 'Thy will' is for me something to be *recognised*, to be construed, whereas my appetite simply makes demands, simply imposes itself.

February 7th

The more we think of the past *in concreto*, the less meaning there is in declaring it to be immutable. The only thing which is really independent of the present act and the re-creative interpretation, is a certain scheme of events; but this scheme is merely an abstraction.

The *scrutiny* of the past; the *reading* of the past.

The interpretation of the world in terms of technics, in the light of technics. The world to be *construed*, to be *deciphered*.

I would say, to sum up my observations, that the belief in an immovable past is due to an optical error of the spirit. People will say 'the past taken in itself does not move; what changes is our way of thinking about it'. But must we not be idealists here and say that the past cannot be separated from the consideration of the past? They will say again, 'It is an immutable fact that Peter accomplished an action at such a moment of time. Only the interpretation of the action can vary, and that is exterior to the reality of Peter's action or of Peter himself.' But I do in fact suspect that this last assertion is untrue, though I cannot absolutely prove it so. It seems to me that Peter's reality—infinitely transcendent over Peter's action —remains involved in the interpretation which renews and re-creates the action. Perhaps that is an absurd idea; we shall have to see. But I would say without demur that Peter's reality is, in a way that can hardly be specified, one with the power of scrutiny which is applied after the event to his actions, to this datum which is claimed to be immutable. This is infinitely clear upon the highest level, in Christology, but more and more uncertain the further one goes down towards the insignificant. But the insignificant is no more than a limiting case. The importance of the novelist's art in its highest form is that it shows us that the insignificant, strictly speaking, cannot and does not exist.

February 8th

My history is not transparent to me. It is only my history in so far as it is not transparent to me. In this sense, it cannot become part of my system and perhaps it even breaks up my system.

February 11th

All this, I feel, needs to be drawn out. At bottom, 'my history' is not a clear notion. On the one hand, I interpret myself to myself as the object of a possible biography. On the other hand, starting from an intimate experience of myself, I unmask the central illusion in every conceivable biography; I apprehend all biography as fiction (as I hinted at the end of my note on Schloezer's *Gogol*).

February 14th

Must think about autonomy. It seems to me that we can only talk legitimately about autonomy in the order of *administration* and the *administrable*. Knowledge—the act or work of knowing—can this be compared with administration?

February 15th

The administration of an inheritance or estate. Life itself compared to an estate, and treated as capable of being administered or managed. In all this, there is room for autonomy. But the nearer we come to creation, the less we can speak of autonomy, or rather we can only do so at a lower level, the level of exploitation; for instance, the artist exploiting his inspiration.

The idea of autonomous disciplines: this, too, can be interpreted in terms of administration. There is the notion of a plant to be exploited, constituting, as it were, a set of tools, or a capital sum specially earmarked for its use. This idea loses every sort of meaning as one rises to the notion of philosophical thought. Yes, that is how it is. The discipline is being treated as the field or mode of exploitation.

Bring this to bear on the very notion of truth. Shew the postulate or hidden method of representation which is taken for granted by those who think that the mind must be autonomous in its pursuit of the truth. This is still not absolutely clear to me today. It seems to me that we always start from a twofold notion, of a field to be developed, and also of an equipment which will make this development possible. It is as though we would not let ourselves admit that this equipment can be supplemented *ab extra*. We say that it would be cheating; we add that it would anyhow be impossible really to bring it off.

I am tempted to think that the idea of autonomy is bound up with a kind of narrowing or particularisation of the subject. The more I enter into an activity with the whole of myself, the less right have we to say that I am autonomous. (In this sense, the philosopher is less autonomous than the pure scientist, and the pure scientist himself less so than the technician.) Autonomy is bound up with the existence of a sphere of activity which is strictly circumscribed. If this is so, the whole of the Kantian ethic rests upon a monstrous contradiction, a sort of speculative aberration.

My life, considered in the totality of its implications—suppose that this could be done—does not seem to me to be something that can be administered (either by myself or by someone other than me). And to this extent I grasp it as unfathomable (see my note for the 8th of February last). Between the administrator and the administered there must exist a certain proportionality, which is here lacking. In the order of *my life*, administration implies mutilation (a mutilation, I grant, which is in some respects unavoidable but which in other cases is sacrilegious).

And so we are led to transcend the opposition autonomy-heteronomy. For heteronomy is administration by another, but still administration; it is on the same level. In the realms of love or inspiration, the distinction loses all meaning. At a certain depth within me, and in a zone where practical specialisations melt away, the terms autonomy and heteronomy become inapplicable.

February 16th

But am I not, in all this argument, ignoring the great sense of the word autonomy, the idea of a rational spontaneity working out its purpose in the very making of the law? Here, in fact, what becomes of the idea of a reason which is legislating universally for itself? Or, to go still deeper, what metaphysical dignity is it proper to give to the very act of legislation? That is really the crux of the whole problem. It seems to me that legislation is simply the formal aspect of administration, and that therefore it does not transcend it. In that case, what is beyond administration is by definition also beyond legislation.

Autonomy considered as non-heteronomy. I understand by this that it refers, phenomenologically speaking, to heteronomy presupposed and refused. It is the 'by myself!' of the little child who is beginning to walk and rejects the hand outstretched to him. 'I want to run my own life'—that is the radical formula of autonomy. It refers essentially to *action* and implies, as I noted the other day, the notion of a certain province of activity circumscribed in space and time. Everything belonging to the order of interests, whatever they are, can be treated with relative ease as a province, a district marked off in this manner. Furthermore, I can administer, or treat as something to be administered, not only my estate and my fortune, but also everything that can be compared even distantly to a fortune, or, more generally, to a *possession*—something *I have*. But where the category of *having* becomes inapplicable, I can no longer in any sense talk about administration, whether by another or myself, and therefore I cannot talk about autonomy either.

February 21st

As soon as we are in Being we are beyond autonomy. That is why recollection, in so far as it is regaining contact with Being, takes me into a realm where autonomy is no longer conceivable; and this is just as true of inspiration, or of any action which involves the whole of what I am. (The love of a person is strictly comparable to inspiration in this respect.) The more I *am*, the more I assert my being, the less I think myself autonomous. The more I manage to conceive of my being, the less subject to its own jurisdiction does it appear to me to be.[1]

February 26th

Suppose that an absolute addition, an entirely unsought gift has been made to man—whether to some men or to all—in the course of history, in what sense is the philosopher bound, in what sense has he the right or even the power, to refuse to take this gift into account? To invoke autonomy here (or even the principle of immanence, which really comes to the same thing) is to say: 'This addition, within the dialectically regulated course of thought, constitutes a foreign body, a scandal: as a philosopher at least I cannot recognise it.' Is this non-recognition implied in the very notion of philosophy? What is really being done here is to refuse to allow an intrusion to take place in a system regarded as closed. But *in concreto* what does this mean for me, a philosopher? The system is not my thought, it goes beyond that. My thought is merely inserted into a certain limitless development, with which, however, it regards itself as co-extensive in principle.[2]

[1] These propositions have an *axial* character for a metaphysic which inclines to assign to a kind of ontological humility the place which most traditional philosophers since Spinoza have given to freedom. This is at least true in so far as they imply a claim made by the subject to identify himself rationally with a certain Thought immanent in the Whole. It is the very possibility of such an identification which is radically denied in such a metaphysic as the one I am trying to define here. (Note written September 11th, 1934.)

[2] The system goes beyond my thought, I said, and this is not untrue: but more essentially, my thought goes beyond the system. Here it is probably the notion 'in so far as' which ought to be attacked. I should be much inclined to think that the philosopher *in so far as* he is a philosopher, i.e. in proportion as he carries out at the heart of his own reality a discrimination which mutilates it, is really denying himself as a philosopher; that the part played by the minds of the last century that were philosophically most alive, such as Schopenhauer and Nietzsche, was just this: that they

133

A certain subject-unit, or a *qui* playing the part of a subject-unit, becomes a centre of inherence or apprehension for a certain *quid* which he relates to himself or which we treat as if he related it to himself. There is a relation here which is transitive only on the grammatical level (what is more, the verb 'to have' is almost never used in the passive, which is most significant). This relation, which essentially *affects* the subject-unit, tends to pass into it, to be transmuted into a state of the subject-unit, without its being possible for this transmutation or reabsorption to be completely carried out.

In order to *have* effectively, it is necessary to *be* in some degree, that is to say, in this case, to be immediately for one's-self, to feel one's-self, as it were, affected or modified. A mutual interdependence of having and being.

I note that there is a strict parallel between having in one's portfolios drawings by X which one might shew to a visitor, and having ideas on this or that subject which one will put forward on occasion. What one has is really by definition something one can shew. It is interesting to note how difficult it is to make a substantive of τὸ ὄν; τὸ ὄν becomes changed to ἐχόμενον as soon as it is treated as something that can be shewn. But there is a sense in which 'to have consciousness of' means 'to shew to one's-self'. Consciousness as such is not a possession or a manner of having, but it may be enjoyment of something which it treats as a possession. Every action goes beyond possession, but may, after the event, be treated as a possession itself; and this in virtue of a sort of grading down. I note that the secret, as opposed to the mystery, is essentially a possession in that it can be shewn.

We must not overlook the fact that all spiritual possession has its

brought to light the sort of dialectic in virtue of which the philosopher is led to deny himself as a 'Fachmensch', as a specialist. (Note written September, 1934.)

springs in something that cannot be shewn (my ideas are rooted in what I am). But what characterises this non-shewable as such, is the fact that it does not belong to me, it is essentially *unbelonging*. There is therefore a sense in which I do not belong to myself, and this is exactly the sense in which I am absolutely not autonomous.

February 27th

We shew what we have; we reveal what we are (though of course only in part).

Creation considered as the liberation of what cannot be shewn.

But where philosophical creation does not exist, philosophy does not exist either. It cannot, without denying or betraying itself, crystallise into results capable of being simply assimilated and thereby possessed.

March 1st

Could we not make 'having' our starting-point for a definition of desire? To desire is to have and not to have: the psychical or non-objective element of having already exists in its entirety in desire; but it is just by its separation from the objective element that desire becomes a gnawing pain.

March 4th

My deepest and most unshakable conviction—and if it is heretical, so much that the worse for orthodoxy—is, that whatever all the thinkers and doctors have said, it is not God's will at all to be loved by us *against* the Creation, but rather glorified *through* the Creation and with the Creation as our starting-point. That is why I find so many devotional books intolerable. The God who is set up against the Creation and who is somehow jealous of his own works is, to my mind, nothing but an idol. It is a relief for me to have written this. And I declare until further orders that I shall be insincere every time I seem to be making an assertion contrary to what I have just written. I could not get over my discomfort yesterday with X. I was telling him how I disliked denominationalism. He does not understand, and says it is pride. But the opposite is the truth.[1]

March 5th

What I wrote yesterday needs to be qualified. It is true of the stage I am in at present, but I know that this stage is still rudimentary.

I heard once more the *Missa Solemnis*, conducted by Wein-gartner, and was as deeply moved as when I heard it in 1918. There is no work that I feel is more in tune with my thoughts. It is a luminous commentary upon them.

March 8th

Through a phrase from Brahms (in one of the Intermezzi, op. 118, I think) which has been in my head the whole afternoon, I have suddenly come to see that there is a universality which is not of the conceptual order; that is the key to the idea of music. But how hard it is to understand! The idea can only be the fruit of a kind of spiritual gestation. A close analogy with the living creature.[2]

[1] This, in any case, remains absolutely true for me: that every attempt at *Divine psychology*, every claim to imagine God's attitude towards me, inspires me with unconquerable mistrust. It is really quite impossible for me to allow that we can somehow ideally place ourselves in God—I mean put ourselves in his place so as to look at ourselves from thence. I am far from ignoring the serious difficulties, of a metaphysical and theological order, which certainly derive from such an impossibility, but I must confess that the use made by the greater number of theologians of the idea of analogy, for getting over this, seems to me to lie open to the most serious objections. My own position on this point seems to me, I must admit, exposed, delicate, and profoundly unsatisfying. (Note written on September 13th, 1934.)

[2] This, too, must be examined and worked out. Bergson is certainly right; we are here in an order where duration is somehow incorporated with what it is working upon and bringing to its ripeness. But, on what

To return to suicide. At bottom, experience seems to show us that men can be disposed of, got rid of. And so I treat myself also as able to be disposed of. But here we should try exactly to define the limits within which this external experience of the mortality of others can be realised. It is, in fact, more complete when the persons in question have never counted (existed) for me. But 'being disposed of' loses its meaning more and more in the case of persons who, in so far as they have ever really counted in my life, must continue to do so still. The 'notion'(?) expressed by the phrase 'belonging to the past' is not always used in the same sense; it can be weakened indefinitely. It only takes on the full harshness of its sense where we are speaking of an instrument thrown aside, put out of use, cast away. I shall of course be told that a radical distinction must be made between the other man as object (for he really is got rid of), and a whole set of subjective superstructures which my mind builds upon him; they survive the object in so far as my mind itself survives him. But as the Neo-Hegelians saw with admirable lucidity, this is really a most precarious distinction and should be treated with the greatest caution. It can only be applied to the limiting case. It loses its meaning in proportion as the person in question is really mingled with my life. This can only be denied by claiming that the word *mingled* is inapplicable here and that absolute monadism is the truth. If it is not so, and to my mind it manifestly is not so, we must recognise that this is not a possible starting-point where real intimacy exists. Intimacy; that is really the fundamental notion.

But in that case, it is clear that I cannot consider myself able to be disposed of unless I treat myself as a perfect stranger—unless,

one might call the structural aspect of this order of reality, Bergson has perhaps not thrown enough light in spite of everything. (Note written September 13th, 1934.)

indeed, I put aside all possibility of *haunting*, I should come to the conclusion that the more actual and profound my intimacy with myself, the more right I am in believing that the picture I formed of myself as an object which it is in my power to put right out of use is one to be treated with caution, and even absurd in itself. (It goes without saying that when I speak of haunting, I evoke the results which may be brought upon me by a murder of which I am guilty. I do not really get rid of my victim; he remains present with me in the very heart of the obsession with which I saddled myself when I thought to be done with him.) Here again someone will say. 'But the whole point is whether the victim is conscious of this haunting which he brings about in the man who thinks he has blotted him out of his universe.' But here we must return to a close examination of the actual problem of consciousness, and first we must mint afresh the outworn terminology which we generally employ to state it. It is clear that if I stick to a sort of psycho-physical parallelism, I shall be tempted to declare that where the body as such is destroyed, the consciousness itself is no doubt annihilated. It remains to be seen what view we ought to take of this parallelism.

To me the arrangement of the world is of such a kind that it seems expressly to invite us to believe in this parallelism and so in the reality of death. But at the same time a more secret voice, more subtle clues, allow us to feel that this may be nothing but a façade, to be treated and appreciated as a façade. Then freedom springs up in arms against such counterfeits; and as she rouses herself, she discerns in the borders of experience all manner of alliances, all manner of promises—allusions of which one illumines and reinforces another—of a deliverance, a dayspring still beyond our power to imagine.

With regard to death and mortification; we must understand that, for Christians, death compared with life represents not less but more, or at least the way to something more; it is an exaltation, and not, as fatal error would have us believe, a mutilation or denial. If that were so, Nietzsche would be perfectly right; but he is wrong, because he clung to an entirely naturalistic view of life, and from that point of view the problem no longer has any meaning. Life so understood carries with it no *beyond*, no soaring power; it can no longer be transcended.

Undated

ON THE PROBLEM OF BEING

The problem of being tends first of all to be stated as the question : 'What is the ultimate material of the world?' An enquiry which by its very nature proves disappointing. Reflection will shew us, first, that the very notion of material is obscure, ambiguous, and perhaps inapplicable to the world in its entirety; next, and above all, that this material, even supposing we could identify it, might well not be the essential thing. So we see that there is distance, an open gap, between the intellectual hunger (obscure even to itself) which gave birth to the problem, and the terms in which this problem is stated. Even if the problem were or could be resolved, the hunger would perhaps not be satisfied. At this point the hunger would tend to be more directly conscious of itself. In that case there would be room for transition to the notion of an intelligible organisation or structure.

This is one of the possible ways.

But there are others. One is reflection on the idea of appearance, and on the implications of the bare fact that there are appearances. Another way is to reflect on the fact of assertion.

There are some appearances that can be manifestly shewn up as appearances. Hallucination in all its forms, for one. But in this class, one never gets further than correction. Still, there must be a great temptation to run all the lines on here and treat the whole of experience as φαινόμενον. But a very difficult criteriological problem will face us then, the same that faces us when, for instance, we are distinguishing primary and secondary qualities. Reflection will show us in the end that primary qualities are not necessarily endowed with an ontological priority over secondary qualities. Here again an intellectual hunger is at work, a hunger which feels a kind of deep-seated trouble in becoming perspicuous to itself.

The problem of affirmation. All ontology centres on the act of affirmation which is considered not, as a matter of fact, in itself, not primarily as an act, but in its specific intentionality. And it is in this region that we shall find a sort of dangerous neighbourhood appearing between ontology and logic in its strict sense.

March 12th

At no time and in no circumstances can affirmation ever appear as originator of the reality of what it affirms. The formula is here: 'I affirm it because it is.' And this formula is already the translation of a reflection that came before it, but at this stage the expression 'this is' seems to be outside the affirmation and prior to it; the affirmation refers back to something given. But a second reflection is about to arise here. Affirmation in the act of reflecting itself is led to encroach on the private and almost holy ground of 'this is'. At this point I say to myself: but 'this is' itself presupposes an affirmation. Hence we have a regress which seems to be infinite, unless I bring myself to lay down the affirmation itself as origin. But we will not press this point. Let us admit that Being has first laid a sort of siege to the self; by self I mean the subject who affirms. This subject none the less intervenes between the being and the affirmation, in the rôle of a mediator. And then the problem arises which I observed in my notes of January the 19th, for I am inevitably led to ask what is the ontological standing of this self in relation to the being which besieges him. Is he whelmed in it, or does he on the contrary have some sort of command over it? If he commands it, what gives him this mastery and what exactly does it mean?

March 14th

Are we to say that deeper reflection will lead us to recognise that affirmation presupposes a power of positing? a power which somehow foreruns it and hands over to it the substance of what the affirmation asserts? It is very likely that this is the truth, but how can I approach this truth?

It should be noticed, in any case, that the power of positing, by its very essence, goes beyond the problematic (cf. note of last February 6th).

The agony of the present days passes all bounds. The Disarmament Conference is at the point of death. There was the incident at Kehl, and terror reigns there. At times I live with the feeling that death is upon us all, and upon all that we love. As I was on my way to see V—— this afternoon, I had a sort of light on this, in the Rue La Condamine—just this: 'Think that dream is turning into nightmare, and when nightmare has reached its most agonising point, you will awake. That will be the experience which today you call death.' This upheld me. It is a way of being able to bear the haunting idea that Paris will be destroyed.

March 16th

'Mysteries are not truths that lie beyond us; they are truths that comprehend us.' (R. P. Jouve.)

March 31st

About N's suicide. Is it in my power to reduce myself to an absolute impotence? Can I use my will in such a way as to put myself in a state where I can no longer will anything and no longer do anything? Does reality lend itself to this absolute desertion (or at least would-be absolute desertion)? The least we can assert is that reality at any rate seems to be arranged in such a way as to keep up in my mind belief in the possibility of such a step, a belief in its ultimate effectiveness. The whole band of appearances gathered around me encourages me to believe that I can really get rid of myself.

That is how we should express a phenomenology of suicide which consisted in seeing how suicide must necessarily look to my eyes; a complete enfranchisement, but one in which the liberator, in freeing himself from himself, thereby eliminates himself.

But there is room for another mode of reflection, which compared with this is hyper-phenomenological; is this conspiracy of appearances telling the truth? They seem to range themselves together so as to make me think that my freedom is here fundamental. But is this absolute act perpetrated by myself upon myself something that can really happen? If it were, I should, it seems, be right in claiming a sort of *ameitas* (self-causality) for myself, since I should only continue to be by a continuous permission accorded by myself to myself. The whole question is, what sort of reality is mine, in a world whose constitution is such that it permits what I have called an absolute desertion. To my mind, it is clear in any case that such a world excludes even the possibility of participation in the being upon which my reality as subject rests. I am here no more than something that *happened to be*. But to this happening to which I reduce myself, I still attribute the most fundamental power over itself. Is there not here an internal contradiction? In other words, I am my life but can I still think my life?

April 11th

Have realised this once again; for each of us, every moment of our lives, the worst is possible, or what we think is the worst. There is no objective guarantee. This must be reconciled with the idea of God—an all-powerful God. But does not the fact that the worst is possible prove the infinite weakness of God? Between this infinite weakness and this infinite power, it seems that a mysterious junction takes place, a union of seeming opposites beyond the idea of causality.

July 23rd

Afterthoughts on a discussion with R. C ——on the connection between suffering and sin.

My claim is that this connection is, properly speaking, inexperienceable, that is to say, it cannot be transferred to the level of particular experience. In the presence of someone who suffers, I am absolutely unable to say, 'Your suffering is the punishment for an identifiable sin, of which you may not be personally guilty anyhow.' (C—— brought in heredity, but this is beside the mark from a religious point of view.) We are here in the realm of the unfathomable, and this is something we must manage to make philosophically clear. A strange thing; suffering is, in fact, only capable of taking on metaphysical and spiritual meaning in so far as it implies an unfathomable mystery. But on the other hand—and this is the paradox—all suffering is by its very nature '*this* suffering', whence the almost irresistible temptation to find for it an explanation or justification which is also determined and particular. But this is just what we cannot do. The problem from the religious point of view consists in transforming the unfathomable into a positive quantity. There is a whole dialectic here which I see only in part. To give a particular explanation in terms of punishment is to assume that God is 'someone', to place him on the same level as the particular person who suffers; and by this very assumption to incite the person to discussion and revolt. ('Why me and not so-and-so? Why this fault and not that one?' etc.) But it is clear that this level of comparison and discussion is just what we must transcend. This is surely the same as to say that 'this suffering' must be apprehended as the actual participation in an universal mystery, which can be grasped as brotherhood and understood as a metaphysical bond.

We should never forget, on the other hand, that the man who from outside—I am thinking of R. C.—draws my attention to the link between my suffering and my sin, needs to be inwardly qualified to carry out the act. He can only be this if he is himself entirely humble and offers himself as a sharer, as it were, in my sin. Perhaps he must even share in my suffering. In fact, he must become 'another I'. In so far as he is a pure and simple other, he cannot play this part; he is disqualified. We might find a way from here to a philosophical statement about the being of Christ.[1]

July 26th

Having and spatiality. Having relates to taking, but it seems that there no hold is offered except by things that are in space or can be compared with something spatial. These two propositions must be closely examined.

July 30th

I wanted to make a note at Rothau yesterday that the seat of suffering certainly seems to be the point at which Having flows into Being. Perhaps we can only be hurt through our possessions. But is this really so?

Just now, during a wonderful walk above Zermatt, I was think-

[1] To my mind, these remarks are extremely important in the consideration of the metaphysical relationship implied in priesthood, and I do not mean priesthood regarded in a specially denominational way. By these remarks one can, I think, see the abyss that lies between the attitude of the priest and that of the moralist. As soon as the priest begins to turn himself into a moralist, he denies himself as a priest.

ing again very minutely about the essential *mutability* of the past. The notion that events are deposits made in the course of history is at bottom a false one. If we look carefully, we shall see that there is no historical deposit. The past remains relative to our reading it in a certain way. I felt an idea forming in my mind that there is a reciprocal tension between the past and the mode of attention that is concentrated upon it. If this is so, the expressions 'accomplished once and for all' and 'plain and simply happening' would mask a positive paralogism. I cannot help thinking that this looks like the beginning of a road to which I have not yet really committed myself. Perhaps this will provide us with the means of throwing new lights upon death. But I do not see clearly as yet; I only have a kind of presentiment. We must look at the positive implications of a critique of the idea of historical deposit.

August 13th

Knowing as a mode of having. The possession of a secret. Keeping it, disposing of it—and here we get back to what I wrote on the 'shewable'. The absolute opposition of secret and mystery—mystery being that which by its very essence I cannot dispose of. Knowledge as a mode of having is essentially communicable.

August 14th

The twofold permanence implied in having. (I am still taking the fact of having a secret as my typical case.) A secret is itself something that resists duration, something upon which duration cannot bite, or which is treated as such. But it must be the same for the subject, for the *qui*, otherwise the secret would destroy itself. The secret is obviously comparable with the object kept, with the content preserved in that which contains it. I think that this comparison is always possible as soon as we find ourselves in the realm of Having. But—and this is worth noticing—the analysis of the spatial act of keeping is reflected on the spiritual level; I noticed this a long time ago.

We should ask ourselves to what extent we *have* a feeling, under what conditions a feeling can be treated as a possession. Only from the social point of view, I think, and in so far as I am in dialogue with myself.

Consider presence as something of which I cannot dispose in any way; which I cannot possess. There is a constant temptation either to turn it into an object, or to treat it as an aspect of myself. It is as though we were not equipped for thinking about it. There are numberless ways of applying this principle.

Mental 'having'. Some people are so made that they can put their hand on a required piece of the contents of their mind as if it were an object or paper that was efficiently classified. They have constituted themselves on the pattern of the classifications which they have made of their objects of study. But it may also be said conversely that these classifications are only the tangible symbols of the order they have inaugurated in themselves. In any case, the correspondence between the outward and the mental order tends to be as strict as possible. The body comes in here as a principle of disturbance, whose possibilities we cannot fathom. The order which I have set up within me depends on something over which, in the last analysis, I have no power.

When I am placed in 'normal' conditions, my mental possessions conform to their nature of being possessions; but the moment the conditions change, this ceases to be the case. To tell the truth, it seems that the conditions themselves somehow depend on me and so tend also to look like possessions. But this is to a great extent an illusion.

August 15th

I am again preoccupied by the question what it means to possess qualities. The word 'also' seems to me only to have meaning in the

146

order of Having. Perhaps the recourse to the category of Having for thinking of qualities is an expedient, a makeshift necessary if we are to conceive (or persuade ourselves that we conceive) the juxta-position of qualities. I am tired this evening—but it seems to me that there is here a track worth following.

August 16th

What I am trying to say is this. From the moment when the category of 'also', of 'in addition' is introduced, the category of Having creeps imperceptibly in as well. This would be valid even for a single quality, in so far as we are unable to help imagining it in our own minds as *added*—to nothing (within an ideal something which contains it). I feel that important metaphysical conclusions may be drawn from this, notably with regard to the impossibility of thinking of God according to the mode of Having, as *possessing*. In this sense any doctrine of the Attributes would tend inevitably to lead us astray. The *I am that I am* of Scripture would be truly the most adequate formula from an ontological point of view.

Here we ought to ask what is the relation between Having and passivity. I think that we are passive, and offer a hold, in exact proportion as we share in the order of Having. But this is no doubt only one aspect of a deeper reality.

Could not Having be thought of as somehow a way of being what one is not?

It is clear that all these reflections, which seem to be so abstract, are founded for me on a curiously immediate experience of ad-herence to one's possessions (which are exterior without being really so). We must keep returning to the type-case, which is cor-poreity, the fact of having a body, typical having, absolute having. And, beyond corporeity, we must grasp my relation to my life. The ontological meaning of sacrifice of life, of martyrdom. I have already noted this, but we must continually return to it. At the present moment, I also glimpse the need to emphasise at once the apparent identity and the real opposition of martyrdom and suicide: the one an affirmation of self,[1] the other a ruling out of self.

The ontological foundation of Christian asceticism. But this detachment (poverty, chastity, etc.) must not be mere amputation; everything which is shaken off must be simultaneously found again at a higher level. I think all the Gospel texts should be read again in the light of these reflections.

September 27th

I have just re-read these last notes. Must analyse the idea of *belonging*. My body belongs and does not belong to me; that is the root of the difference between suicide and martyrdom. Must lay bare the metaphysical foundations of a study which aims at discovering the limits within which I have the right to dispose of my body. It would be absurd to condemn self-sacrifice on the ground that my body or my life do not belong to me. I must ask myself in what sense, and within what limits, I am the master of my life.

The idea of belonging seems to presuppose the idea of organism, at least in so far as organism is implied in the fact that there is a 'within' in it. But this idea of the 'within' is not clear. If we look into it, we find that in fact it is not purely spatial. The best example here is that of a house, or of anything that can be compared to a house; for instance, a cave.

I thought of this in the Luxemburg, from which I return with this formula: 'Having is the function of an order which carries

---

[1] This formula is clearly inadequate. What is affirmed in martyrdom is not the self, but the Being to which the self becomes a witness in the very act of self-renunciation. But one can conversely say that in suicide, the self affirms itself by its claim to withdraw from reality. (Note written September 27th, 1934.)

with it references to another *qua* another.'[1] It must in fact be seen that the hidden thing, the secret, is *ipso facto* something that can be shewn. Tomorrow I should like to try to examine the counterpart of this from the point of view of being. It is manifest to me that being really implies nothing of the kind. Perhaps even, in the order of being, the Other tends to melt away and be denied.

September 28th

It should be asked whether the distinction between *within* and *without* is not denied by being as such. It is connected with the problem of appearance. We must see whether, when we bring in the idea of appearance, we are not unconsciously shifting our ground to the level of having. When we ask ourselves what is the link between being and the appearances it presents, we are really asking how they can be integrated into it. And the moment the notion of integration comes up, we are back on the level of having. Being, it seems, can never be a sum.

October 7th

I return to the category of having in so far as it is implied in the fact, for a subject, of having (i.e. of carrying with it) predicates. It is not essential to make the distinction between keeping for one's-self and giving out. Having includes the possibility of this alternation and rhythm. Examine the relation between this and the act of consciousness. Does not consciousness also imply this double possibility? There is probably no fundamental difference between being conscious of something and manifesting it to others (i.e. making them conscious of it). The *other* is already there when I am conscious for myself, and expression is, I suppose, only possible be-

---

[1] The connecting link is the fact that the distinction between within and without implies effects of perspective, which are only possible where the distinction is drawn between the *same* and the *other*.

cause this is so. We must pass from there to the infra-conscious and super-conscious. Can we distinguish them? Perhaps this should be correlated with what I wrote on the implications of the question *what am I?* (cf. my note of March 12th).

Could we not say that there is no problem except the problem of Having and what we treat as Having? This would link up with my theory of the ontological mystery. In the sphere of the problematic, the difference between within and without is important; but it melts away as soon as we enter the realm of mystery.

October 11th

Examine the relations between having and being able. To say 'I have the power to . . .' means '*the power to* is numbered among my attributes and endowments'. But that is not all. 'To have' is 'to have power to', since it is clearly in a sense 'to have the disposal of'. Here we touch on one of the most obscure and fundamental aspects of having.

October 13th

I must relate my notes of the last few days to what I said earlier about functional behaviour. A function is, by its very essence, something that one has; but in proportion as my function swallows me up, it becomes me, and substitutes itself for what I am. Function must be distinguished from act, since act clearly escapes from the category of having. As soon as there is creation, in whatever degree, we are in the realm of being; that is what we must manage to make fully intelligible. One difficulty arises from the fact that creation, in the finite sense of the word, is no doubt only possible in the midst of a kind of having. The more creation can shake this off, the nearer it is to absolute creation.

(1) It is instructive to see how philosophers, in the course of history, have for the most part instinctively turned away from Having. This is no doubt because the notion contains much that is ambiguous, obscure, and almost impossible of elucidation.

(2) The moment that a philosopher's attention has turned to Having, this attitude can only appear to him to be unjustifiable. A phenomenological analysis of Having might well be a useful introduction to a renewed analysis of Being. By 'phenomenological analysis' I mean the analysis of an implicit content of thought, as opposed to a psychological analysis of 'states'.

(3) It seems:

(*a*) that we can only speak of Having where a certain *quid* is related to a certain *qui*, treated as a centre of inherence and apprehension, which is in some degree transcendent;

(*b*) that, more strictly, we cannot express ourselves in terms of Having except when we are moving on a level where, in whatever manner or in however analogical a sense, the opposition of *without* and *within* retains its meaning;

(*c*) that this order is manifested to our thought as essentially involving the reference to another *qua* other.

(4) The order of having is the order of predication or the characterisable. But the metaphysical problem which faces us here is to what extent a genuine reality, a reality as such, lends itself to characterisation; and also whether being is not essentially uncharacterisable, though of course it will be understood that the uncharacterisable is not the same as the indeterminate.

(5) The uncharacterisable is also that which cannot be possessed. This brings us back to presence. We return to the difference between the Thou and the He. It is clear that the Thou, treated as He, comes under the jurisdiction of a characterising judgment. But it is

no less clear that the Thou treated as Thou stands on a different level. Examine praise from this point of view.

The opposition of desire to love is a very important illustration of the opposition of Having to Being. Desire is, in fact, having and not having. Desire may be regarded as autocentric and heterocentric at once (the polarity of the same and the other). But love transcends the opposition of the same to the other by planting us in Being.

Another essential application: the difference between autonomy and freedom (cf. my note of February 16th).

October 23rd

I notice for the first time today that there is, in content, the idea of potential action (it can pour out, spread abroad, etc.). There is in content what there is in possession, a potency. Content is not purely spatial.

October 27th

Must examine, more closely than I have done as yet, the nature of the relative dependency of being and having: our possessions swallow us up. The metaphysical roots of the need to preserve. Perhaps this links up with what I have written elsewhere about alienation. The self becomes incorporated in the thing possessed; not only that, but perhaps the self is only there if possession is there too. But the self disappears in the full exercise of an act, of any creation whatever. It only reappears, it seems, when there is a check in creation.

October 29th

I must develop what I said about the uncharacterisable. We cannot think of a character without attaching it to a subject by the link expressed by the verb *to belong*. But this supposes a sort of pattern whose nature we must try to make clear. We are here in an order which essentially carries with it the use of the expression 'also'; this character is chosen *among* others. We are not, however, faced with a collection, as phenomenalism would have us believe, there is always the transcendence of the *qui*. But is not this transcendence a function of the attitude which I take up in face of the *qui*? Is it not a projection? All this is still very misty in my mind; it is an idea that needs bringing into focus.

To think of somebody else is in a manner to affirm myself in face of this somebody else. To put it more accurately, the other is on the far side of a chasm, and there is no isthmus between us. But this chasm or separation is something that I only realise if I stop and stand outside myself—picture myself, if you like that better.

October 30th

Here is my view. The world of the Same and the Other is the world of the identifiable. In so far as I remain its prisoner, I surround myself with a zone of separation. Only on condition that I take my stand in this zone can I think of myself according to the category of Having. To identify is in fact to recognise that something, or someone, has, or has not, such-and-such a character, and, conversely, such-and-such a character is relative to a possible identification.

All this can only have meaning or interest if we manage to conceive of something beyond this world of the Same and the Other; a beyond which reaches out to the ontological as such. This is where the difficulties begin.

One thing we can see immediately; that the question 'What am I?' has no equivalent on the level of Having. To this question I cannot, by definition, give an answer for myself (cf. my notes of last March).

II

OUTLINES OF A PHENOMENOLOGY OF HAVING[1]

The first point I want to make this evening is that the ideas which I am about to put before you are in my opinion nuclear ideas. They contain the germ of a whole philosophy. I will confine myself to the mere adumbration of a great part of it; for if it is sound, others will probably be in a position to elaborate its various branches in forms which I cannot imagine in detail. It is also possible that some of these tracks, whose general direction I hope to indicate, may turn out to lead nowhere.

I think I should tell you, first of all, how it was that I came to ask myself questions about Having. The general consideration was grafted, as it were, on to inquiries which were more particular and concrete, and I think it is essential to begin by referring to them. I apologise for having to quote from myself, but it will be the simplest way of sharing with you the interests which occasioned these researches, otherwise they must seem to you hopelessly abstract. (The written summary you have received will have given you their general sense.)

In the *Journal Métaphysique* I had already begun to state the following problem, which seems at first to be of a purely psychological order. How, I asked, is it possible to identify a feeling which we have for the first time? Experience shows that such an identification is often extremely difficult. (Love may appear in such disconcerting shapes as to prevent those who feel it from suspecting its

[1] Paper delivered to the Lyons Philosophical Society in November, 1933.

real nature.) I observed that an identification of this sort can be realised in proportion as the feeling can be compared with something I *have*, in the sense that I *have* a cold or the measles. In that case, it can be limited, defined and intellectualised. So far as this can be done, I can form some idea of it and compare it with the previous notion I may have had about this feeling in general. (I am, of course, just giving you a skeleton at present, but never mind.) On the other hand, I went on to say, in proportion as my feeling cannot be isolated, and so distinguished, I am less sure of being able to recognise it. But is there not really a sort of emotional woof running across the warp of the feeling I *have*? and is it not consubstantial with what I *am*, and that to such a degree that I cannot really set it before myself and so form a conception of it? This is how I got my first glimpse of something which, though it was not a clear-cut distinction, was at least a sort of scale of subtle differences, an imperceptible shading-off from a feeling I have to a feeling I am. Hence this note written on March 16th, 1933:

'Everything really comes down to the distinction between what we have and what we are. But it is extraordinarily hard to express this in conceptual terms, though it must be possible to do so. What we *have* obviously presents an appearance of externality to ourselves. But it is not an absolute externality. In principle, what we *have* are things (or what can be compared to things, precisely in so far as this comparison is possible). I can only *have*, in the strict sense of the word, something whose existence is, up to a certain point, independent of me. In other words, what I have is added to me; and the fact that it is possessed by me is added to the other properties, qualities, etc., belonging to the thing I have. I only have what I can in some manner and within certain limits dispose of; in other words, in so far as I can be considered as a force, a being endowed with powers. We can only transmit what we have.'

From this point I went on to consider the extremely difficult question of whether there was anything in reality which we cannot transmit and in what manner it could be thought of.

Here, then, is one approach, but it is not the only one. I cannot, for instance, concentrate my attention on what is properly called *my* body—as distinct from the body-as-object considered by physiologists—without coming once more upon this almost impenetrable notion of having. And yet, can I, with real accuracy, say that my body is something which I have? In the first place, can my body as such be called a thing? If I treat it as a thing, what is this 'I' which so treats it? 'In the last analysis,' I wrote in the *Journal Métaphysique* (p. 252), 'we end up with the formula: My body is (an object), I am—nothing. Idealism has one further resource: it can declare that I am the act which posits the objective reality of my body. But is not this a mere sleight-of-hand? I fear so. The difference between this sort of idealism and pure materialism amounts almost to nothing.' But we can go much deeper than this. In particular, we can show the consequences of such a mode of representation or imagination for our attitude towards death or suicide.

Surely killing ourselves is disposing of our bodies (or lives) as though they are something we *have*, as though they are things. And surely this is an implicit admission that we belong to ourselves? But almost unfathomable perplexities then assail us: what is the self? What is this mysterious relation between the self and ourself? It is surely clear that the relation is quite a different thing for the man who refuses to kill himself, because he does not recognise a right to do so, since he does not belong to himself. Beneath this apparently negligible difference of formulae, may we not perceive a kind of gulf which we cannot fill in, and can only explore a step at a time?

I limit myself to these two pointers. There may be others, and we shall notice them as they arise, or at least some of them.

It now becomes necessary to make an analysis. I must warn you that this analysis will not be a *reduction*. On the contrary; it will show us that we are here in the presence of a datum which is opaque and of which we may even be unable to take full possession. But the recognition of an *irreducible* is already an extremely important step in philosophy, and it may even effect a kind of change in the consciousness which makes it.

We cannot, in fact, conceive of this irreducible without also conceiving of a Beyond, in which it is never resolved; and I think that the double existence of an irreducible and the Beyond goes far towards an exact definition of man's metaphysical condition.

We should first notice that the philosophers seem to have always shown a sort of implicit mistrust towards the notion of having (I say 'notion', but we must ask whether this is a suitable expression, and I really think it is not). It almost looks as if the philosophers had on the whole turned away from having, as if it were an impure idea, essentially incapable of being made precise.

The essential ambiguity of having should certainly be underlined from the very beginning. But I think that we cannot, at present, exempt ourselves from going on to the enquiry I am suggesting today. I was prosecuting this enquiry when I first came across Herr Gunter Stern's book *Ueber das Haben* (published at Bonn by Cohen, 1928). I will content myself with quoting these few lines:

'We have a body. We have. . . . In ordinary talk we are perfectly clear about what we mean by this. And yet nobody has thought of turning his attention upon what, in common parlance, is intended by the word "have"; no one has attended to it as a complex of relations, and asked himself in what having consists, simply as having.'

Herr Stern rightly observes that when I say 'I have a body', I do not only mean 'I am conscious of my body': but neither do I mean 'something exists which can be called my body'. It seems that there must be a middle term, a third kingdom. Herr Stern then plunges into an analysis steeped in Husserl's terminology. I will not follow him there, especially as I know (for he has told me so himself) that the results of his enquiry have now ceased to satisfy him. It is now time, I think, to proceed to the most direct explanation we can manage; and we must take care not to have recourse to the language of German phenomenologists, which is so often untranslatable.

It may be asked why, in these circumstances, I have myself made use of the term *phenomenology*.

I reply that the non-psychological character of such an enquiry as this must be emphasised as strongly as possible; for it really concerns the content of the thoughts which it is trying to bring out, so that they may expand in the light of reflection.

I should like to start with the clearest examples I can, where having is plainly in its strongest and most exact sense. There are other cases where this sense (or perhaps we should more properly call it this emphasis) is weakened almost to vanishing point. Such limiting cases can and should be practically neglected (having headaches, for instance, having need, etc.—the absence of the article is a revealing sign here). In cases of the first type, however, that is, in significant cases, it seems that we are right to distinguish two kinds, so long as we do not forget afterwards to ask ourselves about the relations between them. Having-as-possession can itself develop varieties that are very different, and arranged, as it were, in a hierarchy. But the possessive index is as clearly marked when I say, 'I have a bicycle,' as it is when I assert, 'I have my own views on that,' or even when I say (and this takes us in a slightly different direction), 'I have time to do so-and-so.' We will provisionally set aside having-as-implication. In all having-as-possession there does seem to be a certain content. That is too definite a word. Call it a certain *quid* relating to a certain *qui* who is treated as a centre of inherence or apprehension. I purposely abstain from the use of the word subject, because of the special meanings, whether logical or epistemological,

158

which it connotes: whereas it is our task—and difficult for this very reason—to try to blaze a trail for ourselves across territory outside the realms either of logic or of the theory of knowledge.

Notice that the *qui* is from the first taken as in some degree transcendent to the *quid*. By transcendent I just mean that there is a difference of level or degree between the two of them, but I make no attempt to pronounce on the nature of that difference. It is as clear when I say, 'I have a bicycle,' or 'Paul has a bicycle', as when I say 'James has very original ideas about that'.

This is all perfectly simple. The position becomes more complicated when we observe that any assertion about having seems to be somehow built on the model of a kind of prototypical statement, where the *qui* is no other than *myself*. It looks as if having is only felt in its full force, and given its full weight, when it is within 'I have'. If a 'you have' or a 'he has' is possible, it is only possible in virtue of a kind of transference, and such a transference cannot be made without losing something in the process.

This can be made somewhat clearer if we think of the relation which plainly joins possession to power, at any rate where the possession is actual and literal. Power is something which I experience by exercising it or by resisting it—after all, it comes to the same thing.

I should be told here that having is often apt to reduce itself to the fact of containing. But even if we admit that this is so, the important point must still be made, that the containing itself cannot be defined in purely spatial terms. It seems to me always to imply the idea of a potentiality. To contain is to enclose; but to enclose is to prevent, to resist, and to oppose the tendency of the content towards spreading, spilling out, and escaping.

And so I think that the objection, if it is one, turns on a closer examination, against the man who makes it.

At the heart of having, then, we can discern a kind of *suppressed* dynamic, and suppression is certainly the key-word here. It is this which lights up what I call the transcendence of the *qui*. It is significant that the relation embodied in having is, grammatically, found to be intransitive. The verb 'to have' is only used in the passive in exceptional and specialised ways. It is as though we saw passing before us a kind of irreversible progress from the *qui* towards the *quid*. Let me add that we are not here concerned with a mere step taken by the subject reflecting upon having. No, the progress seems to be carried out by the *qui* itself: it seems to be within the *qui*. Here we must pause for a moment, as we are drawing close to the central point.

We can only express ourselves in terms of *having* when we are moving on a level where, in whatever manner and whatever degree of transposition, the contrast between within and without retains a meaning.

This is completely applicable to having-as-implication, of which it is now time to say a few words. It is really perfectly clear that when I say, 'Such-and-such a body has such-and-such a property,' the property appears to me to be inside, or, as it were, rooted in the inside, of the body which it characterises. I observe, on the other hand, that we cannot think of implication without also thinking of force, however obscure the notion may be. I think that we cannot avoid representing the property or character as defining a certain efficacy, a certain essential energy.

But we are not at the end of our investigations.

Reflection will, in fact, now bring before our eyes the existence of a kind of dialectic of internality. *To have* can certainly mean, and even chiefly mean, *to have for one's-self*, to keep for one's-self, to hide. The most interesting and typical example is *having a secret*. But we come back at once to what I said about content. This secret is only a secret because I keep it; but also and at the same time, it is only a secret because I could reveal it. The possibility of betrayal or discovery is inherent in it, and contributes to its definition as a secret.

160

This is not a unique case; it can be verified whenever we are confronted with having in the strongest sense of the word.

The characteristic of a possession is being shewable. There is a strict parallel between having drawings by X in one's portfolios, which can be shewn to this or that visitor, and having ideas or opinion on this or that question.

This act of shewing may take place or unfold before another or before one's-self. The curious thing is that analysis will reveal to us that this difference is devoid of meaning. In so far as I shew my own views to myself, I myself become someone else. That, I suppose, is the metaphysical basis for the possibility of expression. I can only express myself in so far as I can become someone else to myself.

And now we see the transition take place from the first formula to the second one: we can only express ourselves in terms of having, when we are moving on a level implying reference to another taken as another. There is no contradiction between this formula and my remarks just now on 'I have'. The statement 'I have' can only be made over against *another* which is felt to be other.

In so far as I conceive myself as having in myself, or more exactly, as mine, certain characteristics, certain trappings, I consider myself from the point of view of another—but I do not separate myself from this other except after having first implicitly identified myself with him. When I say, for instance, 'I have my own opinion about that,' I imply, 'My opinion is not everybody's'; but I can only exclude or reject everybody's opinion if I have first, by a momentary fiction, assimilated it and made it mine.

Having, therefore, is not found in the scale of purely interior relations, far from it. It would there be meaningless. It is found, rather, in a scale where externality and internality can no longer be really separated, any more than height and depth of musical tone. And here, I think, it is the tension between them that is important.

We must now return to having-as-possession in its strict sense.

Take the simplest case, possession of any object whatever, say a picture. From one point of view we should say that this object is exterior to its possessor. It is spatially distinct from him, and their destinies are also different. And yet this is only a superficial view. The stronger the emphasis placed on having and possession, the less permissible is it to harp upon this externality. It is absolutely certain that there is a link between the *qui* and the *quid*, and that this link is not simply an external conjunction. But in so far as this *quid* is a thing, and consequently subject to the changes and chances proper to things, it may be lost or destroyed. So it becomes, or is in danger of becoming, the centre of a kind of whirlpool of fears and anxieties, thus expressing exactly the tension which is an essential part of the order of having.

It may be said that I can easily be indifferent to the fate of this or that object in my possession. But in that case, I should say that the possession is only nominal, or again, residual.

It is, on the other hand, very important to notice that having already exists, in a most profound sense, in desire or in covetousness. To desire is in a manner to have without having. That is why there is a kind of suffering or burning which is an essential part of desire. It is really the expression of a sort of contradiction; it expresses the friction inseparable from an untenable position. There is also an absolute balance between covetousness and the pain I feel at the idea that I am going to lose what I have, what I thought I had, and what I have no longer. But if this is so, then it seems (a point we had noticed before) that having in some way depends upon time. Here again we shall find ourselves confronted with a kind of mysterious polarity.

There is certainly a two-fold permanency in having: there is the permanency of the *qui*, and the permanency of the *quid*. But this permanency is, of its very nature, threatened. It is willed, or at least wished, and it slips from our grasp. The threat is the hold exerted by the other *qua* other, the other which may be the world itself, and before which I so painfully feel that I am I. I hug to myself this thing which may be torn from me, and I desperately try to incorporate it in myself, to form myself and it into a single and indissoluble complex. A desperate, hopeless struggle.

This brings us back to the body, and corporeity. The primary object with which I identify myself, but which still eludes me, is my own body. We may well think that we are here at the very heart of the mystery, in the very deepest recesses of having. The body is the typical possession. Or is it?

Before pursuing this further, let us return once more to having-as-implication. In this, the characteristics to which I have been drawing attention seem to disappear. Let us go right to one extreme end of the ladder which links up abstract and concrete, and consider the statement, 'A certain geometrical figure has a certain property'. I confess that I cannot, without recourse to pure sophistry, find in this anything at all like that tension between external and internal, that polarity of the same and the other. It is therefore a proper question whether, in taking Having into the very heart of essences—for what I have just said of the geometrical figure seems to me to cover also the living body or species exhibiting certain characteristics—we are not making a sort of unconscious transference which is in the last analysis unjustifiable. That point I will not press, at any rate not now, for it seems to me of secondary interest. But I think that the setting-up of my body as the typical possession marks an essential stage in metaphysical thought.

Having as such is essentially something that *affects* the *qui*. It is never reduced, except in a completely abstract and ideal way, to something of which the *qui* can have the disposal. Always there is a sort of boomerang action, and nowhere is this clearer than in the case of my body, or of an instrument which is an extension of it, or which multiplies its powers. Perhaps this has some analogy with the dialectic of the master and the slave as Hegel has defined it in *The Phenomenology of the Mind*. This dialectic has its spring in the tension without which *real having* does not and cannot exist.

The point we are discussing now lies at the very heart of the world of every day, the world of daily experience with its dangers, its anxieties, and its techniques. At the heart of experience, but also at the heart of the unintelligible. For the fact must be faced, that this tension, this fateful double action, may at any moment turn our lives into a kind of incomprehensible and intolerable slavery.

Before going further, let us once again sum up the position in which we stand.

Normally, or (if you prefer it) usually, I find myself confronted with things: and some of these things have a relationship with me which is at once peculiar and mysterious. These things are not *only external*: it is as though there were a connecting corridor between them and me; they reach me, one might say, underground. In exact proportion as I am attached to these things, they are seen to exercise a power over me which my attachment confers upon them, and which grows as the attachment grows. There is one particular thing which really stands first among them, or which enjoys an absolute priority, in this respect, over them—my body. The tyranny it exercises over me depends, by no means completely, but to a considerable degree, upon the attachment I have for it. But—and this is the most paradoxical feature of the situation—I seem, in the last resort, to be annihilating myself in this attachment, by sinking myself in this body to which I cling. It seems that my body literally devours me, and it is the same with all the other possessions which are somehow attached or hung upon my body. So that in the last analysis—and this is a new point of view—Having as such seems to have a tendency to destroy and lose itself in the very thing it began by possessing, but which now absorbs the master who thought he controlled it. It seems that it is of the very nature of my body, or of my instruments in so far as I treat them as possessions, that they should tend to blot me out, although it is I who possess them.

But if I think again, I shall see that this kind of dialectic is only possible if it starts from an act of desertion which makes it possible. And this observation at once opens up the way to a whole new region.

And yet, what difficulties we find! What an array of possible objections! In particular, could it not be said, 'In so far as you treat the instrument as pure instrument, it has no power over you. You control it yourself and it does not react upon you.' This is perfectly true. But there is a division or interval, hardly measurable by thought, between having something, and controlling or using it: and the danger we are speaking of lies just in this division or interval. Spengler, in the very remarkable book he has just published on *The Decisive Years* and the state of the world today, somewhere notices the distinction that I am getting at here. In speaking of investments or shares in companies, he emphasises the difference between pure having (*das blosse Haben*), and the responsible work of direction which falls to the head of the undertaking. Elsewhere he insists upon the contrast between money, treated as an abstract, in the mass (*Wertmenge*), and real property (*Besitz*), in a piece of land, for example. There is something in this to throw indirect light upon the difficult piece of thinking which I am now trying to explain. 'Our possessions eat us up,' I said just now: and it is truer of us, strangely enough, when we are in a state of inertia in face of objects which are themselves inert, but falser when we are more vitally and actively bound up with something serving as the immediate subject-matter of a personal creative act, a subject-matter perpetually renewed. (It may be the garden of the keen gardener, the farm of a farmer, the violin of a musician, or the laboratory of a scientist.) In all these cases, we may say, having tends, not to be destroyed, but to be sublimated and changed into being.

Wherever there is pure creation, having as such is transcended or etherialised within the creative act: the duality of possessor and possessed is lost in a living reality. This demands the most concrete illustration we can think of, and not mere examples taken from the category of material possessions. I am thinking in particular of such pseudo-possessions as *my ideas and opinions*. In this case, the word 'have' takes on a meaning which is at once positive and threatening. The more I treat my own ideas, or even my convictions, as something *belonging* to me—and so as something I am proud of (unconsciously perhaps) as I might be proud of my greenhouse or my stables—the more surely will these ideas and opinions tend, by their very inertia (or my inertia towards them, which comes to the same thing) to exercise a tyrannical power over me; that is the principle of fanaticism in all its shapes. What happens in the case of the fanatic, and in other cases too, it seems, is a sort of unjustified alienation of the subject—the use of the term is unavoidable here—in face of the thing, whatever it may be. That, in my opinion, is the difference between the ideologist, on the one hand, and the thinker or artist on the other. The ideologist is one of the most dangerous of all human types, because he is unconsciously enslaved to a part of himself which has mortified, and this slavery is bound to manifest itself outwardly as tyranny. There, by the way, may be seen a connexion which deserves serious and separate examination. The thinker, on the other hand, is continually on guard against this alienation, this possible fossilising of his thought. He lives in a continual state of creativity, and the whole of his thought is always being called in question from one minute to the next.

This throws light, I think, on what I have left to say. The man who remains on the plane of having (or of desire) is *centred*, either on himself or on another treated as another; the result is the same in either case, so far as the tension or polarity goes which I was emphasising just now. This point needs a much more detailed development than I can give it at present. The notion of the self, and of one's-self, should really be firmly seized upon. We should then realise that, contrary to the belief of many idealists, particularly the philosophers of consciousness, the *self* is always a thickening, a sclerosis, and perhaps—who knows?—a sort of apparently spiritualised expression (an expression *of* an expression) of the body, not taken in the objective sense but in the sense of *my* body in as far as it is mine, in so far as my body is something I have. Desire is at the same time auto-centric and hetero-centric; we might say that it appears to itself to be hetero-centric when it is really auto-centric, but its appearing so is itself a fact. But we know very well that it is possible to transcend the level of the self and the other; it is transcended both in love and in charity. Love moves on a ground which is neither that of the self, nor that of the other *qua* other; I call it the Thou. I should think a more philosophical designation would be better, if it could be found; but at the same time I do think that abstract terms here might betray us, and land us once more in the region of the *other*, the *He*.

Love, in so far as distinct from desire or as opposed to desire, love treated as the subordination of the self to a superior reality, a reality at my deepest level more truly me than I am myself—love as the breaking of the tension between the self and the other, appears to me to be what one might call the essential ontological datum. I think, and will say so by the way, that the science of ontology will not get out of the scholastic rut until it takes full cognisance of the fact that love comes first.

Along these lines, I think, we can see what is to be understood by the uncharacterisable. I said that, underlying our mental picture of things, as subjects possessing predicates or characteristics, there must be a transference. It seems plain to me that the distinction between the thing and its characteristics cannot have any metaphysical bearing: it is, shall we say, purely phenomenal. Notice, too, that characteristics can only be asserted in an order which admits of the use of the word 'also'. The characteristic is picked out from others; but at the same time, we cannot say that the thing is a collection of characteristics. Characteristics cannot be juxtaposed, and we do not juxtapose them except in so far as we ignore their specifying function and treat them as units or homogeneous entities; but that is a fiction which does not bear examination. I can, strictly speaking, treat an apple, a bullet, a key, and a ball of string as objects of the same nature, and as a sum of units. But it is quite different with the smell of a flower and its colour, or the consistency, flavour and digestibility of a dish. In so far, then, as characterisation consists in enumerating properties, placing one beside the other, it is an absolutely external proceeding; it misleads us, and never, in any circumstances, gives us the least opportunity of reaching the heart of that reality which we are trying to characterise. But, speaking philosophically, the really important point to recognise is that characterisation implies a certain setting of myself in front of the other, and (if I may say so) a sort of radical banishment or cutting-off of me from it. I myself bring about this banishment, by myself implicitly coming to a *halt*, separating myself, and treating myself (though I probably am not conscious of so doing) as a thing bounded by its outlines. It is only in relation to this implicitly limited *thing* that I can place whatever I am trying to characterise.

It is plain that the will to characterise implies, in the man who is exerting it, a belief at once sincere and illusory that he can make abstraction from himself *qua* himself. The Leibnizian idea of *characteristica universalis* shows us how far this *pretention* can go. But I am inclined to think that we forget how untenable, metaphysically speaking, is the position of a thought which believes that it can place itself over against things in order to grasp them. It can certainly develop a system of taking its bearings by things, a system of increasing and even infinite complexity: but its aim is to let the essence of things go.

To say that reality is perhaps uncharacterisable is certainly to make an ambiguous and apparently contradictory pronouncement, and we must be careful not to interpret it in a way which conforms with the principles of present-day agnosticism. This means:–If I adopt that attitude to Reality, which all efforts to characterise it would presuppose, I at once cease to apprehend it *qua* Reality: it slips away from my eyes, leaving me face to face with no more than its ghost. I am deceived by the inevitable coherence of this ghost, and so sink into self-satisfaction and pride, when in fact I ought rather to be attacked by doubts of the soundness of my undertaking.

Characterisation is a certain kind of possession, or claim to possession, of that which cannot be possessed. It is the construction of a little abstract effigy, a *model* as English physicists call it, of a reality which will not lend itself to these tricks, these deceptive pretences, except in the most superficial way. Reality will only play this game with us in so far as we cut ourselves off from it, and consequently are guilty of self-desertion.

I think, therefore, that as we raise ourselves towards Reality, and approach it more nearly, we find that it cannot be compared with an object placed before us on which we can take bearings: and we find, too, that we are ourselves actually changed in the process. If, as I believe, there is an ascending scale of dialectic, in a sense not so essentially different as one might suppose from the Platonic doctrine, then this dialectic is two-fold, and relates not only to reality but also to the being who apprehends it. I cannot, at this time, go into the nature of such a dialectic. I will be content to point out that such a philosophy would give a totally new direction to the doctrine, for example, of the Divine Attributes. I confess that, to myself at any rate, the attributes of God are exactly what certain post-Kantians have called *Grentzbegriff*. If Being is more uncharacterisable (i.e. more unpossessable and more transcendent in every way) in proportion as it has more Being, then the attributes can do no more than express and translate, in terms that are completely inadequate, the fact that Absolute Being is as a whole rebellious to descriptions which will never fit anything but what has less Being. They will only fit an object before which we can place ourselves, reducing ourselves, to some extent, to its measure. and reducing it to ours. God can only be given to me as Absolute Presence in worship; any idea I form of Him is only an abstract expression or intellectualisation of the Presence. I must never fail to remember this, when I try to handle such thoughts; otherwise the thoughts will suffer distortion in my sacrilegious hands.

And so we come at last to what is for me the essential distinction—the central point of my essay on *The Ontological Mystery*, to be published in a few days— the distinction between problem and mystery, already presupposed in the paper you have just heard.

I venture to read now a passage from a paper delivered last year to the Marseilles Philosophical Society. It will appear in a few days from now as the appendix to a play, *le Monde Cassé*.[1]

'In turning my attention to what one usually thinks of as ontological problems, such as Does Being exist? What is Being? etc., I came to observe that I cannot think about these problems without seeing a new gulf open beneath my feet, namely, This I, I who ask questions about being, can I be sure that I exist? What qualifications have I for pursuing these inquiries? If I do not exist, how can I hope to bring them to a conclusion? Even admitting that I do exist, how can I be assured that I do? In spite of the thought which comes first into my head, I do not think that Descartes' *cogito* can be of any help to us here. The *cogito*, as I have written elsewhere, is at the mere threshold of validity; the subject of the *cogito* is the epistemological subject. Cartesianism implies a severance, which may be fatal anyhow, between intellect and life; its result is a depreciation of the one, and an exaltation of the other, both arbitrary. There is here an inevitable rhythm only too familiar to us, for which we are bound to find an explanation. It would certainly not be proper to deny the legitimacy of making distinctions of order within the

[1] Published by Desclée de Brouwer.

unity of a living subject, who *thinks* and strives to *think of himself*. But the ontological problem can only arise beyond such distinctions, and for the living being grasped in his full unity and vitality.

This leads us to ask what conditions are involved in the idea of working out a problem. Wherever a problem is found, I am working upon data placed before me; but at the same time, the general state of affairs authorises me to carry on as if I had no need to trouble myself with this Me who is at work: he is here simply presupposed. It is, as we have just seen, quite a different matter when the inquiry is about Being. Here the ontological status of the questioner becomes of the highest importance. Could it be said, then, that I am involving myself in an infinite regress? No, for by the very act of so conceiving the regress, I am placing myself above it. I am recognising that the whole reflexive process remains within a certain assertion which I *am*—rather than *which I pronounce*—an assertion of which I am the place, and not the subject. Thereby we advance into the realm of the metaproblematic, that is, of mystery. A mystery is a problem which encroaches upon its own data and invades them, and so is transcended *qua* problem.'

We cannot now go on to make further developments, indispensible though they are. I will limit myself to one example in order to give definiteness to my conceptions, and that shall be the mystery of evil.

I am naturally inclined to consider evil as a disorder which I look into; I try to make out its causes, the reason for its existence, and even its hidden ends. How is it that this machine is so defective in its functioning? Or is this apparent defect due to a defect, not apparent but real, in my own vision, a kind of spiritual presbyopia or astigmatism? If so, the real disorder would lie in myself, and yet would remain objective in relation to the mental censorship which unmasked it. But evil simply recognised, or even contemplated, ceases to be evil *suffered*, in fact I think it simply ceases to be evil. I only really grasp it as evil in proportion as it touches me; that is, where I am involved in it in the sense that one is involved in business. This being involved is fundamental, and I can only discount it by an act of the mind, legitimate in some cases, but fictional, and which I must not allow to deceive me.

Traditional philosophy has tended to reduce the mystery of evil to the problem of evil. That is why, when it touches realities of this kind—evil, love and death—it so often gives the impression of being a game, or a kind of intellectual sleight-of-hand. The more idealist the philosophy, the more strong the impression; for the thinking subject is then more deeply intoxicated with an emancipation which is in fact deceptive.

I ought now (though there is hardly time) to go over the whole of the first part of my paper, and try to shew how light can be thrown upon it by these distinctions. It seems clear to me that the realm of having is identical with the realm of the problematic—and at the same time, of course, with the realm where technics can be used. The metaproblematic is in fact metatechnical. Every technic presupposes a group of previously made abstractions which are the condition of its working; it is powerless where full-blooded Being is in question. This point might be drawn out in several directions. At the root of having, as also at the root of the problem or the technic, there lies a certain specialisation or specification of the self, and this is connected with that partial alienation of the self which I mentioned earlier. And this brings us to the examination of a distinction which, to me, seems extremely important and with which I will end this already overloaded lecture—I mean the distinction between autonomy and freedom.

It is essential to note that autonomy is above all the negation of a heteronomy presupposed and rejected. 'I want to run my own life' —that is the radical formula of autonomy. It is here that we can see that tension between the Same and the Other, which is the very pulse of the world of having. We should further recognise, I think, that autonomy bears on any realm which admits of administration, however conceived. It in fact implies the idea of a certain sphere of activity, and can be more closely defined when this sphere can be closely circumscribed in space and time. Anything in the nature of interests, whatever the interests are, can be treated with relative ease as a sphere or district with fixed boundaries. And further, I can, to a great extent, treat my own life as capable of being administered by another or by myself (myself here meaning the not-other). I can administer anything which admits the comparison, however indirect, with a fortune or possession. But it is quite different when the category of having can no longer be applied, for then I can no longer talk of administration in any sense, and so cannot speak of autonomy. Take, for example, the realm of literary or artistic talents. To a certain extent a talent may be administered, when its possessor has taken the measure of it, when his talent resides in him as a possession. But for genius, properly so-called, the idea of such administration is a complete contradiction; for it is of the essence of genius to be always outrunning itself and spilling over in all directions. A man *is* a genius, but *has* talent (the expression 'to *have* genius' is literally meaningless). I really think that the idea of autonomy, whatever we may have thought of it, is bound up with a kind of reduction or particularisation of the subject. The more I enter into the whole of an activity with the whole of myself, the less legitimate it is to say that I am autonomous. In this sense, the philosopher is less autonomous than the scientist, and the scientist less autonomous than the technician. The man who is most autonomous is, in a certain sense, most fully involved. Only this non-autonomy of the philosopher or the great artist is not heteronomy any more than love is hetero-centricity. It is rooted in Being, at a point either short of self or beyond self, and in a sphere which transcends all possible possession; the sphere, indeed, which I reach in contemplation or worship. And, in my view, this means that such non-autonomy is very freedom.

It is not our business here even to outline a theory of freedom, if only because we should have to begin by asking whether the idea of a theory of freedom did not imply contradiction. Here I will point out just one thing: the self-evident truth that in the scale of sanctity and of artistic creation, where freedom glows with its fullest light, it is never autonomy. For the saint and the artist alike, auto-centricity and the self are entirely swallowed up in love. We might perhaps seize this opportunity to show that most of the defects of Kant's philosophy are essentially bound up with the fact that he had no suspicion of all this; he never saw that the self can and should be transcended without there being any need for heter-onomy to replace autonomy in consequence.

I must come to a conclusion, and this is not easy. I will simply return to my preliminary formula. I said then that we should end by the recognition of an irreducible, but that we should also find something beyond this irreducible; and I said that such a duality seemed to me part of the very nature of man's metaphysical condi-tion. What is this irreducible? I do not think that we can, properly speaking, define it, but we can in some measure locate it. It is the ontological deficiency proper to the creature, or at least to the fallen creature. This deficiency is essentially a kind of inertia, but apt to turn into a sort of negative activity, and it cannot be eliminated. On the contrary, our first task is to recognise it. It makes possible a certain number of autonomous and subordinate disciplines; each of them certainly representing danger to the unity of the creature in so far as it tends to absorb it, but each also having its own worth, and partial justification. And therefore it is also necessary that these activities and autonomous functions should be balanced and harmonised by the central activities. In these, man is recalled into the presence of mystery, that mystery which is the foundation of his very being, and apart from which he is nothingness: the grand mystery of religion, art and metaphysic.

PART TWO
FAITH AND REALITY

I

SOME REMARKS ON THE IRRELIGION OF TODAY[1]

I shall do my best today to define the attitude of mind which regards the religious question simply as obsolete. This attitude demands a careful definition.

It is not necessarily the same thing to say that the religious question is obsolete and to deny that a religious datum persists, provided that the datum belongs to the realm of feeling. By definition, this datum could not be obsolete; but a custom or idea can be obsolete, and so can a belief in so far as it can be treated as an idea. There would also be no point in denying that religion needs explanation when regarded as a fact, i.e. as a body of institutions, rites, etc.; it would indeed be absurd to try. (It is even worth noticing that with a certain type of mind, the greater its separation from any kind of religious life, the greater also is its curiosity about the origin of so strange and diverse a set of phenomena, and about the reason for its obviously important place in human history.) When people say 'The religious question is obsolete', they mean 'there is no longer any point in asking whether the assertions of religion correspond with anything in reality. There is no point in asking whether a Being exists having the attributes traditionally connected with the word God; nor whether salvation, as believers call it, is anything but a certain form of subjective experience which they clumsily interpret in terms of myth. Everybody,' they add, 'will realise why.' I shall here quote a passage from Bertrand Russell, as it seems to me

[1] Lecture delivered on December 4th, 1930, to the *Fédération des Associations d'Étudiants chrétiens*.

most significant. 'That Man is the product of causes which had no prevision of the end they were achieving; that his origin, his growth, his hopes and fears, his loves and his beliefs, are but the outcome of accidental collocations of atoms; that no fire, no heroism, no intensity of thought and feeling can preserve an individual life beyond the grave; that all the labours of the ages, all the devotion, all the inspiration, all the noonday brightness of human genius, are destined to extinction in the vast death of the solar system, and that the whole temple of Man's achievement must inevitably be buried beneath the débris of a universe in ruins—all these things, if not quite beyond dispute, are yet so nearly certain, that no philosophy which rejects them can hope to stand.'[1]

Russell's private religious beliefs do not, of course, concern us here. The interest of the passage lies rather in its being a typical statement of the negative creed implied in the attitude we set out to examine. There are undeniably some people who claim that you can found a religion even upon this cosmic despair. I must say that I cannot see how this can be maintained without a shocking misuse of terms, and one day I will explain why.

Perhaps it will throw a little light on the tortuous path down which I am going to take you, if I mention at once that I propose to work from three consecutive points of view—three distinct positions, or three steps in a scale. They are: (1) the point of view of pure rationalism, or the philosophy of Enlightenment; (2) applied science, or rather, the philosophy of applied science; (3) the philosophy founded on the supremacy of Life, or the Vital Principle.

First, let us look at the peculiar idea of modernity involved in the sort of rationalism we are trying to describe. 'Today,' they say, 'it is no longer possible to believe in miracles or the Incarnation.' 'A man of 1930 cannot possibly accept the doctrine of the resurrection of the body.' These are examples taken at random. The interesting

[1] *Philosophical Essays*, p. 60.

thing about them, to me, is their emphasis on the *date*, which is treated as a point of view, one might almost say a specially favourable position for seeing things—call it, if you like, an *observatory*. They seem to be representing Time or History as a space containing fields of unequal quality; and accordingly they use epithets like 'advanced' and 'retrograde' to imply approval and disapproval; such epithets are a striking feature of the political psychology of our own country. They will be quite ready to admit the fact that the latest phase in time may show a falling-back by comparison with the previous stage. This is to be expected, because enlightened minds may find themselves mixed up with reactionary ones at some particular point in time. A power-problem may arise, and the reactionaries may get the upper hand for the moment, so that there is an apparent setback. But they assure us that it will not last; sooner or later the human mind will set out again on its victorious march towards the light. 'The light.' A word (or conception in the vaguest sense of the term) whose importance cannot be over-estimated. I believe that if we really thought about it, we should find it to be the expression—secularised and stripped to the last ounce of meaning—of an idea worked out by the Greeks and still more by the Fathers of the Church. We will not press the point at present. Their manner of presenting this idea of progressive enlightenment is two-fold: sometimes it is ethical-political (the word obscurantism being very significant here) and sometimes technical-scientific. The two aspects are closely bound up with each other.

The first point to notice is this. A philosophy of enlightenment is almost bound to make capital of the popular trick of comparing humanity, considered throughout the whole of its history, with a single person passing from childhood to adolescence, from adolescence to manhood, and so on. The enlightened mind regards itself as an adult, who can no longer allow himself the pleasure of repeating the nursery stories that so delighted his childish age. But this is an over-simplified picture, and open to the gravest objections. We might well ask whether childhood has not its own peculiar values —a happy trustfulness, a peculiar candour—which the grown man should preserve at all costs, unless he is to land up at a dogmatism dictated by experience and unable to bear him any fruit but jejune cynicism. Many great truths come into play in this connection, and have been admirably expounded by such writers as Péguy.

And there is a second point, still more important. Most people would agree without question that the progress of enlightenment cannot take place without a progressive elimination of the anthropocentric element. They enlist on their side the wonders of modern astronomy, thus: 'Before Copernicus and Galileo', they say, 'it was perfectly natural to think that the Earth was the centre of the Universe, and that man occupied a special position in what they still called Creation. But astronomy has put the Earth and Man in their proper perspective. Now we can see that the place they occupy is almost infinitesimal compared with the immense size of the visible universe.' All this seems aimed at taking down the simple-minded and ridiculous pride of mankind, which thought itself the supreme expression and perhaps ultimate purpose of the cosmos.

But please notice at once that this philosophy only *seems* to be satirising human pride, in spite of its foundation of positive cosmology. It is in fact exalting it. There is a shift of position, and what an extraordinary one it is! It is true that Man regarded as an object of science is thrust back into the ranks, a mere object among an infinite crowd of other objects. But Man still possesses one thing that claims to transcend the material world to which he is reduced —Science. We will not call it Human Science, for these philosophers are doing their best to dehumanise and deracinate Science, and consider it by itself in its intrinsic movement. So they will talk to us of Mind and Thought (in capitals). It would be a mistake not to take the capitals seriously, because they exactly express the attempt to depersonalise Mind and Thought. They are no longer somebody's mind, or somebody's thought; they are no longer presences. They are a sort of ideal system, with a free range and flexibility of their own, as the philosophers will be at pains to point out. A writer like M. Brunschwicg—who has done more than anyone now alive to build up this rationalism (this spirituality, as he, in my opinion, quite wrongly, calls it)—such a man, I say, as M. Brunschwicg, is very far from believing that this development of Mind or Science is the unfolding in Time of an absolute Principle, existing for itself through all Eternity, like Aristotle's *Nous* or Hegel's *Absolute Mind*. To him, *Nous* and *Absolute Mind* are just metaphysical fictions. The Mind of his own panegyrics is still called God, but it is devoid of all attributes which can give the word any meaning. 'No doubt', he concedes at the end of his book on *The Progress of Consciousness*, 'No doubt a God who has no point of contact with any uniquely important event in space or time, a God who has taken no initiative and assumed no responsibility for the physical aspect of the Universe; who has willed neither the ice of the poles nor the heat of the tropics; who cares neither for the hugeness of the elephant nor the minuteness of the ant; neither for the destructive action of the microbe nor the constructive reaction of the globule; a God who never dreams of punishing the sins of ourselves or our ancestors; who knows no more of perjured men than of rebellious angels; who grants success neither to the prediction of the prophet nor to the miracle of the magician; a God who has no dwelling-place either in Earth or Heaven, who can be perceived at no special point in history, who speaks no language and can be translated into none: this God, to the primitive mentality or the coarse supernaturalism so clearly professed by William James, is what he would call an abstract ideal. But for a thought which has travelled further away from its own beginnings, a thought which has become subtler and more highly trained, this

God is one who abstracts himself from nothing and for whom nothing is abstract, since concrete reality is only what it is through its intrinsic truth-value.' An important passage, worthy of serious consideration. We are aware throughout of the far more terrible pride of the man who thanks God that he is free from the primitive mentality, and rejoices in his adult status without misgiving. Remember the phrases I have quoted to you already, 'In our time it is no longer permissible ...'; 'A man of 1930 could not allow ...' and so on.

But take care. If, in the eyes of a Christian philosopher like Saint Bonaventure, Man appeared to be the centre of the Universe, he was so only as being an image of God. *'Esse imaginem Dei,'* he writes, *'non est homini accidens, sed potius substantiale, sicut esse vestigium nulli accidit creaturae.'* (To be an image of God is not accidental to man but of his essence, just as it cannot be an accident to a footprint to have been imprinted.) Plainly, the 'ridiculous anthropocentric attitude' is really just applied theocentrism. To Saint Augustine, Saint Thomas and Saint Bonaventure, God is the centre, and God alone. But today it is the human mind, dehumanised, stripped of all power, all presence, and all existence, and then put in God's place to act as His substitute.

It is plainly very difficult to think one's way into such a philosophy. Its initiates are few. I am sure that most people who think the religious question obsolete would not subscribe to it, but would prefer to adopt an agnosticism modelled on Spencer or a materialism such as Le Dantéc's. This is, of course, worse from a speculative point of view, but it finds more numerous and firmer footholds in our minds. What are the footholds of a doctrine like M. Brunschwicg's? Pride, first of all, and I am not afraid to say so. I shall be contradicted; they will say that it is not personal pride, for the Mind they are telling us about is not the Mind of an individual. My first answer is, that it is, or tries to be, the Mind of everybody.

And we know very well, from Plato onwards, what a deal of flattery democracy will allow itself—and this idealism, after all, is simply transposed democracy. And that is not all. The idealist is bound in the end to substitute himself for the Mind—and then we have an individual to deal with. Let us confront him with the (as he thinks) shocking spectacle of a Christian astronomer. How can an astronomer believe in the Incarnation or go to Mass? The idealist's only hope is to put up a distinction. As an astronomer, this monster (or rather this amphibian) is a man of the twentieth century and the idealist can greet him as a contemporary. As a man who believes in the Incarnation, however, and goes to Mass, he is behaving like a mediaeval—or a child; and this is a pity. When we ask the philosopher to justify his extraordinary dichotomy, he may call upon Reason and Mind till he is black in the face, but he will not convince us; especially when we see that he does not scruple to use psychological and even sociological arguments to account for these survivals in the astronomer, while he absolutely forbids us turn such arguments or analyses upon himself. He is a man of 1930 from top to toe. And yet he is still invoking an Eternal Mind, but a Mind which has none the less been born; who Its next incarnation will be, Heaven only knows. Frankly, I find all this extremely incoherent. If a Marxist, for example, were to tackle the idealist and tell him plainly that his Mind was a purely bourgeois product begotten of economic leisure, the idealist would have to take refuge in the realm of completely bloodless abstractions. I think myself that idealism of this kind cannot help being cornered, with concrete religious philosophy hemming it in on one side, and historical materialism on the other. For it is in fact impotent when confronted with history—any real history, even if it is just the history of a single life. It has no feeling for tragedy, and (what is worse) no feeling for flesh and blood either. Personally, I think that people who substitute the Cartesian concept of matter for the richly confused idea of the *flesh* which is embedded in all Christian philosophy are doing anything but progressing in their metaphysics. There is an almost untouched task here, and pure metaphysicians would do well to focus all their attention upon it, or so I think: the task of describing the evolution and progressive confusion of the notions of flesh and fleshly existence in the history of philosophical thought.

At bottom, this idealism is a purely professorial doctrine, and falls directly under Schopenhauer's partially unjust criticism of the academic philosophers of his day. (It was partially unjust, because there is a real feeling for concreteness and human drama in such writers as Schelling and Hegel.)

In point of fact, philosophical idealism would very likely have had no appreciable effect upon the development of human thought, had it not found a redoubtable ally in all forms of applied science. I believe that the spirit of applied science is really in itself the most serious obstacle, for many perfectly candid minds, to the acceptance of the notion of religious life, or rather religious truth.

Some rather complicated considerations arise here, and you must forgive me if my analysis seems somewhat over-subtle. I think we have reached the crux of the whole problem.

By 'applied science' I mean, in a general way, any branch of learning which tends to guarantee to man the mastery of a definite object. And so any applied science can obviously be regarded as manipulation, as a way of handling or moulding a given matter. (The matter itself may belong to the mind, as in the science of history or psychology.)

Several points here are worth considering. (1) A science can be defined by the various handles which its object offers it. But conversely, an object itself is only an object in virtue of the handles it offers us, and this is true upon the most elementary level, of simple external perception. For this reason there is a parallel between advance in science and advance in objectivity. An object is more of an object, more *exposed* if I may put it like that, when the sciences under which it falls are more numerous or more developed.

(2) An applied science is in its very nature perfectible. It can always be brought to a higher and higher point of accuracy and adjustment. I would myself add that the inverse is also true, and that nowhere else but in the realm of applied science can we speak of perfectibility and progress in an absolutely strict sense. In this realm alone can perfection be measured, since it is equivalent to output.

(3) This last point is perhaps most important of all. We are becoming more and more aware that all power, in the human sense of the word, implies the use of applied science. The simple-minded optimism of the masses today is founded on this fact. No one could deny that the existence of aeroplanes and wireless sets seems to the vast majority of our contemporaries to be the proof or palpable gauge of progress.

But we should notice the reverse side too—the price paid for such victories. From the scientific point of view, the world in which we live is apt to look at one moment like a mere field for development, and at the next like a subjugated slave. Any newspaper article about a disaster is full of the implicit suggestion that the monster we thought we had tamed is breaking out and taking its revenge. This is the point where applied science links up with idealism. Man is treated now not as Mind but as technical power, and appears as the sole citadel of orderly arrangement in a world which is unworthy of him; a world which has not deserved him, and has to all appearance produced him quite haphazard—or rather, he has wrenched himself out of it by a violent act of emancipation. That is the full meaning of the Prometheus myth. I dare say a great many technicians would shrug their shoulders to hear so strange a mythology laid at their door. But if they are simply technicians and nothing more, what can they do about it? Nothing. They can only immure themselves in the fortress of their own specialised knowledge, and refuse, in fact if not in words, to tackle the problem of unifying the world or reality. Some attempts at synthesis will, of course, be made, because the desire to unify is in fact irresistibly strong, indeed it may be the very foundation of intellectual life. But if you compare these syntheses with the sciences themselves, they will always look relatively adventitious. 'They seem to be rather in the air,' we should say; an everyday phrase which wonderfully expresses the lack of footholds offered by pure synthesis compared with specialised science. From now onwards a shadow seems to spread over reality and make it more and more obscure. We can now only make out that there are different regions; they are still in the light, but the way from one to another is obscured. And that is not the worst. We cannot be fooled by words. The scientific power must belong to somebody, surely? since somebody must exercise it. But who is this 'subject'? We come back again to our former conclusions. The subject will himself be seen as the object of possible sciences. The sciences are distinct and multiple, joined by hardly definable connections. It naturally follows—and experience fully proves—that the sciences themselves are less effective *as* sciences in proportion as they come to bear on realms where these water-tight compartments can no longer hold. That is why the sciences of psychology and psychiatry at present show such disappointing results.

But now we are faced with an appalling and quite unavoidable problem. The subject who lies in his turn at the mercy (if I may so phrase it) of applied science cannot be a source of clarity or a centre of radiation; on the contrary, he can only enjoy a reflected light, a light borrowed from objects, since the sciences to be applied to him will inevitably be constructed on the model of the sciences directed upon the external world. They will therefore be the same in character, although transposed and inverted. To the admirable criticism of Bergson, the most lasting part of his work, I need only allude; I am sure there is no need for me to go into details. But it might be worth making just one further observation. Where the sciences thus extend their sway in all directions, there is one part of the subject—and therefore of concrete reality—which cannot be overrun, namely, the immediate feelings of pleasure and pain. And hand-in-hand with the amazing development of science, there goes, as we should expect, an intensification of the most immediate and also most elementary part of our affective life: call it the desire for a 'good time' if you will. I do not mean that this connection is an absolute rule or that it can be made good in every case. But in practice we do find that the two things go together, and a little general observation and thought will convince us that this is so. We do find in fact that unusually high development of the applied sciences goes with great impoverishment of our inner lives. The lack of proportion between the apparatus at the disposal of humanity and the ends it is called upon to realise seems more and more outrageous. I am sure to be told that the individual in the scientific state tends to be subordinated to social ends which go far beyond him; but is this really so? We have often heard the sociological sophistry that the whole contains more than the sum of its parts. But the truth is that although it undoubtedly contains something other than they do, all the evidence seems to show that the difference falls on the debit side and is expressible by a minus sign. There is no reason why a society of dunces, whose individual ideal is the spasmodic jigging of the dance-hall or the thrill of the sentimental and sensational film, should be anything more than a dunce society. It is obviously the inferior or rudimentary qualities in these individuals which draw them together. There is the difference, by the way, between a society like this and a community like the Church; for there the individuals do not swarm together mechanically, but do form a whole which transcends them. Such a community, however, is only possible because its members have each of them managed to keep inviolate that inner citadel called the soul, to which all sciences as such are opposed. To my mind, the most serious objection that can be raised to such a doctrine as Marxism is this: that it can maintain itself only in the struggle for its own supremacy; as soon as it is supreme, it destroys itself and makes way for nothing better than coarse hedonism. That is why many of the young people whom you see among you today, professing to be Communists, would, I am sure, go over to the Opposition at once if Communism were to win the day.

These criticisms bring us indirectly to the definition of an order which stands in sharp and complete contrast to the world of applied sciences. Pure religion, religion as distinct from magic and opposed to it, is the exact contrary of an applied science; for it constitutes a realm where the subject is confronted with something over which he can obtain no hold at all. If the word transcendence describes anything whatever, it must be this—the absolute, impassable gulf which opens between the soul and Being whenever Being refuses us a hold. No gesture is more significant than the joined hands of the believer, mutely witnessing that nothing can be done and nothing changed, and that he comes simply to give himself up. Whether the gesture is one of dedication or of worship, we can still say that the feeling behind it is the realisation of the Holy, and that awe, love and fear all enter into it simultaneously. Notice that there is no question here of a passive state; to assert that would be to imply that the activity of the technician, as he takes, modifies or elaborates, is the only activity worthy of the name.

We must, of course, recognise that we are in a state of utter confusion today about this point and many others. It is almost impossible for us to avoid a picture of activity which would be in some sense physical. We can hardly help seeing it as the starting-up of a machine, a machine of which our bodies are the spring and perhaps also the model. We have completely lost sight of the classical idea, taken up and enriched by the Fathers of the Church, that contemplation is the highest form of activity: and it might be worth while to ask ourselves why. The moralistic point of view in all its forms, with its belief in the almost exclusive value of works, seems to be very largely responsible for discrediting the contemplative virtues. Kantianism still more, by bringing in constructive activity as the formal principle of knowledge, has had the same disastrous tendency; it refuses all positive reality to the contemplative virtues, were it only by the fatal separation which it made for the first time between theoretical and practical reason. I admit, of course, that no true contemplation can be practised except from within a realist metaphysical system—and will not here go into the nature of the realism in question, which is not, of course, necessarily the same as St. Thomas's.

There is no reason, then, to deny that worship can be an act: but this act is not simple apprehension. It is in fact extremely difficult to define, particularly the aspect which is not mere apprehension. We might say that it was the act of simultaneously throwing one's-self open and offering one's-self up. They would grant us that as a psychological description: but opening to what? offering to what? Modern subjectivism is at once up in arms, and we are back at the first formulation. But I think it is beyond dispute that if pure subjectivism ought really to be considered as a standpoint attained once for all by the modern mind, then the religious question would indeed have to be regarded as obsolete. One contemporary example is of particular use here. It is quite obvious that religion is impossible in such a universe as Proust's; and if, here and there, we come across something which belongs to the religious category, this just means that cracks have appeared in the structure of Proust's universe.

But I think that this subjectivism cannot be for one moment

regarded as an established position. I have only time to indicate the general directions of my reasons for thinking this, and will not go into details today. My own position on this point agrees almost completely with that of M. Jacques Maritain, and has common ground also with the German theories of intentionality held by contemporary phenomenologists. I believe that Descartes and his disciples only opposed realism because they had a partly materialist notion of it. 'Despite their claim to treat of sense and intelligence,' says Maritain, 'Descartes and Kant never came beyond the threshold, because they spoke of them in the same way as they did of other things, and had no knowledge of the realm of mind.' I should like to add a parallel observation: they made illegitimate borrowings from optics in their epistomology, with effects that can hardly be exaggerated. Here is another example of science made the starting-point for the effacement of spiritual reality.

I think, then, that it is only by leaning on unfounded postulates of this sort that one is led to treat worship, for example, as a mere attitude having no link with any reality whatever. But if we go behind them, if that is, we climb resolutely up the hill down which modern philosophy has been slipping for more than two centuries, then I believe it is possible for us to recover the basic idea of sacred knowledge: and this alone can restore its reality to contemplation.

I am a little ashamed to offer you superficial and hasty outlines of such very complicated and important ideas. But I cannot hope to do more than reconnoitre such an enormous territory. As Peter Wust, the German metaphysician, writes: 'If we consider the evolution of the theory of knowledge from Plato and St. Augustine, through the Middle Ages, and up to the present time, we feel that we are witnessing a more and more successful process of secularisation being applied to that holy part of the human mind which can only be called the *intimum mentis*.' He goes on to say that we moderns have to proceed by way of a metaphysic of knowledge to the slow and painful *recovery* of something which was *given* in the Middle Ages through a mysticism veiled in mystery and awe. I think we could put this more simply by saying that we may have lost touch with the fundamental truth that knowledge implies previous *askesis*—purification, in fact—and that when all is said and done, knowledge in its fulness is not vouchsafed except where it has first been deserved. And here once more I think that the progress of applied science, and the habit of considering knowledge itself as a technical operation which leaves the knower wholly un-affected, has powerfully militated against a clear view of these matters. The *askesis* or purification must chiefly lie, it is clear, in progressively detaching ourselves from speculative thought in so far as it is purely critical and simply the faculty of making objections. 'Truth is perhaps wretched,' said Renan, and Claudel was angry with the phrase—because it sums up with terse cynicism what I should like to call the *Philosophy of the But*. When Barrés in his *Notebooks* speaks of 'the mournful melancholy of Truth', he is speaking from the heart of this philosophy. It is the root of every kind of pessimism; and sacred knowledge (as I called it) is its flat negation. A negation which is not always a starting-point, but perhaps more often, and certainly in Claudel's own case, the fruit of a heroic struggle.

Here again, I think, we touch on one of the most sensitive points of our subject—call it a nerve-centre, if you will. For most people, to say that the religious question is obsolete is the same as to say that the incurable imperfection of the world is now an established truth. And here we cannot overestimate the practical importance of the kind of negative apologetics which atheists habitually use: they seize every chance to show that the universe falls below our demands and can never satisfy them, and that the metaphysical expectation which we feel within us, whether it be inheritance or survival, can never be fulfilled by things as they are.

But—and this is surprising—their insistence on the imperfection of the world goes hand in hand with a complete inability to think of evil as evil, or sin as sin. Here again we see the technical approach at work. The world is treated as a machine whose functioning leaves much to be desired. Man is luckily at hand to correct some of the faults; but for the moment, unfortunately, the whole is not in his control. It should be added that these faults or defects of working are nobody's fault: for there is nobody there to blame. Only man is *somebody*: otherwise there is simply an impersonal mechanism. And even Man is quite prepared to treat himself like the rest, by the process of inversion or internalisation of which I spoke above; to sink himself into this depersonalised cosmos. He is quite prepared to see in himself certain defects of working, which must be curable by taking various measures, and applying various kinds of individual or social therapeutic action.

This presents us with a most illuminating connection: the relation between worship on the one hand and consciousness of sin on the other; for sin cannot be dealt with by any form of science, but only by the supernatural action of grace. May I draw your attention to the fact that the relation implied in science is here reversed? For not only does the reality involved in worship elude all possible control by the human subject, but also the subject seems, inversely, to pass under the control of an incomprehensible choice emanating from the mysterious depths of Being.

This body of facts can alone give meaning to the notion of salvation. Salvation is quite meaningless in an intellectual climate dominated by the belief in a natural order which it is the business of science to restore, wherever it is found to have been accidentally upset.

The idea of an order or natural course of life, to be re-established if necessary by suitable means, brings us to the third and perhaps the most central battlefield of the debate. Here the basic idea is neither the progress of enlightenment nor the advancement of technical science, but the march of Life itself, taken, not as a value, but as a source of values or a basis for evaluation.

A little while ago I heard of a characteristic remark made by one of the people most at the centre of international social work. 'I don't object to mysteries on principle,' he said, 'in fact there may *be* mysteries for all I know. But I can't feel any personal interest in, for instance, the doctrine of the Trinity. I don't see what it has to do with me or what use it can be to me.' Now this seems to me a most significant attitude. The worthy man could have become passionately interested in a discussion of fiscal justice, or the principles of social security, for he would have recognised its 'vital' character: but he thinks the Trinity is merely a subject for idle speculation. The word 'vital', taken in its literal sense, is what should occupy us here. Notice that there is a very obvious connection between the idea of life (or the primacy of the Vital) and my earlier remarks about the spirit of applied science. For the mastery of objects is still, after all, relative to life considered as something of intrinsic value, something which is its own justification. I will not harp on the origin of this idea, and will merely remind you that Nietzsche gave the completest expression to it. In Nietzsche the idea of life slides into the will to power, an idea which at first glance may appear more precise. But in other writers the idea retains its rich vagueness (and therefore, it must be added, its basic ambiguity). The single point I want to stress is this. To many minds it is life which is the unique criterion or beacon of all values (and some of these who so believe think themselves Christians; here indeed is food for thought!). For instance, take the elementary distinction between right and wrong. In their eyes, an action will be right if it tells in favour of life, wrong if it tells against it.

Notice at once that from this point of view life is something on which we neither need nor can pass judgment. Questions about the value of life are no longer in order, for life is itself the principle of all value. But here an ambiguity at once arises before us, presenting us with inextricable difficulties. What life are we talking about? Mine? Yours? Or life in general?

First of all, it is clear that this doctrine, which seems to have no rational basis, can only be justified by being immediately self-evident. But to what is the self-evidence attached if not to my own feelings about *my own life*, and the special sort of warmth I feel radiating from it? Is it not linked up with the irreducible datum of my own self-love?

Unfortunately it is also perfectly clear that the people who claim to use Life as their criterion of values, especially where conflicts arise, are by no means referring to my life *qua* mine, but to life in general. For instance, a Swiss schoolmaster friend of mine who believes in the primacy of Life (though he would not interpret it in the least like Nietzsche) will be at pains to point out to his pupils that the practice of chastity, or, in a very different sphere, the practice of co-operation, is bound up with Life itself, and that if we flout these great duties we are flouting Life, etc. Two points are immediately apparent here. First, my friend has begun by defining Life in a tendentious way so that it is coloured by certain spiritual needs in himself, though he has no direct awareness of them. Secondly, if we take life generally, yet vaguely in the mass, we cannot draw from it the same doctrine as we can from the immediate though restricted intuition felt exclusively about my life in direct experience.

A philosophy of Life is therefore destined by its own nature to be ambiguous. It either simply claims to translate certain biological truths into general terms; in which case, the field of such truths being enormous, it might be used to justify contradictory theories. (I need not remind you, perhaps, of the extraordinary actions which one of our most notorious contemporary writers claims to justify by parallels in the animal kingdom.) Or else it will make a bold but unjustifiable projection, and, ceasing to consider life as a phenomenon or group of phenomena which are biologically observable, will see instead a kind of spiritual force or current; in which case it will at once lose its experimental status. I think, for my own part that there is something unprincipled in this attempt to eat one's cake and have it too; here is a doctrine which presents as the expression of empirical data what is really only a free choice of the mind.

The more concrete our examples, the more hopeless the confusion we find.

If any axiom is implied in the scattered and unformulated philosophy which colours or underlies present-day literature, it seems to be this: 'I am the same as my life. I am my life. To say that my life will one day be spent means that on that day I myself shall be entirely spent.' The writers suppose that only a body of fictions, which should be regarded as pure survivals, stand between me and this fundamental identity. Do not let us ask how this error or mistake is metaphysically possible, for that enquiry would take us too far out of our way. The claim they are making is that life somehow secretes spiritual poisons which may block its stream at any moment, and that it is the task of consciousness to dissolve these poisons and flow, as far as it can, with the stream it has thus cleared.

Now these are certainly metaphors, and I am sure they originate in the philosophy of applied science of which I spoke just now. That is not important here. The important thing to see here is where we shall be led by so understanding the relation between ourselves and our lives or (to put it more accurately) by holding this view of intellectual honesty. I think that we here touch upon the most serious problem raised by the literature of the last few years, and especially by M. Gide. I can only approach it from one direction.

It should be noted that this concern for perfect sincerity corresponds incontestably and explicitly with the desire for freedom. I refer you to such books as *Les Nourritures Terrestres*—an extraordinarily significant piece of evidence. But what is the price of freedom? Nothing less than a complete renunciation of all claims to master my life. For mastering my life is in effect subordinating it to some principle. Even supposing that this principle is not a passively acquired heritage, it will still represent a phase of my past in fossilised form. This phase of my past has no right to govern my present. But if I am to shake off the yoke of the past, there is only one way of doing it—by giving myself over to the moment and forbidding myself any form of commitment, any kind of vow. Surely you will agree with me that this liberty, in the cause of which I am putting constant constraint on myself, has nothing in it, no *content*; in fact it is the refusal of all content whatsoever. I am well aware that M. Gide—not the Gide of today, the rationalist who is perhaps rather like Voltaire, but the Gide of *Les Nourritures Terrestres*—will praise the fulness of the unclouded instant, savoured in all its novelty. But it is all too clear that dialectic has the last word here: it teaches us that novelty cannot be savoured except by the unconscious reference to a past with which it is contrasted; and that, strangely enough, there is a satiety of novelty; one can be weary of the succession of one new thing after another for the very reason that they are all new.

And this brings us within sight of another fact, too important to pass over, though it is difficult to speak of it without smacking of the stale old sermons you have so often heard before. But our recent experiences have brought the old truths into terrible relief—would it were not so!—the truth that nothing comes nearer to despair, the rejection of being and suicide, than a certain way of extolling Life as the pure present moment. There is obviously no need for us to declare, like that young and impetuous Catholic apologist, M. Jean Maxence, that 'Kant calls to Gide, and Gide to André Breton, and Breton leads Jacques Vaché to suicide.'[1] That really is rather too sweeping a way of describing the genealogies of

[1] *Positions*, p. 218.

195

thought: indeed, in passing from Kant to Gide, M. Maxence is making out a case which cannot be upheld. I do not think that despair is the necessary outcome of Gide's doctrine of the moment; but only because the soul does not lack resources and sometimes has defences of which it is itself unaware. The story of M. Gide and his works proves this well enough. In my opinion, this doctrine of the Instant is not only a *limiting* position, but also a *literary* position carrying with it literary advantages; and on the whole it is recognised as such, at least implicitly. A man who really lived by it would be destined, is destined, and will be destined to the worst of spiritual catastrophes.

I will draw a single conclusion from these observations. We can find no salvation for mind or soul unless we see the difference between our being and our life. The distinction may be in some ways a mysterious one, but the mystery itself is a source of light. To say 'my being is not identical with my life' is to say two different things. First, that since I *am* not my life, my life must have been given to me; in a sense unfathomable to man, I am previous to it; *I am* comes before *I live*. Second, my being is something which is in jeopardy from the moment my life begins, and must be saved; my being is a stake, and therein perhaps lies the whole meaning of life. And from this second point of view, I am not *before* but *beyond* my life. This is the only possible way to explain the ordeal of human life (and if it is not an ordeal, I do not see what else it can be). And here again, I hope very much that these words will not stir up in our minds memories of stereotyped phrases drowsily heard in the torpor too often induced by a Sunday sermon. When Keats— certainly not a Christian in the strict meaning of the word—spoke of the world as a 'vale of soul-making', and declared in the same letter of April 28th, 1819 (p. 256 Colvin's edition) that 'as various as the Lives of Men are—so various become their souls, and thus does God make individual beings, Souls, Identical Souls, of the sparks of his own essence', he had the same idea as mine, though in his inimitable style it takes on far greater splendour and freshness. This brings me to my last point.

I realise perfectly that the words 'grace' and 'salvation' give some of you a heartbreaking feeling of staleness. There is nothing new in them for voice or vision. The air around them has been breathed so long that it has become stifling. Now this is at the bottom of all the surrealist experiments of the day—this need to escape to something completely unknown. They contain nothing, I believe, that is not partially justifiable, so long as we turn away our eyes from the self-hatred and devilish perversion so often cloaked by the desire for novelty.

But two observations are necessary here. Grace and salvation are no doubt commonplaces, like their peers, birth, love and death. They can none of them be tricked out anew, for they are all unique. The first time a man falls in love, or knows that he is to be a father or to die, he cannot feel he is hearing stale news. He would more likely feel that it was the first time anyone had ever loved or had a child or prepared for death. It is the same with genuine religious life. Sin, grace and salvation, as words, may be old stuff; as facts they are not, since they lie at the very heart of our destiny.

But that is not my only answer. There is another yet. I believe most deeply that in the sphere of religion, too, the need for renewal is legitimate up to a point; that is, as far as it concerns forms of expression. And on this note I would end my lecture. I am sure that the reputation enjoyed by some modern schools of thought, and the human reverence commanded by or corresponding to this reputation, has been shown to have a destructive effect on spiritual development. But I believe that there is also a danger in thinking that philosophico-theological ideas such as we find in St. Thomas Aquinas, for instance (not doctrine, for that is another story), are suitable for everybody in our day, just as they stand. I am inclined to say that they are suited to some minds but not to all; and that the profoundly true intuitions expressed in the Thomist formulae would gain greatly in force and intelligibility if they could be presented in fresh terms; in words that were newer, simpler, more moving, and more closely in tune with our own experience and (if you will forgive the word) our own ordeal. But this presupposes a refashioning which would only be possible after an immense preliminary work of criticism and reconstruction. Today we are nearly buried under the rubble. Till the rubble has been cleared away it is hopeless to think of building. It is a thankless task, appallingly thankless, yet I think that it must be done; only thus can religious life recover its soaring power. It is needed by the already convinced Christians, who would otherwise sink into the lethargy of devitalised doctrine. It is needed still more by those who are as yet unbelievers; who are feeling their way and surely longing to believe, and end their agonising struggle, if they would only admit it; who fear that they may be yielding to temptation if they surrender to the mounting faith and hope they feel in their hearts. It is sheer madness to call this speculative labour a mere luxury. It is, I repeat, a necessity, demanded not only by reason but also by charity. I think that those who say (in perfect good faith) that Christianity is first and above all a social matter, a doctrine of mutual help, a sort of sublimated philanthropy, are making a grievous and dangerous mistake. Their use of the word 'Life' is (as we have seen before) charged with ambiguity. I think that the man who says 'It doesn't matter what you think so long as you lead a Christian life' is committing the worst of offences against Him who said 'I am the Way, the Truth, and the Life'. The Truth. It is on the ground of Truth that we should fight our first battle for religion; on this field only can it be won or lost. In the issue of that fight, man will show whether he has indeed betrayed his mission and his destiny; we shall see, then, whether or no loyalty must remain the standard of a little chosen band of saints, advancing to their certain martyrdom, and indefatigably praying as they go for those who have chosen the shadows.

II

SOME THOUGHTS ON FAITH[1]

I wish to make one thing clear from the start: not the point of view from which I hope to treat the subject—you can gather that for yourselves—but the personal attitude I intend to take up, and the kind of support I hope to obtain from my hearers.

In point of fact, it is not my desire to speak to you simply as a Catholic, but rather as a Christian philosopher. Let me put it like this. It so happens that I have come to the Christian faith late in life, and after a winding and intricate journey. This journey I do not regret, for many reasons and especially because I can still recall it vividly enough to feel a particular sympathy with those who are yet on the road, following out, often with great difficulty, tracks resembling those which I stumbled along in my time.

This metaphor cannot be avoided; but of course it is clumsy and in some ways even scandalous. I can in no sense boast of having *arrived*. I am convinced that I see more clearly than I did, though 'convinced' is a word at once too weak and too intellectual. That is all. Perhaps it would be better to say this; the freer and more detached parts of me have struggled up into the light, but there is still much of me that lies in shadow, untouched by the almost level rays of the dawning sun: much of me is still, as Claudel would put it, unevangelised. This part of me can still have a fellow-feeling for groping souls, travellers and seekers. But even this view is superficial. For I believe that no man, however enlightened and holy he is, can ever really arrive until the others, *all* the others, have started out

---

[1] Lecture addressed to the *Fédération des Étudiants Chrétiens*, February 28th, 1934.

to follow him. That is a great truth, and applies to philosophy as well as to religion, though philosophers have on the whole neglected it, for reasons which I will not go into at present.

I can now explain the general direction of the task I have set myself today. I want to make it my business to *reflect* before those who follow in my footsteps, and so perhaps to stretch out a helping hand to them as they climb the dark hill of Destiny, our common fate. We never climb alone, though we often seem to do so; belief in loneliness is the first illusion to dispel, the first obstacle to overcome; in some cases the first temptation to conquer. There is no need for me to say that I chiefly address myself to the less fortunate among you; to those who despair of ever reaching the summit of the mountain, or (what is worse) are persuaded that there is no summit and no ascent, and that the adventure of Life is reduced to tramping miserably about in the mists; the process will go on till death, when total extinction will devour or dedicate its incomprehensible vacuity.

First, then, I will put myself in the place of those wandering travellers who have ceased to believe even in a goal to be attained— I mean a metaphysical goal, not a social one—and who have ceased to attach any meaning to the word 'destiny'.

These wanderers are legion, and we must not deceive ourselves with the belief that they can be rallied by explanation or encouragement; yet I think there is one sort of meditation which has a rousing force. I think there is something which has greater power than art or poetry in the tragic state of the world's struggle today. A concrete metaphysic, in tune with the deepest notes of our personal experience, may have a decisive part to play for many souls. In the short time allowed to me, I will try to indicate some roads that a few people may not disdain to follow.

I want to attempt to draw out the more or less implicit idea of faith formed in the minds of those who honestly believe as a certainty that they do not possess it. For the sake of analysis, I think we shall have to distinguish several cases to which unbelief as we know it can always be more or less accurately reduced. I shall purposely neglect the case (which is anyhow very rare) of those who reply to our questions, 'To me the word *faith* is meaningless; I do not even understand what it could denote.' The man I am thinking of would be bound, if we pressed him, to adopt one of the following positions:

(1) Either he would join the ranks of those who think that faith is simply a weakness and a form of credulity, and congratulate themselves on being free of it.

(2) Or else, far from deriding it, he will say that faith is a boon to its possessor, but that this boon is denied to himself. The second case is ambiguous and must be further subdivided into three possibilities:

(*a*) He may mean 'Faith is admittedly a convenient deception, but unfortunately it does not deceive me'. In this case he is really preening himself on a sort of superiority, which is balanced by the admission of the painful price exacted by it. But fundamentally he despises what he seems or pretends to envy, so he is in the same case as the unbeliever who regards faith as a mere weakness.

(*b*) Faith may also be regarded as a pleasant idiosyncrasy, rather like a feeling for music. But this second alternative is itself ambiguous. For the man of faith is in fact making assertions about reality, which the music-lover, of course, is not. Are these assertions valid? The unbeliever whose case we are at present considering would no doubt say 'Yes, they are valid for the man who makes them'. But this is equivalent to saying that they are false, for the man who makes these assertions claims that they are for everybody and not only for himself.

(c) Last of all comes the case, more frequent than most people imagine, of the unbeliever who regards faith as a real communion with a higher reality for the man who has it, but confesses that this reality is unfortunately not revealed to him. In this case, the unbeliever speaks of faith almost as a blind man speaks of sight.

I find it particularly easy to describe the last case, since for many years it was my own. I even wrote that I believed in the faith of others although I had none myself. But I have realised since then that this was a contradictory attitude, and that it was anyhow a deep delusion to think that I could really believe in the faith of others if I had none of my own. The fact is that when we have already come as far as this, we are in an open and expectant state of mind which either implies faith or is faith. At any rate, I wrote during the same period, 'I do not truly know whether I have faith or not: I do not know what I believe.'

And so today I am inclined to think that the state expressed by this confession of uncertainty is really, though not consciously, the state of the man who thinks he can roundly declare himself to be without faith.

FAITH A FORM OF CREDULITY

Now let us return to the first two cases I described, and particularly to the idea that faith is a form of credulity. Does it and can it correspond to the believer's idea of his faith or to his experience of it?

We at once meet with a difficulty, a paradox. Faith is a virtue: can this be squared with interpreting faith as credulity?

At first sight we should say 'Certainly not'. Virtue is a power, but credulity is a weakness, a relaxation of judgment. It seems then that the believer and the unbeliever are using the same word for two unrelated things. I foresee that the unbeliever will reply something like this: 'The believer holds that faith is a virtue because it implies a kind of humility. But to us, it is just this humility which seems so despicable, for it touches a part of our nature that we think it is wrong to humiliate, namely our judgment. And whence comes this need of humbling the judgment? From radical cowardice. Life in the world presents us with a terrible picture. Yes, but the truly wise man, whose wisdom is also heroism, is not afraid to look the world in the face. He knows that, outside himself and his own reason, he has no hope of finding any refuge from the misrule which governs the world. The believer, on the other hand, fancies that there is an ultimate refuge beyond the world, in which he puts his trust and to which he makes his prayer. He fancies that the God he invokes is pleased by his worship; and so he comes to treat as a virtue what we unbelievers know very well to be nothing better than escapism and voluntary blindness.'

FAITH AN ESCAPE

This is the centre of the problem. We have, I think, managed to grasp the idea of faith as it is held by the unbeliever when the unbelief is absolute and takes the form of rejection, almost of disgust. But we are bound to ask ourselves about the position to which such a judgment refers.

Observe in the first place that the interpretation of faith as escape is a pure construction, and in many cases does not correspond with the facts. For instance, I can assure you from my own experience that my faith was born at a time when I was in an exceptional state of moral stability and personal happiness. Otherwise I might have been suspicious of it. To what does this invention of the unbeliever correspond?

We might do well here to consider the penetrating remarks made by Scheler in his book *Resentful Man*. The unbeliever, he said, takes it for granted that all true values must be universal, and such that they are admitted by everyone. He says that something which can be neither demonstrated nor communicated, and which does not force itself irresistibly upon all reasonable creatures, whoever they may be, has no more than a purely subjective significance and may therefore be legitimately set aside. But what is the reason for this concern for widespread universality? Why this appeal to the judgment of the first comer, whoever he may be? Scheler inclines to the view that it is due to a grudge so deep-seated that it is unconscious; the grudge felt all too often by the *have-nots* towards the *haves*. Whatever he may say, whatever interpretation he strives to put on this destitution which he wants to call emancipation, it must be admitted that, now and then, the unbeliever will see himself as a *have-not* and the believer as a *have*.

UNBELIEF BASICALLY EMOTIONAL

There is, then, an emotional element lurking beneath the apparently objective and rational assertion or claim made by the unbeliever; and what is more, deeper thought on the matter will show us that it could not be otherwise.

Let us examine once more the assertion of the militant unbeliever. It comes down to this. 'I know there is nothing there: if you try to persuade yourself to the contrary, it is just because you are too cowardly to face this terrible truth.' *I know there is nothing there.* Try to take in the monstrosity of that assertion. It is offered, or at least should normally be offered, as the conclusion of infinite research. In fact, such research is impossible. Our position in the universe does not allow us even to begin it. So weak is our position that we cannot even value the life of one of our fellow-men and judge whether it repays his trouble in living it. So if the pessimists seem to be reporting the results of a research, they are just deceiving us. It is an unconscious imposture. 'Pessimism', I wrote at the time when I was unsure whether I believed or not, 'can only be a philosophy of disappointment. It is a purely polemical doctrine, and the pessimist who holds it is making an attack upon himself or upon an opponent

outside himself. It is the philosophy of "Do you? Well, I don't".'
The unbeliever, then, who is really the same as the absolute pessimist, must not be held up as the defender of objective truth. There
is in fact no attitude more subjective, and more insidiously subjective, than his own.

SCEPTICISM

But are we not therefore driven into a kind of despairing scepticism? Are we not forced to say simply that certain persons have the
faculty of belief, as a given body has a given property, and that
others have not? that this faculty may indeed be enviable, but that,
after all, this leads us nowhere and brings us to no conclusion, and
that we cannot know whether the delusion lies with the believers or
the unbelievers?

This position seems to be quite untenable, and I should like to
say clearly why.

What does this scepticism really imply?

It finally comes down to saying to the believer, 'Perhaps you can
see something that I can't, but the mistake may just as well be on
your side. No judgment between us is possible. All the same,
perhaps you suppose that you can see someone who is not really
there.'

THE CONTRADICTIONS OF SCEPTICISM

The whole question here is whether, in voicing this doubt, one
is not unconsciously substituting, for the reality of faith, an entirely
imaginary notion which is not in the least like the deep and undeniable experience of the believer.

When I say to my man, 'You thought you saw someone, but I
think you were mistaken and that there was no one there,' we are
both of us on the level of objective experiment, and this implies by
definition that there are points of reference, verifications, and an

impersonal (or rather depersonalised) check. My assertion can only make sense if there are means of ascertaining that the other man's belief did not correspond with reality, i.e. if an observer X, assumed to be normal and endowed with a normal sensory apparatus and a sane judgment, could be put in our place and arbitrate between us. But it is easy to see that such a substitution is quite inconceivable here, and that we cannot even imagine its being made.

If we think about it, indeed, we shall see that the substitution can only be made on a level, or on a spiritual plane, where our individuality is specialised, and momentarily reduced, for certain practical purposes, to a partial or partialised expression of itself. For instance, I can very well say to someone whose sight is better than mine, 'Come and stand here and tell me if you see so-and-so.' Or to someone with a more subtle sense of taste, 'Come and taste this and tell me what you think of it.' Even in more complex cases, which nevertheless only employ some elements of the personality (normalis-able elements we might call them), I could say to somebody else, 'Put yourself in my place—what would you do?' But I can no longer do it in cases where the *whole* of a person is involved: no one can put himself *in my place*. And faith, when it is most real and most like itself (for we must of course not consider its degraded or mech-anical expressions here) is most sure to issue from the whole being of a man and to *involve* him.

This is not all. We must notice that the object of faith is simply not manifested with the characteristics which distinguish any em-pirical person. It cannot figure in experience, since it entirely com-mands and transcends experience. If I am in some ways led to regard it as outside myself, it appears to my consciousness still more essentially as being within myself, more inward to me than I can be to myself, I who invoke or assert it. This means that the distinction between internal and external, and the categories of outside and inside, vanish as soon as faith comes on to the scene. An essential point this,: though the psychology of religion by its very definition ignores it, since it equates faith with a simple state of the soul, a purely internal event. Much could profitably be drawn from this, but I cannot attempt it now. If I were forced to use a metaphor, I should say that the believer thinks of himself as within a reality which at once penetrates and enfolds him.

From this new point of view the sceptic's attitude becomes meaningless. For if he says, 'Perhaps there is nobody there, where you think there is somebody,' he is appealing, either actually or by implication, to a corrective experience which by definition would leave outside itself the very thing which is in question: for the object of faith is assumed to transcend the conditions implied in all experience. We must recognise, therefore, that as faith is revealed in its pure nature, it will triumph more and more over the sceptics, who can only question the value of faith because they begin with a picture of it which caricatures it.

It might also be said that scepticism tends to treat belief and unbelief as attitudes which, although of course they are mutually exclusive, are nevertheless related to each other as two alternative suppositions; and thereby fails to appreciate their essential incommensurability. It is not enough to say that the believer's universe is not the same as the unbeliever's. We must understand that it overflows it in all directions and integrates it, just as the world of the seeing man overflows and integrates the world of the blind man.

UNBELIEF A REFUSAL

But there is something else no less important. As the soul approaches more nearly to faith, and becomes more conscious of the transcendence of her object, she perceives more and more clearly that she is utterly incapable of producing this faith, of spinning it of her own substance. For she knows herself, she realises more and more clearly her own weakness, impotence and instability; and thus

207

she is led to a discovery. This faith of hers can only be an adherence, or, more exactly, a response. Adherence to what? Response to what? It is hard to put into words. To an impalpable and silent invitation which fills her, or, to say it in another way, which puts pressure upon her without constraining her. The pressure is not irresistible: if it were, faith would no longer be faith. Faith is only possible to a free creature, that is, a creature who has been given the mysterious and awful power of withholding himself.

And so the problem stated at the beginning of this lecture appears under a new guise. From the point of view of faith and of the believer, unbelief, at any rate when it is explicit, begins to look like a refusal, refusal moreover which can take on many different forms. I will merely observe here that very often, perhaps most often, it takes the form of inattention, of turning a deaf ear to the appeal made by an inner voice to all that is deepest in us. It should be noticed that modern life tends to encourage this inattention, indeed almost to enforce it, by the way it dehumanises man and cuts him off from his centre, reducing him to a collection of functions which have no power of intercommunication. We must add that where religious faith seems to survive in a man who is thus department-alised, it is apt to become debased and to look like mere routine to an outside observer. Unbelief will this time have a shred of justification, though here again it rests on nothing but a misunderstanding.

This inattention or distraction is indeed a kind of sleep, from which we can each of us awake at any time. The inattentive man may be awakened just by meeting somebody who radiates genuine faith—which, like a light, transfigures the creature in whom it dwells. I am one of those who attach an inestimable value to personal encounters. They are a spiritual fact of the highest importance, though unrecognised by traditional philosophy, for reasons which are perfectly clear but irrelevant to our present discussion. The virtue of such encounters is to rouse the inattentive to a reflection or return upon themselves, to make them say 'Am I really sure that I don't believe'? This is enough: if the soul really asks herself this question in all sincerity, rejecting all angry prejudices and parrot imaginings, she will be brought to recognise, not indeed that she already believes, but that she is in no case to say that she does not believe. Or perhaps it would be truer to say that the assertion of unbelief, made just then, would almost inevitably be tainted with pride, and that completely honest and careful introspection could not fail to unmask this pride. 'I do not believe' ceases to look like 'I cannot believe' in its own eyes, and tends to turn into 'I will not believe'.

HAS HEROISM AN INTRINSIC VALUE?

Fom this last point of view, the spiritual position of a man like André Malraux may be regarded as specially significant, one might almost say typical. His absolute pessimism about the world as it stands has, as its reverse side, the (no doubt originally Nietzschean) idea that what matters most is, not the wretchedness of man, but his greatness, not that he must do without succour and be resigned to doing without, but that he must not even desire it. To a Malraux, man has not grown to manhood or reached his full stature until he has taken full account of his own tragic position. In the eyes of the author of *La Condition Humaine*, this alone makes heroism possible. We stand here on the backbone of a steep ridge which keeps apart some of the most courageous minds of our generation. But we at once notice something that may well disturb us. What exactly does it mean to assign an intrinsic value to heroism? It seems plain to me that the value is here attached to a kind of ardour and to the entirely subjective feelings about it of the man who is striving to act heroically. But there is no valid or objective reason why heroic ardour should be put higher on the list than any other sort, for instance, erotic ardour. You can only justify the hierarchy by bringing in an entirely new scale of considerations, which have nothing to do with either heroism or ardour; for instance, social utilitarianism. But as soon as we get on to that ground, we contradict the Nietzschean idea from which we started. To a logical Nietzschean, social utility is an idol, one might almost say a low-grade idol. Of course I am perfectly prepared to admit that in a book like *La Condition Humaine* charity breaks out in two or three places; but it comes like a voice from another world. I think you can only link heroism and love together if you slur over the facts; they are irreducible except in a single case, the heroism of the martyr. I take that word in its strictest sense, *witness*. But in a philosophy which turns on refusal, there is no place for witness, since witness refers to a higher reality acknowledged in worship.

THE DEBASEMENT OF THE WORD 'WITNESS'

Like so many other important ideas, the notion of witness has become considerably debased. The first thing that occurs to us when we hear the word is the witness we may be called upon to give when we have been present at some event. And so we develop a tendency to think of ourselves as recording-machines, and to treat witness as the mere playing-over of the record. Hence we forget the really important point about witness; its attestation. That is the essential here. Yes, but what is attesting? Not simply establishing a fact; nor simply asserting. When I attest, I bind myself, but I do it of my own free will, since attestation given under the yoke of constraint would be useless and would deny its own nature. In this sense it brings into being the closest and most mysterious union of necessity and liberty. There is no act more essentially human than this. At the root of it there is the recognition of a certain datum: but at the same time there is something else quite different. In attesting, I really proclaim, *ipso facto*, that I should be going back on myself, and—yes—even annulling myself, were I to deny this fact, this reality of which I have been the witness. The denial, of course, may take place, as mistake, contradiction or betrayal, and it is a betrayal indeed. It is extremely important to show how degrees in attestation are conceivable. Its spiritual value becomes more and more noticeable where it has to do with those invisible realities which do not beat upon us with the immediate, strident and irresistible obviousness of the objects of sense-experience. We see here a paradox which cannot be too strongly insisted upon. The realities to which religious attestation refers are certainly transcendent: but from another point of view they look as if they really needed that humble and beggarly witness, the believer who attests them. There could surely be no better example of the incomprehensible, or perhaps rather supra-intelligible polarity which lies at the heart of faith.

FAITH AND ATTESTATION

Indeed, the closeness of the link between faith and attestation becomes fully apparent as soon as we touch upon the intermediary idea of fidelity. There cannot be faith without fidelity. Faith in itself is not a movement of the soul, a transport or ravishment: it is simply unceasing attestation.

Yet here once more we must turn back to the unbelievers. They cannot resist interrupting us here with a question—always the same one, and we come up against it at every stage of the unending dispute—'What about the people who can only witness to the injustice they have fallen prey to, the manifold suffering they have undergone, the abuses they have seen? How can they give their witness in favour of a higher reality?' Once more the stumbling-block is the problem of evil. I have already given a partial answer to this question, but I should like to point out also that the great witnesses have certainly never been recruited from the fortunate of this world, but far more from the suffering and the persecuted. If there is one single conclusion forced upon us by the spiritual history of mankind, it is that the growth of faith is hindered, not by misfortune, but by satisfaction. There is a close kinship between satisfaction and death. In all domains, but especially perhaps in the domain of the spirit, the man who is satisfied, and admits himself to have everything he needs, is already beginning to rot. Satisfaction is what so often gives birth to the *taedium vitae*, the secret disgust, which we may all have felt at times, one of the most subtle of all the forms of spiritual corruption.

But of course this does not mean that a philosophy of attestation and faith need necessarily be a cult of moral pain. The quality which is furthest from satisfaction is not pain, but joy. The neo-pagan critics of Christianity have never had the least conception of this. They fail to see the close kinship which joins joy to faith and hope, and to the thankfulness of the witnessing soul who glorifies God. We must make a new use here of the distinction that M. Bergson so admirably drew between the Closed and the Open. Satisfaction is something that happens within doors, in a *closed* creature; but joy can only unfold beneath the open sky. It is radiant in its very nature; it is like the sun at noonday. But we must not let a spatial metaphor deceive us. The distinction between open and closed only takes on its full meaning when we are speaking of faith. Or, to go deeper still, when we are speaking of the free act of the soul, as she wills or refuses to acknowledge that higher principle which momently creates her and is the cause of her being, and as she makes herself penetrable or impenetrable to that transcendent yet inward action without which she is nothing.

PETER WUST ON THE NATURE OF PIETY

Peter Wust writes, 'We should assign the first beginnings of philosophy to the primitive emotion (*Uraffect*) called Astonishment.'[1] It is true to say that modern philosophy from its beginning tried to put methodical doubt in the place of astonishment, and saw in it a point *a priori* to all rational speculation. But this is simply a clear indication of the way in which fundamental metaphysical relations were already being overthrown at that period. Doubt is really no more than a *second a priori* of philosophical thought, if I may so phrase it; a phenomenon of reaction, a kind of recoil, which can only take place when our deepest being has been somehow split by an ontological mistrust so deep-rooted as to be almost a *habitus* of the soul. Mistrust or trust towards Being; those, to Wust, are the two main directions which every mind inclined to speculation must choose between. Even this is not enough; the opposition is of wider importance. It does not only concern the metaphysician's solutions of the theoretical problem of reality, but the whole of culture considered in all its expressions.[2]

The human mind, since Descartes, has been familiar with the idea of a scientific philosophy (i.e. one without presuppositions). But this implies, for the same reasons, a monstrous (*ungeheuerlich*)

[1] *Dialektik des Geistes*, p. 212.
[2] At first sight we might here be tempted to reply by reminding Wust of the high place accorded by Descartes to Admiration in his theory of the passions. But did he ever think of it as a metaphysical starting-point? or, still more, as what we might call a sensitive zone where Being acknowledged as such grips the creature whom admiration stirs? It would seem rash to claim that he did.

upsetting of speculative balance.[1] 'Scientific' philosophising is surely just setting one's-self the almost inhuman task of denying, absolutely and in the very depths of the soul, all pre-eminence and all positive hegemony of values. The philosopher has to say, at the very beginning of his enquiry, that he does not know whether there is such a thing as order or whether chaos is equally possible. He bears witness—or rather is thought to do so—that Yes and No are equally indifferent to him. In his eyes, this indifference is the sacred badge of the philosopher.

But we should ask whether this indifference is genuine or even possible. Wust thinks that an analysis which went deeper than that of Descartes would show us that astonishment at ourselves is the basis of doubt.

My doubt betrays my consciousness of my own contingent character and—still more implicitly—of the hidden gravitation of my own deepest being to a *centre* or an absolute *middle point* of being (not indeed apprehended but surmised) where the metaphysical insecurity of the creature may at last find rest. This insecurity and instability, contrasting so strangely with the everlasting repose and immutable order of Nature, is the central mystery, and the philosophy of Wust might be said to be an exhaustive inquiry into it. Nowhere else today, I think, could we find a more resolute attempt to define the metaphysical position of humanity; and to relate it, on the one hand, to the order of Nature which it breaks through and transcends, and on the other hand to a supreme Reality which enfolds it on every side, though it never violates the relative independence that is the prerogative of the creature. For this Reality is itself free and freely sows the harvest of freedoms.

Astonishment, as we see it, for example, in the eyes of a child, is the shaft of light which breaks through the enfolding clouds of our natural sleep, that sleep which holds under its sway whatever is

[1] *Loc. cit.,* p. 213.

absolutely subject to the Law. Astonishment is the rising of 'the sun of the spirit blazing on the horizon of our being and filling us wholly with *supra-vital* delight, as its first rays gild and discover the exquisite panorama of creation and the eternal order that rules it'.[1]

How can we fail to see in this the inspiration running through the whole work of our own Claudel? Perhaps indeed it must direct all truly Catholic theories of knowledge.

> *Wretched? How can I say without impiety*
> *That the truth of the things His highest hand has fashioned*
> *Is a wretched truth? Can I say without absurdity*
> *That a world which wears His likeness and works to His glory*
> *Is less than myself, and my most imagination*
> *Overtops it, and finds in it nothing to lean on?*[2]

Claudel has emphasised the ὕβρις, the impious pride, at the root of such doubt, and Wust himself never tires of denouncing it. Reviving the tradition of the great Doctors, so harshly broken by the 'scientific' philosophy engendered by the *Cogito*, he reminds us of the great truth which Jacques Maritain has stressed in our own time and country with such force: that knowledge is in itself a mystery. The great mistake of idealism perhaps lies in its initial assumption that the act of thinking is transparent to itself, whereas it is nothing of the kind. Knowledge is in fact unable to give an account of itself. When it tries to think itself, it is led irresistibly either to be content with metaphorical and material expressions which caricature it, or to treat itself as an absolute and self-sufficient datum, enjoying a priority to its object so startling that it becomes impossible to understand how it can be so entirely incapable, as far as one can see, of creating that object in all its unimaginable richness.

But of course we can never be content just to say that knowledge

[1] *Loc. cit.,* p. 206. [2] *Le Soulier de Satin,* 1st day, Scene VI.

is a mystery; we must add that it is a gift, perhaps, in a way, a grace; and that is Wust's claim when he attributes to it a 'naturally charismatic'[1] quality; though this is gradually hidden from the conscious mind by the increasing secularisation of the knowing process. Once the secularisation is complete—and it is going on everywhere in the modern world—it must give rise to all the excesses of a self-intoxicated reason, cut off at once from belief and being, and bound to regard itself as an exploiting power whose actions are only censored by itself. And the world, too, in whose bosom this 'Promethean' power is at play, is stripped of all the attributes originally given to it by those unsophisticated minds for whom knowledge was not yet distinct from worship.

It must be made absolutely clear that the philosophy of Wust is not to be construed as fideism. He explains himself on this point with perfect clarity in the *Dialectic of the Spirit*.[2] 'The fideist', he says, 'is at the antipodes of the simple faith of the child; his faith is really the faith of despair.'[3] But of what does he despair, if not of his own poor human reason? and that because he began by presuming too much upon it. It would be no paradox to maintain that the fideist is a 'fallen Gnostic'. (The word 'gnostic', of course, is here used to describe those who put an absolute value on their needs or claims to know.) Wust, faithful to his love of dialectical oppositions and reconciliations (a heritage from Fichte, probably), also observes that the same 'Lucifer-like' point of consciousness closely unites the two attitudes, however opposed their indices may appear to a superficial consideration.

But the genuine Christian keeps his distance from both pitfalls equally. When he witnesses to his trust in the universal Order, his witness should not be interpreted as mere surface optimism, but

[1] *Naivität und Pietät*, p. 184.   [2] Cf. especially pp. 620 *et seq.*
[3] 'The fideist', he says, 'makes a desperate leap into the eternal night of Godhead.'

recognised as the result of his reverence for the whole of Reality. It may easily seem irrational *to us*, at least to some extent, but nothing justifies our attributing existence *in itself* to this irrationality. 'The mind that throws itself upon Reality like a child knows that every personal creature is saved in so far as he surrenders without stint and without despair to the inner wooing of that Love whose voice he hears unceasingly in the depths of his soul.'[1]

I think it is impossible to exaggerate the importance of the part played in Wust's philosophy by this Platonic Idea of Childhood. It would obviously be absurd to set against it the alarming 'facts' of all the Freudian case-histories. However precociously the spirit of mistrust and cunning and perversity arises in the mind of a child, the Idea nevertheless has unbreakable validity. For it is a Witnessing Idea, one might almost say a Judging Idea; or better still, perhaps, an absolute *a priori* of human sensibility. One could quote the admirable passage where Wust is asking what it is that we find missing in the Stoic sage, and the sage as Spinoza, and even Schopenhauer conceives him, however near they come to sanctity. He replies that the lack in all of them is the lack of supreme and innocent delight in existence (*Daseinsfreude*), of the idealism and optimism so opposed to the tragic outlook. Despite their greatness and heroic dignity, despite the serene smile that plays over their lips (and what indescribable subtlety it has, the smile of the Buddhist monks of Ling-Yang-Tsi!), they lack that final security in existence, that armour of proof which guards the simple child, his serene trust and innocence. The sages renowned in history are still not innocent children in the strange and deep sense of the Gospel: 'Verily, I say unto you, Whosoever shall not receive the Kingdom of God as a little child, he shall not enter therein' (Mark x. 15). 'This is the only possible way for the wise man to attain supreme wisdom; however deeply he has drunk at all the springs of human

[1] *op. cit.*, p. 622.

knowledge, however fully his spirit has supped of the bitter experience of the world.'[1]

But someone may ask, is there any real reason why these sages, whether Buddhist or Stoic, should not recapture the soul of the child? One fact prevents them, according to Wust; they have broken away from the filial relationship with the Supreme Spirit, and this alone is what enables a man to have a child-like attitude towards the ultimate secret of things. This relationship is automatically destroyed by the triumph of naturalistic philosophy, which depersonalised the supreme principle of the universe: for to this view necessity can only appear as either fate or blind chance; and a man weighed down by such a burden is in no state ever to regain his vanished delight and absolute trust. He can no longer cling to the deep metaphysical optimism, wherein the primal simplicity of the creature in the morning of life joins the simplicity of the sage— better here to call him the saint—who, after journeying through experience, returns to the original point of the circle; the happy state of childhood which is almost the lost paradise of the human mind.[2]

Of course, we may ask whether this Paradise can indeed be regained; how can we imagine the recovery of a state which after all does seem related to non-experience as such? Wust's answer to this question is chiefly, as we have seen before, that there is an active principle of order and love (an It, an *Es*, over against the Me, the *Ich*) working continuously in the depth of our being. It is therefore a metaphysical impossibility for the Me ever completely to break its moorings and sever itself from its ontological roots. And therefore, if I have understood him rightly, a positive conversion remains

[1] *Naivität und Pietät*, p. 110.
[2] Wust, of course, explicitly recognises the Fall as a fact (cf. *Dial. des Geistes*, p. 311, for an example), but it is far from incompatible with the deeper optimism here in question.

possible to the end. The self, renouncing the 'Promethean' pride whose only end is death, and avoiding also the opposite extreme of agnostical and desperate pessimism, at last makes confession of that *docta ignorantia* described by Nicolas of Cusa at the dawn of our age. Let me say once more that this is not the act of spiritual suicide encouraged by certain kinds of fideism, but the glad acceptance, made in a spirit of devout humility, of the limits set by supreme Wisdom to the manner of knowledge with which It has endowed the human mind.

Perhaps this is a good place to observe that the theories of the Unknowable which flourished in the West during the second half of the nineteenth century, and to which numbers of minds 'formed by contact with the positive sciences' still give their allegiance, are no better than beggarly caricatures of this wise doctrine, so accurately based upon man's *middle state*. Our neglect of it brought us to the perilous chances of an overweening metaphysic. Except for a narrow circle which has kept itself perpetually in touch with the eternal springs of knowledge and spirituality, the irreparable results of the ontological insolvency of Western thought have hardly begun to make themselves felt, continuing as they have for two and a half centuries, and that in spheres apparently quite remote from pure speculation. Peter Wust is certainly right to blame it upon a pride so inveterate that it can no longer be consciously felt. But I think that I should put more emphasis than he does on the way the 'moderns' absolutely refuse a hearing to all attempts to establish any connection between being and value. There is no surer way to the very denial of reality as such. This 'devaluation' of being means turning it into a *caput mortuum*, a mere abstract residue. It is then the easiest thing in the world for the idealist critic to prove that it is a mere fiction of conceptual imagination, which a stroke of the pen will abolish without making the least difference to anything.

This point of view enables us more fully to appreciate Peter

Wust's eminently reconstructive critique of the idea of piety. The idea is alive, and even worked out to an infinite degree, among all spiritually-minded men who have considered their own deepest experience. But contemporary philosophers, especially in France (with two or three exceptions), seem to think that the idea applies only to an 'attitude', and that the 'attitude' will at most only be interesting to 'behaviour' specialists. Wust, who owes much to Scheler on this as on many other points, saw very clearly that there is serious danger in treating piety as an attitude or state; far from this, we should see in it a real relation of the soul to its own spiritual context, and also of course to itself. This is the way to recover the sense of religion as a *bond* (*ligamen*), so fundamental and yet so frequently neglected.

According to Wust, there is a close correspondence between simplicity and piety on the one hand as the *habitus* of the soul, and surprise and reverence on the other, as fundamental emotions or affections. The latter are related to the former much as the act is to the potency in Aristotle's metaphysic. This simply means that the soul's overwhelming sense of reverence before the harmony of the universe presupposes that such a soul has previously been attuned to this harmony. Wust recalls a passage in Goethe where he speaks of piety as 'original virtue' (*Erbtugend*) which therefore has its seat in a sphere unreachable by our immediate consciousness of ourselves. As Wust rightly observes, what he calls *Naivität* (the French *naïveté* is certainly not quite an accurate equivalent), differs from piety chiefly in the degree of its actualisation. Piety is the prolongation and enrichment on the side of will of that spiritual candour which he, like many of his predecessors from Schiller onwards, calls by the name of *Naivität*.

But even within piety we should distinguish complementary sides or rather aspects. In so far as piety is, properly speaking, a *link*, it re-enacts on a higher level that universal principle of cohesion which governs nature and corresponds with what Claudel calls the *family-arity* of all things with one another. But this very cohesion implies a certain self-affirmation in the terms it joins or draws together; without this it is done away with, and disappears. This cohesion, then, does not only draw things together but also keeps them at their proper distances. We find the same characteristic on the higher level which we are considering now. 'There is one kind of piety which a person shows towards himself, where the factor of *distance* appears with its essential characteristics. There is also a piety towards beings of the same nature as ourselves, with whom we cultivate spiritual relations.'[1] There is even a form of piety towards beings of an infra-human order. But piety reaches its highest point when it is given to the Creator Spirit (*Urgeist*), since He is the absolute centre of all ties woven between particular beings.

Wust very strongly emphasises the special importance to be attached to piety towards one's-self. 'Piety towards one's-self is the great law of love,' he says,[2] 'which we apprehend in the depths of our nature, because each of us is *this* creature who has been given *this* shape and has occupied *this* place in the order of creation; the moment we have apprehended this law, it is incumbent upon us to assert it with all our might. And the bliss of our soul lies in never resisting that silent appeal which mounts up from the depths of our being.'

I feel that here, once more, the philosopher of Cologne is stressing a profound truth doggedly ignored by the great majority of lay philosophers. He is really distinguishing, in the clearest possible manner, a love of self—perhaps mystical, certainly spiritual—from the egoism which is just an extension of the will to live or the instinct of self-preservation. No doubt this instinct is presupposed by piety towards one's-self. But the specific object of piety is to protect the soul against the danger of pride inseparable from the act

[1] *Naivität und Pietät*, p. 128.   [2] *Loc. cit.*, p. 129.

of its natural self-affirmation. 'Its particular aim', as he finely puts it, 'is to maintain religious awe in the self towards the metaphysical deeps of its own reality, that mysterious reality with which God has endowed it. For our self is a holy temple of the Spirit, built by God's own hand, a wonderful inner universe with its own laws of gravity, still more marvellous than those we can see in the full vitality of the external universe with its infinity of mechanisms. It is a sanctuary, a Holy of Holies into which we may not enter, though it is ours, without a hidden and holy fear. We *may* not, I said. But also we *cannot*, in this Holy of Holies, enter the place of the altar with the eternal lamp of the most sacred mysteries burning before it. There is indeed a sense in which we are given to ourselves; and this is the meaning of our relative *aseitas*. But we are only entrusted to ourselves as works of art from the studio of an eternal Master. We are not our *own* masterpieces. That is why we are only left to ourselves as infinitely precious heirlooms, which we must treat as we would treat the treasure of our bliss.'[1]

These metaphors, at least when they are translated out of the German, may seem rather grandiloquent; but we must not be put off by this. The idea in itself, I think, is extremely important. It is only because they have lost sight of this idea that the lay philosophers can reproach a believer with the 'selfishness', for instance, which they believe him to show by working for his own salvation. They do not see that the self-love enjoined by the Christian religion—enjoined, not merely allowed—is inseparable from the sense of close duality between what I am in my workaday life, and that hidden reality generally called the soul, which has been given to me, and of which I must give an account on the last day. Could we not say, in terms a little different from Wust's, that the non-Christian philosopher of today starts, perhaps sometimes unconsciously, from an assumption which may have dreadful consequences, namely, that

[1] *Loc. cit.*, pp. 132-133.

I am the same as my life? He must then go on to say that the soul itself is only a more highly wrought expression of that hidden life, a sort of efflorescence, of which we cannot strictly say that it is given to me, since it is *in fact myself*. Once this fatal assumption is granted —and its origins may easily be discovered in a certain type of biological philosophy prevalent in the nineteenth century—it is clear that the love of self, or charity to the self, must be regarded simply as an extension of the life-instinct.

But the assumption just cannot be allowed, I think, without ignoring some of the most urgent demands of genuine spiritual life —all those demands described in Wust by the admirable but untranslatable word *Distanzierung*, which so well expresses the fact that I am not on an equal footing with myself, because what is deepest in me is not of me. 'Piety towards one's-self,' he says again, 'surrounds the self like a delicate membrane, which must be kept safe from harm if we want to protect our souls from being laid open to great dangers.'[1] Such personal facts as restraint and tact are bound up with this need, and also a reverence for the self which may accompany the highest form of spiritual dignity. But between this feeling and the dangerous pride which springs from an exaggerated awareness of my personal independence, there is only a thin dividing line; we must realise that it is not easy to draw it. And yet the distinction holds, since reverence for one's-self is really concerned with 'values which are, as it were, a heavenly trust within us which we are bound to defend whenever a hostile power threatens to profane them'.

Wust, as we see, most explicitly repudiates the thesis that reverence for one's-self is defined as a sort of egocentric formalism, giving an absolute status to an out-and-out principle of freedom, divorced from all the spiritual contents in which it may be embodied. And it is in the name of these same values, of which it is in some sense the

[1] *Naivität und Pietät*, p. 133.

guardian and keeper, that the self is bound to resist the intrusions and encroachments of other personalities lacking in the sense of piety, lest they should work it harm.

If this is so, then we must agree that the conceptions of contemporary monadism miss an important truth. It is generally said today, without preliminary enquiry, that it is just a lack in us, a pure deficiency, which prevents us from being able to plunge into the spiritual being of another. Whereas in fact we should see that this inability is simply the price we pay for our spiritual dignity as free creatures. 'Our soul in its ultimate depths is a secret, and this is the inner chamber of the soul which we are, up to a certain point, obliged to preserve religiously. Reverence for ourselves forbids us to unveil the sanctuary of our souls with a rash and impious hand, and to do so would be a real profanation and show an unforgivable lack of modesty.'[1]

This is perhaps the place to observe, more explicitly than even Wust himself, how much all naturalist interpretations of modesty are at fault, whether they are founded on a particular view of society or a view of life. A modesty which is entirely of the spirit, the modesty of the soul shown in such a passage as I have just quoted, can plainly only be justified by the notion of the individuality as its own treasure-house: it overflows all the categories which modern philosophy has taught us to use and be content with. Against this modesty, in fact, the most active and most opposite powers of our age have made alliance, and it is worth thinking for a moment about this surprising confederacy.

Not only does a social imperative bid us share our spiritual riches so that everyone can make his own use of them—here we see the completely material picture of invisible possessions now generally painted—and a kind of diffuse philosophy tends to identify the spiritual and communicable: but also, rising from the other horizon,

[1] *Loc. cit.*, p. 136.

a call to sincerity (of which the most striking phrases were certainly invented by Nietzsche) forbids us to allow any veils between ourselves and our 'souls', lest hypocrisy should grow up in their shade.

We must recognise that there is a problem here, and I am not sure that Peter Wust sees how serious it is. The word *soul*, which I have just used, with such an anti-Nietzschean ring, only retains its fulness of meaning, it seems, when one's privacy of relation with himself has been safeguarded. I should like to describe it as linked, if not with notion, at least with the consciousness of a dialogue between the most active and critical 'voices' of the orchestra within us and a ground-bass whose value would be changed and even lost if it ever quite touched them. We should lose and not gain by bringing in here the notion of the unconscious: the unconscious and even the subconscious are irrelevant in this context, and besides, we know the intellectual disasters following the rash use made of them by certain disciples of W. James. I am trying to make just two points here; first, that we can only speak of the soul where there is a sense of what might be called the *scoring* of the spiritual orchestra, and secondly, that sincerity in its most aggressive sense must necessarily oppose the very existence of the hierarchies assumed in such *orchestration*, since it must regard them as the results of prejudice or complacency, and say that they cannot stand up to 'the light of truth'. The whole question is really whether this criticism does not presuppose the confusion of two spheres in fact irreducible to one another. Does not this process of spreading out the spiritual life to view deny its most specific character, the very inwardness that makes it what it is? just as the dissection and flattening out of a flower-head with all its organs side by side destroys the corolla and makes it no longer a flower?

And yet we cannot deny that the difficulty is still a very serious one; for nothing can be put to more dangerous use than this idea of a personal hierarchy valid only for the individual, whose duty to

225

himself requires him to uphold it within him. I think myself that the solution can only be found by deepening our conceptions of transparency and purity. But here a preliminary distinction must be made. Men's minds have never before been so ready as they are now rashly to identify an exclusively formal process of cleaning-up—which in all its forms can take place at the surface of the soul, since it has no interest in its structure or life—with something quite different, a manner of being which conditions activity, and is to be perceived as immediately as we can perceive, for instance, the correct tuning of an instrument. But if we follow this road, I think we shall have to recognise that the problem of purity, taken in its human and not merely formal meaning, cannot be stated without the help of those ontological categories which we thought we were rid of for ever. The conception of purity generally held today in one sort of philosophy of art (and even of life perhaps) rests on the complete separation of form and content. But one has only to turn back to Wust's 'Witnessing Idea' to realise that when we take the 'purity' of a child as our standard, this is just the state of things which we cannot accept. We shall then have no other expedient than to allege the mythical nature of this so-called purity, and once more the 'discoveries' of the psycho-analysts will be on the side of this refutation of popular optimism. But we cannot help asking whether these would-be objective investigations are not really dedicated from the start to a kind of pseudo-Schopenhauerian and certainly atheist dogma, which rules and directs their practice before making use of their results. Even suppose—and this is just an inverted form of simplicism—that we consent to ascribe this 'purity' of spirit to a preconception, a milk-and-water notion held by adults and somewhat suspiciously romanticised: we shall still have to ask whether the criticism also applies to the holy soul which through trials has learnt how to safeguard or even to win a purity, if not of *feeling* (that may be impossible), at least of *will* and, still more precious, of *vision*. Here, we may be sure, the critic will be tempted to quarrel with the sheer notion of asceticism and self-improvement, as though every work done on one's-self and every labour of reform within implied a falsehood, *were* indeed an incarnate falsehood. A condemnation all the more surprising, if we think of it, since the sincerity he preaches itself requires a kind of asceticism, because it is entirely directed against a willing blindness in us perhaps bound up with the state of our nature.

The idea of sincerity as it has raged, especially in France, for the last ten years, seems to me to be deprived of all value by a single fact: that it is essentially a weapon but will not admit it, and the apparent disinterestedness which it vaunts is nothing but a cloak for its overwhelming desire for negative justification. If so, we cannot be too careful of those dangerous—and from one aspect at least positively reckless—alliances between sincerity and purity which seem to have been made in our time. Where sincerity becomes that indiscretion against the self so rightly condemned by Wust, it is explicitly turned against the only kind of purity which has a genuine spiritual value. Of course this does not mean, as I said before, that purity flourishes in a carefully preserved artificial twilight. Quite the reverse. It cannot be a mere coincidence that men of great purity seem to give out a light which shines on themselves as well as others. The halo, only discernible to the eye of the spirit, is one of those facts from which any metaphysician worthy of the name can draw almost unlimited wisdom. But this light which (mystics apart) the greatest of the painters have used with mysterious power to crown their achievements—painters, I think, much more than writers[1]—this light which is life because it is Love, cannot be too

[1] One can hardly help asking whether literary activity as such is not always in some degree—except where it is purely lyrical—turned *against* a certain fundamental purity of the soul. This is surely not the case in music or the plastic arts.

sharply distinguished from the diabolical lucidity that may some-times be brought to bear upon appalling perversities, where the man who describes them has not the least desire to bring them to an end—a light, indeed, which can illuminate the deepest shadows without taking away one jot of their suffocating gloom.

Everything depends, I suppose, upon the hidden intention guiding the soul's vision of itself. Diabolical lucidity, I said; for therein hatred of the self is sometimes at work, but hatred of sin never. Hatred of the self; for the negative need of 'justification' tends to blot out all difference, all dividing lines, and to prove that sin does not exist since it is simply me, and covers the country of my being from boundary to boundary.

There is a lust for sincerity which is simply an exaltation of all the negative powers at my command; perhaps the most utterly Satanic of all forms of suicide, where extreme pride, in its boundless perversion, imitates extreme humility. If the soul thus surrenders to the 'demon of knowledge' without first submitting itself to any training or purification of the will, it is, though not of course with full awareness, setting up an idolatry for itself whose effects must be disastrous, because such idolatry encourages and upholds the satis-faction in despair of which we have seen such distressing examples around us.

Lust for sincerity, idolatry of inward knowledge, perverse exalta-tion combined with a belittling analysis of the self—these are just so many synonyms for a single evil: the blindfolding which makes it possible for the self to disregard that universal loving will at work everywhere, outside it and within. Piety towards one's-self cannot be separated for a moment from piety towards others, as we well know: this is why we can say that piety in its universal nature is the bond which for ever unites man, the whole of nature, and the whole of the spiritual world. This principle of unity is entirely spiritual, since it is a principle of love, and it stands over against the chain of pure necessity underlying the union of merely natural phenomena. Wust even goes so far as to speak (rather vaguely, I think) of piety as the synthetising factor of an other-worldly *chemistry*, underlying the attraction at work between souls and their surroundings. Here, as elsewhere, he lets himself slide into a way of speech too directly borrowed from German early nineteenth-century idealism; he is certainly going too far towards the pantheism which he will nevertheless reject at any price. And yet, however suspect we find the metaphors which he cannot help using, we do find in his work a sense (and it may be quite accurate historically) of the relation which brings together public life, taken in its coherent unity, and man's piety in the face of nature, as it flourished in ancient Rome and even in the Middle Ages. Is he not generally right in his contention that social relations become less close when the peasant and the craftsman give place to the tradesman (and the workman), and that when man loses contact with the soil and with real things, he is apt to be cut off from the very roots of his existence, so that even his culture becomes endangered?[1]

The peasant, for the very reason that he depends on nature, is bound to show patience towards nature; and because its details have become familiar to him, he unconsciously builds up a treasure-house of objective experience, and so comes little by little to welcome the gifts of the earth as the wages of his labour and patience. For him there is no question of the 'crucifixion of nature', the result of technical advancement where nothing but intellect and pure egoism are needed, so that we can see the 'stigmata', so to speak, of the physical and mathematical sciences imprinted upon the modern world. Rightly or wrongly, Wust blames upon the philosophical doctrine of Kantianism the initial responsibility for the attitude implied by the sciences, and for the pillaging of nature by man which

[1] *Naivität und Pietät*, p. 133.

begins as soon as his relation with nature ceases to be the relation between two beings capable of mutual respect and adaptation. In the eyes of Wust, the mechanical science of nature is a sort of technique of burglary. Modern man, he says, has the mark of Cain upon him, and a 'Luciferean' character pervades the culture of those who have lost all piety towards the external world.

It is not altogether easy to decide the worth of such an accusation; it seems to me that it contains some out-of-date sentimentality. Remarks of this kind often seem extremely useless, anyhow, because one cannot see that there is any way of 'getting back to Nature'. Among other objections to Wust's theory, there is nevertheless one which is not as cogent as it looks. How, it may be asked, can we hope to establish those relations between man and nature which rested upon an anthropomorphic interpretation now exploded?

We must answer that modern thought is on this point also adopting the most questionable metaphysical hypotheses as though they were axioms. Some minds may think they are completely free of the kind of ideology which started with Auguste Comte, and yet they will say, as though it were self-evident, that man advances from an infantile to an adult state of knowledge, and that the characteristic mark of the higher stage, which the 'intellectual leaders' of today have reached, is simply the elimination of anthropomorphism. This presupposes the most curious temporal realism, and perhaps especially the most summary and simplicist picture of mental growth. Not only do they make a virtue of disregarding the positive and irreplaceable value of that original candour in the soul, not only do they make an idol of experience, by regarding it as the only way to spiritual dedication, but they also say in so many words that our minds are telling the time differently, since some are 'more advanced', that is—whether or not this is admitted—nearer to a 'terminus'. And yet, by an amazing contradiction, they are forbidden to actualise that terminus even in thought. So that progress no longer consists in drawing nearer to one's end, but is described by a purely intrinsic quality of its own; although they will not consider its darker sides, such as old age and creaking joints, because they no doubt think that they are moving in a sphere where thought is depersonalised, so that these inevitable accidents of the flesh will be automatically banished.

But the moment we allow, with Christian theology, that man is in some degree an image of God, not only is there no longer any question of our giving a negative verdict to anthropomorphism, but it is even clear that such a condemnation would entail sure spiritual danger. Peter Wust says, 'It was fundamentally false, the view which prevailed among modern philosophers, when they fixed their eyes upon the infinitude of the mechanical universe; when there dawned upon them the opinion that Man must be expelled from the centre of the universe and was no more than an insignificant speck on the infinite extent of the cosmic whole.'[1] That is true, but would it not be more accurate to say that it is the very idea of a 'centre of the universe' which is questioned by modern philosophy? The universe, especially since Kant, does not seem to include anything which can be treated as a centre, at least in the theoretical sense of the word. But by a very strange inversion, modern philosophy has come to substitute in the place of this real centre (now no longer conceivable) an imaginary focus existing in the mind. One could even maintain, without being paradoxical, that the 'Copernican revolution' has resulted in the setting-up of a new anthropocentric theory; though it differs from the old in no longer considering man as a being, but rather as a complex of epistemological functions. This anthropocentric theory also excludes all attempts to 'picture' things in the likeness of man— perhaps even to 'picture' them at all. The sense of analogy disappears at the same time as the sense of form. With them, the con-

---

[1] *Naivität und Pietät*, p. 161

crete itself is swallowed up in the *active* gulf of science—active because it actively devours. Today a new choice of alternatives might be said to have arisen, between the dehumanised anthropocentric theory on the one hand, which tends to be favoured by idealist theories of knowledge; and a theocentric theory on the other, which, though it is fully realised by the heirs of mediaeval philosophy, seems to be only vaguely perceived by the lay philosophers. They have broken with all the speculation started by Kant, but they nevertheless will not acknowledge in its fulness that ontological need which lies at the very heart of our lives, and may even be the final secret of which our lives are the dark and wearisome childbed.

This theocentricism is surely the thing to be emphasised if we want to see piety in its proper place in the whole spiritual economy. 'Piety,' as Fichte had already said, 'forces us to respect whatever has a human countenance;' 'but here', adds Wust, 'it becomes the link which joins the huge and universal society of souls in a terrestrial and super-terrestrial union seen wholly and simultaneously; a *Civitas Dei*, in the Augustinian sense, or a visible or invisible Church of God whose members, suffering, militant, and triumphant are linked by the filial relation which binds them all together to their Heavenly Father—all, without exception, bidden to take their places at the eternal Supper of the Spirit.'[1]

Although the expression again leaves something to be desired in the way of strict terminology, I think we have nothing but praise for the universalism which stamps these declarations and gives them their pure and majestic tone. They are chiefly magnificent in their emphasis on the absolute precedence given, in this realm, to piety towards the 'Eternal Thou'. 'The paradox of the finite mind', he writes, 'is its subjection to the continued polarity brought to bear upon him by the *I* and the *Thou*. He tries to vanquish it in his

[1] *Naivität und Pietät*, p. 151.

compulsion to become a pure *I*, but he can only become a pure *I* by gravitating, with ever-increasing intensity, round the universal *Thou* of being and of all ontological community.'[1]

Perhaps it would be a good plan to discount this sort of language (as it is rather too directly derived from Fichte) and try to get at the inward and concrete significance of the notion expressed.

In Wust's view, if we think that we can enter into more immediate possession of ourselves and our proper reality by progressively cutting ourselves off from the particular communities in which we are at first involved, we are labouring under an illusion engendered by pride. He follows Tönnies in clearing up the disastrous confusion which the sociological school of our time had countenanced, by reminding us to make a clear distinction between community and society.

By community, Tönnies understood a union founded upon kinship and love—a union in which its members are joined in an almost organic embrace. Society, on the other hand, implied for him a type of union founded upon mere intellect divorced from love, a purely selfish calculation. But the pessimistic philosophy of culture professed by Tönnies did not give him scope to see all the inferences to be drawn from this distinction, nor even perhaps to explain it with perfect clarity. (It was also, perhaps, a little rash of him to put such a high value on the 'ties of blood'.) There is genuine community wherever man has kept the lifelines of his being intact: wherever he strongly asserts 'the natural inclination to love, which is itself love, and which goes down to the very depths of his soul'. An atmosphere, one might call it, but also a presence. Wust, in a bold metaphor, compares it to a battery which never needs recharging, or a pump which draws up 'the eternal powers of the spirit in the autonomous organisation of our own personalities'. Although he may sometimes seem to do so, he never really condones

[1] *Naivität und Pietät*, p. 139.

233

the excesses of the metaphysic of the *Es* or Impersonal Mind; on the contrary, he never ceases to warn us against them. He even refuses, in a page which I wish I could quote entirely, to admit the existence of that *nature in God* still found in some theistic philosophies—perhaps in the later Schelling—like a survival of those very mistakes which they claimed to have uprooted. The term nature must not, of course, be taken here to mean essence; 'in that sense, God obviously has a nature, since whatever is, has, and must have, an essence.' Wust's problem is whether there is a trans-personal sphere in the reality of the absolute Spirit, and so an 'impersonal'[1] element, from which would spring, as by a natural process, the personal activity functioning on the pattern of the blind principle, the pure It, which rules nature. In other words, is Spinozan ontology valid? Wust objects, in terms reminiscent of Renouvier, that 'it always means ignoring the necessary precedence of *personality* over *thinghood*. It is inconceivable that any sphere in God, however small, should be opaque to the light of Absolute Personality, a fact not so much *central* as *unique*. The Logos can be no stranger, even in the least degree, to the spirituality of the divine Person; He is one with it for ever in close and unbreakable identity.'

But this does not mean that we can treat God's unfathomable abyss of love (*Liebesabgrund*) as a nature (irrational this time) existing in Him as a second and irreducible principle. 'It is only *to us* that the Eternal Love of the Creator, causing him to go outside his own blessed self-sufficiency, seems like an irrational principle. To *us* It may appear in an impersonal guise, at one remove from the Godhead. But in fact It simply shows us a new aspect of His entirely personal Essence, the spirituality of the Absolute Person of God revealed along the lines of His free activity.'[2] This being so, we can see why all finite spiritual activity whatsoever, as soon as it is turned in a positive direction (towards order), can only be founded upon

[1] *Naivität und Pietät*, p. 34.　　　　[2] *ibid.*, p. 163.

love; not so much an echo of God's eternal Love as a vague but irresistible answer awakened by It. In thus categorically asserting the precedence of love over order, Wust removes even the possibility of our making an idol of the intellect. And thereby he makes it equally impossible for us to make an idol of the eternal truths, an idolatry which so limits the theistic affirmation as to rob it of its most positive value. We should observe that Wust, all through this part of his work, bases himself on the Augustinian theory, and makes use of the well-known formula *omnia amare in Deo*, so clearly the nodal point of all his views of piety; he especially throws a flood of light upon the central fact that piety towards ourselves is really nothing but a form of the fear of God. It only degenerates into selfishness and the root of all error when it is unduly separated from the highest form of piety, and turns its activity towards the 'sphere of immanence' (i.e. towards the most deceptive kind of autonomy).

It is easy to see that Wust is exhorting us to make a complete spiritual 'reconstruction'—of the whole personality, I think, the intellect as well as the will. It may be said without exaggeration that he achieved this for himself, with a kind of simple heroism, during the last years of his life. As he expressly said at the end of the *Dialection of the Spirit*, there is no question of making a *sacrificium intellectus*; such an abdication of the mind would be a mere act of despair. He seems to be asking of us simply this: that we should cease once for all to make a certain kind of demand—the demand which he uses as a description of 'absolute gnosticism'—and that we should give up the idea of attaining ultimate knowledge capable of being unfolded into an organic whole, since he has shown that such knowledge is incompatible with the fundamental character of Being. And here (at least in my eyes) here in this notion, or rather this intuition of the metaphysical value properly belonging to humility, lies Wust's most original contribution to the speculative thought of our day.

It is plain that its corollary, 'Pride is a source of blindness', is an essential part of the 'library of human wisdom'. It is one of those truisms that lie buried under the dust of ages, and no one troubles to dig them up again because everyone thinks that their spiritual fertility is for ever exhausted. And yet, if we did take the trouble to apply this commonplace of personal ethics to the realm of de-personalised thought (so-called), we might be astonished to see what unexpected horizons unfolded before our eyes.

As we have said before, there is an immense work of critical reconstruction to be done. The astonishingly free-and-easy assumptions of the rival philosophies must be subjected to thorough and constant scrutiny. Only thus can we see through those doctrines which first strip the human mind of all its ontological attributes and powers, and then go on to endow it with some of the more awful prerogatives of that King whom they fondly believe they have dethroned.

Revised October 31, 1965

harper ✦ torchbooks

HUMANITIES AND SOCIAL SCIENCES

American Studies: General

THOMAS C. COCHRAN: The Inner Revolution: *Essays on the Social Sciences in History* TB/1140

EDWARD S. CORWIN: American Constitutional History. *Essays edited by Alpheus T. Mason and Gerald Garvey* TB/1136

A. HUNTER DUPREE: Science in the Federal Government: *A History of Policies and Activities to 1940* TB/573

OSCAR HANDLIN, Ed.: This Was America: *As Recorded by European Travelers in the Eighteenth, Nineteenth and Twentieth Centuries. Illus.* TB/1119

MARCUS LEE HANSEN: The Atlantic Migration: 1607-1860. *Edited by Arthur M. Schlesinger; Introduction by Oscar Handlin* TB/1052

MARCUS LEE HANSEN: The Immigrant in American History. *Edited with a Foreword by Arthur M. Schlesinger* TB/1120

JOHN HIGHAM, Ed.: The Reconstruction of American History TB/1068

ROBERT H. JACKSON: The Supreme Court in the American System of Government TB/1106

JOHN F. KENNEDY: A Nation of Immigrants. *Illus. Revised and Enlarged. Introduction by Robert F. Kennedy* TB/1118

RALPH BARTON PERRY: Puritanism and Democracy TB/1138

ARNOLD ROSE: The Negro in America: *The Condensed Version of Gunnar Myrdal's An American Dilemma* TB/3048

MAURICE R. STEIN: The Eclipse of Community: *An Interpretation of American Studies* TB/1128

W. LLOYD WARNER and Associates: Democracy in Jonesville: *A Study in Quality and Inequality* ‖ TB/1129

W. LLOYD WARNER: Social Class in America: *The Evaluation of Status* TB/1013

American Studies: Colonial

BERNARD BAILYN, Ed.: The Apologia of Robert Keayne: *Self-Portrait of a Puritan Merchant* TB/1201

BERNARD BAILYN: The New England Merchants in the Seventeenth Century TB/1149

JOSEPH CHARLES: The Origins of the American Party System TB/1049

LAWRENCE HENRY GIPSON: The Coming of the Revolution: 1763-1775. † *Illus.* TB/3007

LEONARD W. LEVY: Freedom of Speech and Press in Early American History: *Legacy of Suppression* TB/1109

PERRY MILLER: Errand Into the Wilderness TB/1139

PERRY MILLER & T. H. JOHNSON, Eds.: The Puritans: *A Sourcebook of Their Writings* Vol. I TB/1093; Vol. II TB/1094

KENNETH B. MURDOCK: Literature and Theology in Colonial New England TB/99

WALLACE NOTESTEIN: The English People on the Eve of Colonization: 1603-1630. † *Illus.* TB/3006

LOUIS B. WRIGHT: The Cultural Life of the American Colonies: 1607-1763. † *Illus.* TB/3005

American Studies: From the Revolution to the Civil War

JOHN R. ALDEN: The American Revolution: 1775-1783. † *Illus.* TB/3011

RAY A. BILLINGTON: The Far Western Frontier: 1830-1860. † *Illus.* TB/3012

GEORGE DANGERFIELD: The Awakening of American Nationalism: 1815-1828. † *Illus.* TB/3061

CLEMENT EATON: The Freedom-of-Thought Struggle in the Old South. *Revised and Enlarged. Illus.* TB/1150

CLEMENT EATON: The Growth of Southern Civilization: 1790-1860. † *Illus.* TB/3040

LOUIS FILLER: The Crusade Against Slavery: 1830-1860. † *Illus.* TB/3029

DIXON RYAN FOX: The Decline of Aristocracy in the Politics of New York: 1801-1840. ‡ *Edited by Robert V. Remini* TB/3064

FELIX GILBERT: The Beginnings of American Foreign Policy: *To the Farewell Address* TB/1200

FRANCIS J. GRUND: Aristocracy in America: *Social Class in the Formative Years of the New Nation* TB/1001

ALEXANDER HAMILTON: The Reports of Alexander Hamilton. ‡ *Edited by Jacob E. Cooke* TB/3060

THOMAS JEFFERSON: Notes on the State of Virginia. ‡ *Edited by Thomas P. Abernethy* TB/3052

BERNARD MAYO: Myths and Men: *Patrick Henry, George Washington, Thomas Jefferson* TB/1108

JOHN C. MILLER: Alexander Hamilton and the Growth of the New Nation TB/3057

RICHARD B. MORRIS, Ed.: The Era of the American Revolution TB/1180

R. B. NYE: The Cultural Life of the New Nation: 1776-1801. † *Illus.* TB/3026

---

† The New American Nation Series, edited by Henry Steele Commager and Richard B. Morris.

‡ American Perspectives series, edited by Bernard Wishy and William E. Leuchtenburg.

* The Rise of Modern Europe series, edited by William L. Langer.

‖ Researches in the Social, Cultural, and Behavioral Sciences, edited by Benjamin Nelson.

§ The Library of Religion and Culture, edited by Benjamin Nelson.

ᵒ Not for sale in Canada.

Σ Harper Modern Science Series, edited by James R. Newman.

FRANK THISTLETHWAITE: America and the Atlantic Community: *Anglo-American Aspects, 1790-1850* TB/1107

A. F. TYLER: Freedom's Ferment: *Phases of American Social History from the Revolution to the Outbreak of the Civil War. 31 illus.* TB/1074

GLYNDON G. VAN DEUSEN: The Jacksonian Era: 1828-1848. † *Illus.* TB/3028

LOUIS B. WRIGHT: Culture on the Moving Frontier TB/1053

American Studies: Since the Civil War

RAY STANNARD BAKER: Following the Color Line: *American Negro Citizenship in Progressive Era.* ‡ *Illus. Edited by Dewey W. Grantham, Jr.* TB/3053

RANDOLPH S. BOURNE: War and the Intellectuals: *Collected Essays, 1915-1919.* ‡ *Ed. by Carl Resek* TB/3043

A. RUSSELL BUCHANAN: The United States and World War II. † *Illus.* Vol. I TB/3044; Vol. II TB/3045

ABRAHAM CAHAN: The Rise of David Levinsky: *a documentary novel of social mobility in early twentieth century America. Intro. by John Higham* TB/1028

THOMAS C. COCHRAN: The American Business System: *A Historical Perspective, 1900-1955* TB/1080

THOMAS C. COCHRAN & WILLIAM MILLER: The Age of Enterprise: *A Social History of Industrial America* TB/1054

FOSTER RHEA DULLES: America's Rise to World Power: *1898-1954.* † *Illus.* TB/3021

W. A. DUNNING: Essays on the Civil War and Reconstruction. *Introduction by David Donald* TB/1181

W. A. DUNNING: Reconstruction, Political and Economic: *1865-1877* TB/1073

HAROLD U. FAULKNER: Politics, Reform and Expansion: *1890-1900.* † *Illus.* TB/3020

JOHN D. HICKS: Republican Ascendancy: 1921-1933. † *Illus.* TB/3041

ROBERT HUNTER: Poverty: *Social Conscience in the Progressive Era.* ‡ *Edited by Peter d'A. Jones* TB/3065

HELEN HUNT JACKSON: A Century of Dishonor: *The Early Crusade for Indian Reform.* ‡ *Edited by Andrew F. Rolle* TB/3063

ALBERT D. KIRWAN: Revolt of the Rednecks: *Mississippi Politics, 1876-1925* TB/1199

WILLIAM L. LANGER & S. EVERETT GLEASON: The Challenge to Isolation: *The World Crisis of 1937-1940 and American Foreign Policy* Vol. I TB/3054; Vol. II TB/3055

WILLIAM E. LEUCHTENBURG: Franklin D. Roosevelt and the New Deal: 1932-1940. † *Illus.* TB/3025

ARTHUR S. LINK: Woodrow Wilson and the Progressive Era: 1910-1917. † *Illus.* TB/3023

ROBERT GREEN MC CLOSKEY: American Conservatism in the Age of Enterprise: 1865-1910 TB/1137

GEORGE E. MOWRY: The Era of Theodore Roosevelt and the Birth of Modern America: 1900-1912. † *Illus.* TB/3022

RUSSEL B. NYE: Midwestern Progressive Politics: *A Historical Study of its Origins and Development, 1870-1958* TB/1202

WALTER RAUSCHENBUSCH: Christianity and the Social Crisis. ‡ *Edited by Robert D. Cross* TB/3059

WHITELAW REID: After the War: *A Tour of the Southern States, 1865-1866.* ‡ *Edited by C. Vann Woodward* TB/3066

CHARLES H. SHINN: Mining Camps: *A Study in American Frontier Government.* ‡ *Edited by Rodman W. Paul* TB/3062

TWELVE SOUTHERNERS: I'll Take My Stand: *The South and the Agrarian Tradition. Intro. by Louis D. Rubin, Jr.; Biographical Essays by Virginia Rock* TB/1072

WALTER E. WEYL: The New Democracy: *An Essay on Certain Political Tendencies in the United States.* ‡ *Edited by Charles B. Forcey* TB/3042

VERNON LANE WHARTON: The Negro in Mississippi: 1865-1890 TB/1178

Anthropology

JACQUES BARZUN: Race: *A Study in Superstition. Revised Edition* TB/1172

JOSEPH B. CASAGRANDE, Ed.: In the Company of Man: *Twenty Portraits of Anthropological Informants. Illus.* TB/3047

W. E. LE GROS CLARK: The Antecedents of Man: *Intro. to Evolution of the Primates.* º *Illus.* TB/559

CORA DU BOIS: The People of Alor. *New Preface by the author. Illus.* Vol. I TB/1042; Vol. II TB/1043

RAYMOND FIRTH, Ed.: Man and Culture: *An Evaluation of the Work of Bronislaw Malinowski* ‖ º TB/1133

L. S. B. LEAKEY: Adam's Ancestors: *The Evolution of Man and His Culture. Illus.* TB/1019

ROBERT H. LOWIE: Primitive Society. *Introduction by Fred Eggan* TB/1056

SIR EDWARD TYLOR: The Origins of Culture. *Part I of "Primitive Culture."* § *Intro. by Paul Radin* TB/33

SIR EDWARD TYLOR: Religion in Primitive Culture. *Part II of "Primitive Culture."* § *Intro. by Paul Radin* TB/34

W. LLOYD WARNER: A Black Civilization: *A Study of an Australian Tribe.* ‖ *Illus.* TB/3056

Art and Art History

WALTER LOWRIE: Art in the Early Church. *Revised Edition. 452 illus.* TB/124

EMILE MÂLE: The Gothic Image: *Religious Art in France of the Thirteenth Century.* § *190 illus.* TB/44

MILLARD MEISS: Painting in Florence and Siena after the Black Death: *The Arts, Religion and Society in the Mid-Fourteenth Century. 169 illus.* TB/1148

ERICH NEUMANN: The Archetypal World of Henry Moore. *107 illus.* TB/2020

DORA & ERWIN PANOFSKY: Pandora's Box: *The Changing Aspects of a Mythical Symbol. Revised Edition. Illus.* TB/2021

ERWIN PANOFSKY: Studies in Iconology: *Humanistic Themes in the Art of the Renaissance. 180 illustrations* TB/1077

ALEXANDRE PIANKOFF: The Shrines of Tut-Ankh-Amon. *Edited by N. Rambova. 117 illus.* TB/2011

JEAN SEZNEC: The Survival of the Pagan Gods: *The Mythological Tradition and Its Place in Renaissance Humanism and Art. 108 illustrations* TB/2004

OTTO VON SIMSON: The Gothic Cathedral: *Origins of Gothic Architecture and the Medieval Concept of Order. 58 illus.* TB/2018

HEINRICH ZIMMER: Myth and Symbols in Indian Art and Civilization. *70 illustrations* TB/2005

Business, Economics & Economic History

REINHARD BENDIX: Work and Authority in Industry: *Ideologies of Management in the Course of Industrialization* TB/3035

GILBERT BURCK & EDITORS OF FORTUNE: The Computer Age: *And Its Potential for Management* TB/1179

THOMAS C. COCHRAN: The American Business System: *A Historical Perspective, 1900-1955* TB/1080

THOMAS C. COCHRAN: The Inner Revolution: *Essays on the Social Sciences in History* TB/1140

THOMAS C. COCHRAN & WILLIAM MILLER: The Age of Enterprise: *A Social History of Industrial America* TB/1054

ROBERT DAHL & CHARLES E. LINDBLOM: Politics, Economics, and Welfare: *Planning & Politico-Economic Systems Resolved into Basic Social Processes* TB/3037

PETER F. DRUCKER: The New Society: *The Anatomy of Industrial Order* TB/1082

EDITORS OF FORTUNE: America in the Sixties: *The Economy and the Society* TB/1015

ROBERT L. HEILBRONER: The Great Ascent: *The Struggle for Economic Development in Our Time* TB/3030

FRANK H. KNIGHT: The Economic Organization TB/1214

FRANK H. KNIGHT: Risk, Uncertainty and Profit TB/1215

ABBA P. LERNER: Everybody's Business: *Current Assumptions in Economics and Public Policy* TB/3051

ROBERT GREEN MC CLOSKEY: American Conservatism in the Age of Enterprise, 1865-1910 TB/1137

PAUL MANTOUX: The Industrial Revolution in the Eighteenth Century: *The Beginnings of the Modern Factory System in England* º TB/1079

WILLIAM MILLER, Ed.: Men in Business: *Essays on the Historical Role of the Entrepreneur* TB/1081

PERRIN STRYKER: The Character of the Executive: *Eleven Studies in Managerial Qualities* TB/1041

PIERRE URI: Partnership for Progress: *A Program for Transatlantic Action* TB/3036

Contemporary Culture

JACQUES BARZUN: The House of Intellect TB/1051

JOHN U. NEF: Cultural Foundations of Industrial Civilization TB/1024

NATHAN M. PUSEY: The Age of the Scholar: *Observations on Education in a Troubled Decade* TB/1157

PAUL VALÉRY: The Outlook for Intelligence TB/2016

Historiography & Philosophy of History

SIR ISAIAH BERLIN et al.: History and Theory: *Studies in the Philosophy of History. Edited by George H. Nadel* TB/1208

JACOB BURCKHARDT: On History and Historians. *Intro. by H. R. Trevor-Roper* TB/1216

WILHELM DILTHEY: Pattern and Meaning in History: *Thoughts on History and Society.* º *Edited with an Introduction by H. P. Rickman* TB/1075

H. STUART HUGHES: History as Art and as Science: *Twin Vistas on the Past* TB/1207

RAYMOND KLIBANSKY & H. J. PATON, Eds.: Philosophy and History: *The Ernst Cassirer Festschrift. Illus.* TB/1115

JOSE ORTEGA Y GASSET: The Modern Theme. *Introduction by Jose Ferrater Mora* TB/1038

SIR KARL POPPER: The Open Society and Its Enemies
Vol. I: *The Spell of Plato* TB/1101
Vol. II: *The High Tide of Prophecy: Hegel, Marx and the Aftermath* TB/1102

SIR KARL POPPER: The Poverty of Historicism º TB/1126

G. J. RENIER: History: Its Purpose and Method TB/1209

W. H. WALSH: Philosophy of History: *An Introduction* TB/1020

History: General

L. CARRINGTON GOODRICH: A Short History of the Chinese People. *Illus.* TB/3015

DAN N. JACOBS & HANS H. BAERWALD: Chinese Communism: *Selected Documents* TB/3031

BERNARD LEWIS: The Arabs in History TB/1029

SIR PERCY SYKES: A History of Exploration. º *Introduction by John K. Wright* TB/1046

History: Ancient and Medieval

A. ANDREWES: The Greek Tyrants TB/1103

P. BOISSONNADE: Life and Work in Medieval Europe: *The Evolution of the Medieval Economy, the 5th to the 15th Century.* º *Preface by Lynn White, Jr.* TB/1141

HELEN CAM: England before Elizabeth TB/1026

NORMAN COHN: The Pursuit of the Millennium: *Revolutionary Messianism in Medieval and Reformation Europe* TB/1037

G. G. COULTON: Medieval Village, Manor, and Monastery TB/1022

HEINRICH FICHTENAU: The Carolingian Empire: *The Age of Charlemagne* TB/1142

F. L. GANSHOF: Feudalism TB/1058

EDWARD GIBBON: The Triumph of Christendom in the Roman Empire (*Chaps. XV-XX of "Decline and Fall," J. B. Bury edition).* § *Illus.* TB/46

MICHAEL GRANT: Ancient History º TB/1190

W. O. HASSALL, Ed.: Medieval England: *As Viewed by Contemporaries* TB/1205

DENYS HAY: The Medieval Centuries º TB/1192

J. M. HUSSEY: The Byzantine World TB/1057

SAMUEL NOAH KRAMER: Sumerian Mythology TB/1055

FERDINAND LOT: The End of the Ancient World and the Beginnings of the Middle Ages. *Introduction by Glanville Downey* TB/1044

G. MOLLATT: The Popes at Avignon: 1305-1378 TB/308

CHARLES PETIT-DUTAILLIS: The Feudal Monarchy in France and England: *From the Tenth to the Thirteenth Century* º TB/1165

HENRI PIERENNE: Early Democracies in the Low Countries: *Urban Society and Political Conflict in the Middle Ages and the Renaissance. Introduction by John H. Mundy* TB/1110

STEVEN RUNCIMAN: A History of the Crusades. Volume I: *The First Crusade and the Foundation of the Kingdom of Jerusalem. Illus.* TB/1143

FERDINAND SCHEVILL: Siena: *The History of a Medieval Commune. Intro. by William M. Bowsky* TB/1164

SULPICIUS SEVERUS et al.: The Western Fathers: *Being the Lives of Martin of Tours, Ambrose, Augustine of Hippo, Honoratus of Arles and Germanus of Auxerre. Edited and translated by F. R. Hoare* TB/309

HENRY OSBORN TAYLOR: The Classical Heritage of the Middle Ages. *Foreword and Biblio. by Kenneth M. Setton* TB/1117

F. VAN DER MEER: Augustine The Bishop: *Church and Society at the Dawn of the Middle Ages* TB/304

J. M. WALLACE-HADRILL: The Barbarian West: *The Early Middle Ages, A.D. 400-1000* TB/1061

History: Renaissance & Reformation

JACOB BURCKHARDT: The Civilization of the Renaissance in Italy. *Intro. by Benjamin Nelson & Charles Trinkaus. Illus.* Vol. I TB/40; Vol. II TB/41

ERNST CASSIRER: The Individual and the Cosmos in Renaissance Philosophy. *Translated with an Introduction by Mario Domandi* TB/1097

FEDERICO CHABOD: Machiavelli and the Renaissance TB/1193

EDWARD P. CHEYNEY: The Dawn of a New Era, 1250-1453. * *Illus.* TB/3002

R. TREVOR DAVIES: The Golden Century of Spain, 1501-1621 º TB/1194

DESIDERIUS ERASMUS: Christian Humanism and the Reformation: *Selected Writings. Edited and translated by John C. Olin* TB/1166

WALLACE K. FERGUSON et al.: Facets of the Renaissance TB/1098

WALLACE K. FERGUSON et al.: The Renaissance: Six Essays. Illus. TB/1084

JOHN NEVILLE FIGGIS: The Divine Right of Kings. Introduction by G. R. Elton TB/1191

JOHN NEVILLE FIGGIS: Political Thought from Gerson to Grotius: 1414-1625: Seven Studies. Introduction by Garrett Mattingly TB/1032

MYRON P. GILMORE: The World of Humanism, 1453-1517.* Illus. TB/3003

FRANCESCO GUICCIARDINI: Maxims and Reflections of a Renaissance Statesman (Ricordi). Trans. by Mario Domandi. Intro. by Nicolai Rubinstein TB/1160

J. H. HEXTER: More's Utopia: The Biography of an Idea New Epilogue by the Author TB/1195

JOHAN HUIZINGA: Erasmus and the Age of Reformation. Illus. TB/19

ULRICH VON HUTTEN et al.: On the Eve of the Reformation: "Letters of Obscure Men." Introduction by Hajo Holborn TB/1124

PAUL O. KRISTELLER: Renaissance Thought: The Classic, Scholastic, and Humanist Strains TB/1048

PAUL O. KRISTELLER: Renaissance Thought II: Papers on Humanism and the Arts TB/1163

NICCOLO MACHIAVELLI: History of Florence and of the Affairs of Italy: from the earliest times to the death of Lorenzo the Magnificent. Introduction by Felix Gilbert TB/1027

ALFRED VON MARTIN: Sociology of the Renaissance. Introduction by Wallace K. Ferguson TB/1099

GARRETT MATTINGLY et al.: Renaissance Profiles. Edited by J. H. Plumb TB/1162

MILLARD MEISS: Painting in Florence and Siena after the Black Death: The Arts, Religion and Society in the Mid-Fourteenth Century. 169 illus. TB/1148

J. E. NEALE: The Age of Catherine de Medici [o] TB/1085

ERWIN PANOFSKY: Studies in Iconology: Humanistic Themes in the Art of the Renaissance. 180 illustrations TB/1077

J. H. PARRY: The Establishment of the European Hegemony: 1415-1715: Trade and Exploration in the Age of the Renaissance TB/1045

J. H. PLUMB: The Italian Renaissance: A Concise Survey of Its History and Culture TB/1161

CECIL ROTH: The Jews in the Renaissance. Illus. TB/834

GORDON RUPP: Luther's Progress to the Diet of Worms [o] TB/120

FERDINAND SCHEVILL: The Medici. Illus. TB/1010

FERDINAND SCHEVILL: Medieval and Renaissance Florence. Illus. Volume I: Medieval Florence TB/1090 Volume II: The Coming of Humanism and the Age of the Medici TB/1091

G. M. TREVELYAN: England in the Age of Wycliffe, 1368-1520 [o] TB/1112

VESPASIANO: Renaissance Princes, Popes, and Prelates: The Vespasiano Memoirs: Lives of Illustrious Men of the XVth Century. Intro. by Myron P. Gilmore TB/1111

History: Modern European

FREDERICK B. ARTZ: Reaction and Revolution, 1815-1832. * Illus. TB/3034

MAX BELOFF: The Age of Absolutism, 1660-1815 TB/1062

ROBERT C. BINKLEY: Realism and Nationalism, 1852-1871. * Illus. TB/3038

ASA BRIGGS: The Making of Modern England, 1784-1867: The Age of Improvement [o] TB/1203

CRANE BRINTON: A Decade of Revolution, 1789-1799. * Illus. TB/3018

J. BRONOWSKI & BRUCE MAZLISH: The Western Intellectual Tradition: From Leonardo to Hegel TB/3001

GEOFFREY BRUUN: Europe and the French Imperium, 1799-1814. * Illus. TB/3033

ALAN BULLOCK: Hitler, A Study in Tyranny. [o] Illus. TB/1123

E. H. CARR: The Twenty Years' Crisis, 1919-1939: An Introduction to the Study of International Relations [o] TB/1122

GORDON A. CRAIG: From Bismarck to Adenauer: Aspects of German Statecraft. Revised Edition TB/1171

WALTER L. DORN: Competition for Empire, 1740-1763. * Illus. TB/3032

CARL J. FRIEDRICH: The Age of the Baroque, 1610-1660. * Illus. TB/3004

RENÉ FUELOEP-MILLER: The Mind and Face of Bolshevism: An Examination of Cultural Life in Soviet Russia. New Epilogue by the Author TB/1188

M. DOROTHY GEORGE: London Life in the Eighteenth Century TB/1182

LEO GERSHOY: From Despotism to Revolution, 1763-1789. * Illus. TB/3017

C. C. GILLISPIE: Genesis and Geology: The Decades before Darwin § TB/51

ALBERT GOODWIN: The French Revolution TB/1064

ALBERT GUERARD: France in the Classical Age: The Life and Death of an Ideal TB/1183

CARLTON J. H. HAYES: A Generation of Materialism, 1871-1900. * Illus. TB/3039

J. H. HEXTER: Reappraisals in History: New Views on History & Society in Early Modern Europe TB/1100

A. R. HUMPHREYS: The Augustan World: Society, Thought, and Letters in 18th Century England [o] TB/1105

ALDOUS HUXLEY: The Devils of Loudun: A Study in the Psychology of Power Politics and Mystical Religion in the France of Cardinal Richelieu § [o] TB/60

DAN N. JACOBS, Ed.: The New Communist Manifesto & Related Documents. Third edition, revised TB/1078

HANS KOHN: The Mind of Germany: The Education of a Nation TB/1204

HANS KOHN, Ed.: The Mind of Modern Russia: Historical and Political Thought of Russia's Great Age TB/1065

KINGSLEY MARTIN: French Liberal Thought in the Eighteenth Century: A Study of Political Ideas from Bayle to Condorcet TB/1114

SIR LEWIS NAMIER: Personalities and Powers: Selected Essays TB/1186

SIR LEWIS NAMIER: Vanished Supremacies: Essays on European History, 1812-1918 [o] TB/1088

JOHN U. NEF: Western Civilization Since the Renaissance: Peace, War, Industry, and the Arts TB/1113

FREDERICK L. NUSSBAUM: The Triumph of Science and Reason, 1660-1685. * Illus. TB/3009

JOHN PLAMENATZ: German Marxism and Russian Communism. [o] New Preface by the Author TB/1189

RAYMOND W. POSTGATE, Ed.: Revolution from 1789 to 1906: Selected Documents TB/1063

PENFIELD ROBERTS: The Quest for Security, 1715-1740. * Illus. TB/3016

PRISCILLA ROBERTSON: Revolutions of 1848: A Social History TB/1025

ALBERT SOREL: Europe Under the Old Regime. Translated by Francis H. Herrick TB/1121

N. N. SUKHANOV: The Russian Revolution, 1917: Eyewitness Account. Edited by Joel Carmichael Vol. I TB/1066; Vol. II TB/1067

A. J. P. TAYLOR: The Habsburg Monarch, 1809-1918: A History of the Austrian Empire and Austria-Hungary [o] TB/1187

4

JOHN B. WOLF: The Emergence of the Great Powers, 1685-1715. * Illus.　TB/3010

JOHN B. WOLF: France: 1814-1919: The Rise of a Liberal-Democratic Society　TB/3019

Intellectual History & History of Ideas

HERSCHEL BAKER: The Image of Man: A Study of the Idea of Human Dignity in Classical Antiquity, the Middle Ages, and the Renaissance　TB/1047

R. R. BOLGAR: The Classical Heritage and Its Beneficiaries: From the Carolingian Age to the End of the Renaissance　TB/1125

RANDOLPH S. BOURNE: War and the Intellectuals: Collected Essays, 1915-1919. ‡ Edited by Carl Resek　TB/3043

J. BRONOWSKI & BRUCE MAZLISH: The Western Intellectual Tradition: From Leonardo to Hegel　TB/3001

ERNST CASSIRER: The Individual and the Cosmos in Renaissance Philosophy. Translated with an Introduction by Mario Domandi　TB/1097

NORMAN COHN: The Pursuit of the Millennium: Revolutionary Messianism in medieval and Reformation Europe　TB/1037

G. RACHEL LEVY: Religious Conceptions of the Stone Age and Their Influence upon European Thought. Illus. Introduction by Henri Frankfort　TB/106

ARTHUR O. LOVEJOY: The Great Chain of Being: A Study of the History of an Idea　TB/1009

PERRY MILLER & T. H. JOHNSON, Editors: The Puritans: A Sourcebook of Their Writings
Vol. I TB/1093; Vol. II TB/1094

MILTON C. NAHM: Genius and Creativity: An Essay in the History of Ideas　TB/1196

ROBERT PAYNE: Hubris: A Study of Pride. Foreword by Sir Herbert Read　TB/1031

RALPH BARTON PERRY: The Thought and Character of William James: Briefer Version　TB/1156

BRUNO SNELL: The Discovery of the Mind: The Greek Origins of European Thought　TB/1018

PAGET TOYNBEE: Dante Alighieri: His Life and Works. Edited with intro. by Charles S. Singleton　TB/1206

ERNEST LEE TUVESON: Millennium and Utopia: A Study in the Background of the Idea of Progress. | New Preface by the Author　TB/1134

PAUL VALÉRY: The Outlook for Intelligence　TB/2016

PHILIP P. WIENER: Evolution and the Founders of Pragmatism. Foreword by John Dewey　TB/1212

Literature, Poetry, The Novel & Criticism

JAMES BAIRD: Ishmael: The Art of Melville in the Contexts of International Primitivism　TB/1023

JACQUES BARZUN: The House of Intellect　TB/1051

W. J. BATE: From Classic to Romantic: Premises of Taste in Eighteenth Century England　TB/1036

RACHEL BESPALOFF: On the Iliad　TB/2006

R. P. BLACKMUR et al.: Lectures in Criticism. Introduction by Huntington Cairns　TB/2003

ABRAHAM CAHAN: The Rise of David Levinsky: a documentary novel of social mobility in early twentieth century America. Intro. by John Higham　TB/1028

ERNST R. CURTIUS: European Literature and the Latin Middle Ages　TB/2015

GEORGE ELIOT: Daniel Deronda: a novel. Introduction by F. R. Leavis　TB/1039

ETIENNE GILSON: Dante and Philosophy　TB/1089

ALFRED HARBAGE: As They Liked It: A Study of Shakespeare's Moral Artistry　TB/1035

STANLEY R. HOPPER, Ed.: Spiritual Problems in Contemporary Literature §　TB/21

A. R. HUMPHREYS: The Augustan World: Society, Thought and Letters in 18th Century England °　TB/1105

ALDOUS HUXLEY: Antic Hay & The Giaconda Smile. ° Introduction by Martin Green　TB/3503

ALDOUS HUXLEY: Brave New World & Brave New World Revisited. ° Introduction by Martin Green　TB/3501

HENRY JAMES: Roderick Hudson: a novel. Introduction by Leon Edel　TB/1016

HENRY JAMES: The Tragic Muse: a novel. Introduction by Leon Edel　TB/1017

ARNOLD KETTLE: An Introduction to the English Novel.
Volume I: Defoe to George Eliot　TB/1011
Volume II: Henry James to the Present　TB/1012

ROGER SHERMAN LOOMIS: The Development of Arthurian Romance　TB/1167

JOHN STUART MILL: On Bentham and Coleridge. Introduction by F. R. Leavis　TB/1070

KENNETH B. MURDOCK: Literature and Theology in Colonial New England　TB/99

SAMUEL PEPYS: The Diary of Samuel Pepys. ° Edited by O. F. Morshead. Illus. by Ernest Shepard　TB/1007

ST.-JOHN PERSE: Seamarks　TB/2002

GEORGE SANTAYANA: Interpretations of Poetry and Religion §　TB/9

C. P. SNOW: Time of Hope: a novel　TB/1040

HEINRICH STRAUMANN: American Literature in the Twentieth Century. Third Edition, Revised　TB/1168

PAGET TOYNBEE: Dante Alighieri: His Life and Works. Edited with intro. by Charles S. Singleton　TB/1206

DOROTHY VAN GHENT: The English Novel: Form and Function　TB/1050

E. B. WHITE: One Man's Meat. Introduction by Walter Blair　TB/3505

MORTON DAUWEN ZABEL, Editor: Literary Opinion in America Vol. I TB/3013; Vol. II TB/3014

Myth, Symbol & Folklore

JOSEPH CAMPBELL, Editor: Pagan and Christian Mysteries Illus.　TB/2013

MIRCEA ELIADE: Cosmos and History: The Myth of the Eternal Return §　TB/2050

C. G. JUNG & C. KERÉNYI: Essays on a Science of Mythology: The Myths of the Divine Child and the Divine Maiden　TB/2014

DORA & ERWIN PANOFSKY: Pandora's Box: The Changing Aspects of a Mythical Symbol. Revised Edition. Illus.　TB/2021

ERWIN PANOFSKY: Studies in Iconology: Humanistic Themes in the Art of the Renaissance. 180 illustrations　TB/1077

JEAN SEZNEC: The Survival of the Pagan Gods: The Mythological Tradition and its Place in Renaissance Humanism and Art. 108 illustrations　TB/2004

HELLMUT WILHELM: Change: Eight Lectures on the I Ching　TB/2019

HEINRICH ZIMMER: Myths and Symbols in Indian Art and Civilization. 70 illustrations　TB/2005

Philosophy

G. E. M. ANSCOMBE: An Introduction to Wittgenstein's Tractatus. Second edition, Revised. °　TB/1210

HENRI BERGSON: Time and Free Will: An Essay on the Immediate Data of Consciousness °　TB/1021

5

H. J. BLACKHAM: Six Existentialist Thinkers: *Kierkegaard, Nietzsche, Jaspers, Marcel, Heidegger, Sartre* ⁰
TB/1002

CRANE BRINTON: Nietzsche. *New Preface, Bibliography and Epilogue by the Author*　TB/1197

ERNST CASSIRER: The Individual and the Cosmos in Renaissance Philosophy. *Translated with an Introduction by Mario Domandi*　TB/1097

ERNST CASSIRER: Rousseau, Kant and Goethe. *Introduction by Peter Gay*　TB/1092

FREDERICK COPLESTON: Medieval Philosophy ⁰　TB/376

F. M. CORNFORD: Principium Sapientiae: *A Study of the Origins of Greek Philosophical Thought. Edited by W. K. C. Guthrie*　TB/1213

F. M. CORNFORD: From Religion to Philosophy: *A Study in the Origins of Western Speculation* §　TB/20

WILFRID DESAN: The Tragic Finale: *An Essay on the Philosophy of Jean-Paul Sartre*　TB/1030

PAUL FRIEDLÄNDER: Plato: *An Introduction*　TB/2017

ÉTIENNE GILSON: Dante and Philosophy　TB/1089

WILLIAM CHASE GREENE: Moira: *Fate, Good, and Evil in Greek Thought*　TB/1104

W. K. C. GUTHRIE: The Greek Philosophers: *From Thales to Aristotle* ⁰　TB/1008

F. H. HEINEMANN: Existentialism and the Modern Predicament　TB/28

ISAAC HUSIK: A History of Medieval Jewish Philosophy
TB/803

EDMUND HUSSERL: Phenomenology and the Crisis of Philosophy. *Translated with an Introduction by Quentin Lauer*　TB/1170

IMMANUEL KANT: The Doctrine of Virtue, *being Part II of The Metaphysic of Morals. Trans. with Notes & Intro. by Mary J. Gregor. Foreword by H. J. Paton*
TB/110

IMMANUEL KANT: Groundwork of the Metaphysic of Morals. *Trans. & analyzed by H. J. Paton*　TB/1159

IMMANUEL KANT: Lectures on Ethics. § *Introduction by Lewis W. Beck*　TB/105

QUENTIN LAUER: Phenomenology: *Its Genesis and Prospect*　TB/1169

GABRIEL MARCEL: Being and Having: *An Existential Diary. Intro. by James Collins*　TB/310

GEORGE A. MORGAN: What Nietzsche Means　TB/1198

PHILO SAADYA GAON, & JEHUDA HALEVI: Three Jewish Philosophers. *Ed. by Hans Lewy, Alexander Altmann, & Isaak Heinemann*　TB/813

MICHAEL POLANYI: Personal Knowledge: *Towards a Post-Critical Philosophy*　TB/1158

WILLARD VAN ORMAN QUINE: Elementary Logic: *Revised Edition*　TB/577

WILLARD VAN ORMAN QUINE: From a Logical Point of View: *Logico-Philosophical Essays*　TB/566

BERTRAND RUSSELL et al.: The Philosophy of Bertrand Russell. *Edited by Paul Arthur Schilpp*
Vol. I　TB/1095;　Vol. II　TB/1096

L. S. STEBBING: A Modern Introduction to Logic　TC/538

ALFRED NORTH WHITEHEAD: Process and Reality: *An Essay in Cosmology*　TB/1033

PHILIP P. WIENER: Evolution and the Founders of Pragmatism. *Foreword by John Dewey*　TB/1212

WILHELM WINDELBAND: A History of Philosophy
Vol. I: *Greek, Roman, Medieval*　TB/38
Vol. II: *Renaissance, Enlightenment, Modern*　TB/39

LUDWIG WITTGENSTEIN: The Blue and Brown Books ⁰
TB/1211

Political Science & Government

JEREMY BENTHAM: The Handbook of Political Fallacies: *Introduction by Crane Brinton*　TB/1069

KENNETH E. BOULDING: Conflict and Defense: *A General Theory*　TB/3024

CRANE BRINTON: English Political Thought in the Nineteenth Century　TB/1071

EDWARD S. CORWIN: American Constitutional History: *Essays edited by Alpheus T. Mason and Gerald Garvey*　TB/1136

ROBERT DAHL & CHARLES E. LINDBLOM: Politics, Economics, and Welfare: *Planning and Politico-Economic Systems Resolved into Basic Social Processes*　TB/3037

JOHN NEVILLE FIGGIS: The Divine Right of Kings. *Introduction by G. R. Elton*　TB/1191

JOHN NEVILLE FIGGIS: Political Thought from Gerson to Grotius: *1414-1625: Seven Studies. Introduction by Garrett Mattingly*　TB/1032

F. L. GANSHOF: Feudalism　TB/1058

G. P. GOOCH: English Democratic Ideas in Seventeenth Century　TB/1006

J. H. HEXTER: More's Utopia: *The Biography of an Idea. New Epilogue by the Author*　TB/1195

ROBERT H. JACKSON: The Supreme Court in the American System of Government　TB/1106

DAN N. JACOBS, Ed.: The New Communist Manifesto & *Related Documents. Third edition, Revised*　TB/1078

DAN N. JACOBS & HANS BAERWALD, Eds.: Chinese Communism: *Selected Documents*　TB/3031

ROBERT GREEN MCCLOSKEY: American Conservatism in the Age of Enterprise, 1865-1910　TB/1137

KINGSLEY MARTIN: French Liberal Thought in the Eighteenth Century: *Political Ideas from Bayle to Condorcet*　TB/1114

JOHN STUART MILL: On Bentham and Coleridge. *Introduction by F. R. Leavis*　TB/1070

JOHN B. MORRALL: Political Thought in Medieval Times
TB/1076

JOHN PLAMENATZ: German Marxism and Russian Communism. ⁰ *New Preface by the Author*　TB/1189

SIR KARL POPPER: The Open Society and Its Enemies
Vol. I: *The Spell of Plato*　TB/1101
Vol. II: *The High Tide of Prophecy: Hegel, Marx, and the Aftermath*　TB/1102

HENRI DE SAINT-SIMON: Social Organization, The Science of Man, and Other Writings. *Edited and Translated by Felix Markham*　TB/1152

JOSEPH A. SCHUMPETER: Capitalism, Socialism and Democracy　TB/3008

CHARLES H. SHINN: Mining Camps: *A Study in American Frontier Government.* ‡ *Edited by Rodman W. Paul*
TB/3062

Psychology

ALFRED ADLER: The Individual Psychology of Alfred Adler. *Edited by Heinz L. and Rowena R. Ansbacher*
TB/1154

ALFRED ADLER: Problems of Neurosis. *Introduction by Heinz L. Ansbacher*　TB/1145

ANTON T. BOISEN: The Exploration of the Inner World: *A Study of Mental Disorder and Religious Experience*
TB/87

HERBERT FINGARETTE: The Self in Transformation: *Psychoanalysis, Philosophy and the Life of the Spirit.* ‖
TB/1177

SIGMUND FREUD: On Creativity and the Unconscious: *Papers on the Psychology of Art, Literature, Love, Religion.* § *Intro. by Benjamin Nelson*　TB/45

C. JUDSON HERRICK: The Evolution of Human Nature
TB/545

WILLIAM JAMES: Psychology: *The Briefer Course. Edited with an Intro. by Gordon Allport* TB/1034

C. G. JUNG: Psychological Reflections TB/2001

C. G. JUNG: Symbols of Transformation: *An Analysis of the Prelude to a Case of Schizophrenia. Illus.*
Vol. I: TB/2009; Vol. II TB/2010

C. G. JUNG & C. KERÉNYI: Essays on a Science of Mythology: *The Myths of the Divine Child and the Divine Maiden* TB/2014

JOHN T. MC NEILL: A History of the Cure of Souls
TB/126

KARL MENNINGER: Theory of Psychoanalytic Technique
TB/1144

ERICH NEUMANN: Amor and Psyche: *The Psychic Development of the Feminine* TB/2012

ERICH NEUMANN: The Archetypal World of Henry Moore. *107 illus.* TB/2020

ERICH NEUMANN: The Origins and History of Consciousness Vol. I *Illus.* TB/2007; Vol. II TB/2008

C. P. OBERNDORF: A History of Psychoanalysis in America
TB/1147

RALPH BARTON PERRY: The Thought and Character of William James: *Briefer Version* TB/1156

JEAN PIAGET, BÄRBEL INHELDER, & ALINA SZEMINSKA: The Child's Conception of Geometry ° TB/1146

JOHN H. SCHAAR: Escape from Authority: *The Perspectives of Erich Fromm* TB/1155

Sociology

JACQUES BARZUN: Race: *A Study in Superstition. Revised Edition* TB/1172

BERNARD BERELSON, Ed.: The Behavioral Sciences Today
TB/1127

ABRAHAM CAHAN: The Rise of David Levinsky: *A documentary novel of social mobility in early twentieth century America. Intro. by John Higham* TB/1028

THOMAS C. COCHRAN: The Inner Revolution: *Essays on the Social Sciences in History* TB/1140

ALLISON DAVIS & JOHN DOLLARD: Children of Bondage: *The Personality Development of Negro Youth in the Urban South* || TB/3049

ST. CLAIR DRAKE & HORACE R. CAYTON: Black Metropolis: *A Study of Negro Life in a Northern City. Revised and Enlarged. Intro. by Everett C. Hughes*
Vol. I TB/1086; Vol. II TB/1087

EMILE DURKHEIM et al.: Essays on Sociology and Philosophy: *With Analyses of Durkheim's Life and Work.* || *Edited by Kurt H. Wolff* TB/1151

LEON FESTINGER, HENRY W. RIECKEN & STANLEY SCHACHTER: When Prophecy Fails: *A Social and Psychological Account of a Modern Group that Predicted the Destruction of the World* || TB/1132

ALVIN W. GOULDNER: Wildcat Strike: *A Study in Worker-Management Relationships* || TB/1176

FRANCIS J. GRUND: Aristocracy in America: *Social Class in the Formative Years of the New Nation* TB/1001

KURT LEWIN: Field Theory in Social Science: *Selected Theoretical Papers.* || *Edited with a Foreword by Dorwin Cartwright* TB/1135

R. M. MAC IVER: Social Causation TB/1153

ROBERT K. MERTON, LEONARD BROOM, LEONARD S. COTTRELL, JR., Editors: Sociology Today: *Problems and Prospects* || Vol. I TB/1173; Vol. II TB/1174

TALCOTT PARSONS & EDWARD A. SHILS, Editors: Toward a General Theory of Action: *Theoretical Foundations for the Social Sciences* TB/1083

JOHN H. ROHRER & MUNRO S. EDMONSON, Eds.: The Eighth Generation Grows Up: *Cultures and Personalities of New Orleans Negroes* || TB/3050

ARNOLD ROSE: The Negro in America: *The Condensed Version of Gunnar Myrdal's An American Dilemma*
TB/3048

KURT SAMUELSSON: Religion and Economic Action: *A Critique of Max Weber's The Protestant Ethic and the Spirit of Capitalism.* || ° *Trans. by E. G. French; Ed. with Intro. by D. C. Coleman* TB/1131

PITIRIM A. SOROKIN: Contemporary Sociological Theories. *Through the First Quarter of the 20th Century* TB/3046

MAURICE R. STEIN: The Eclipse of Community: *An Interpretation of American Studies* TB/1128

FERDINAND TÖNNIES: Community and Society: *Gemeinschaft und Gesellschaft. Translated and edited by Charles P. Loomis* TB/1116

W. LLOYD WARNER & Associates: Democracy in Jonesville: *A Study in Quality and Inequality* TB/1129

W. LLOYD WARNER: Social Class in America: *The Evaluation of Status* TB/1013

RELIGION

Ancient & Classical

J. H. BREASTED: Development of Religion and Thought in Ancient Egypt. *Introduction by John A. Wilson*
TB/57

HENRI FRANKFORT: Ancient Egyptian Religion: *An Interpretation* TB/77

G. RACHEL LEVY: Religious Conceptions of the Stone Age and their Influence upon European Thought. *Illus. Introduction by Henri Frankfort* TB/106

MARTIN P. NILSSON: Greek Folk Religion. *Foreword by Arthur Darby Nock* TB/78

ALEXANDRE PIANKOFF: The Shrines of Tut-Ankh-Amon. *Edited by N. Rambova. 117 illus.* TB/2011

H. J. ROSE: Religion in Greece and Rome TB/55

Biblical Thought & Literature

W. F. ALBRIGHT: The Biblical Period from Abraham to Ezra TB/102

C. K. BARRETT, Ed.: The New Testament Background: *Selected Documents* TB/86

C. H. DODD: The Authority of the Bible TB/43

M. S. ENSLIN: Christian Beginnings TB/5

M. S. ENSLIN: The Literature of the Christian Movement
TB/6

JOHN GRAY: Archaeology and the Old Testament World. *Illus.* TB/127

H. H. ROWLEY: The Growth of the Old Testament
TB/107

D. WINTON THOMAS, Ed.: Documents from Old Testament Times TB/85

The Judaic Tradition

LEO BAECK: Judaism and Christianity. *Trans. with Intro. by Walter Kaufmann* TB/823

SALO W. BARON: Modern Nationalism and Religion
TB/818

MARTIN BUBER: Eclipse of God: *Studies in the Relation Between Religion and Philosophy* TB/12

MARTIN BUBER: Moses: *The Revelation and the Covenant* TB/27

MARTIN BUBER: Pointing the Way. *Introduction by Maurice S. Friedman* TB/103

MARTIN BUBER: The Prophetic Faith TB/73

MARTIN BUBER: Two Types of Faith: *the interpenetration of Judaism and Christianity* ° TB/75

ERNST LUDWIG EHRLICH: A Concise History of Israel: From the Earliest Times to the Destruction of the Temple in A.D. 70 º   TB/128

MAURICE S. FRIEDMAN: Martin Buber: The Life of Dialogue   TB/64

LOUIS GINZBERG: Students, Scholars and Saints   TB/802

SOLOMON GRAYZEL: A History of the Contemporary Jews   TB/816

WILL HERBERG: Judaism and Modern Man   TB/810

ABRAHAM J. HESCHEL: God in Search of Man: A Philosophy of Judaism   TB/807

ISAAC HUSIK: A History of Medieval Jewish Philosophy   TB/803

FLAVIUS JOSEPHUS: The Great Roman-Jewish War, with The Life of Josephus. Introduction by William R. Farmer   TB/74

JACOB R. MARCUS The Jew in the Medieval World   TB/814

MAX L. MARGOLIS & ALEXANDER MARX: A History of the Jewish People   TB/806

T. J. MEEK: Hebrew Origins   TB/69

C. G. MONTEFIORE & H. LOEWE, Eds.: A Rabbinic Anthology   TB/832

JAMES PARKES: The Conflict of the Church and the Synagogue: The Jews and Early Christianity   TB/821

PHILO, SAADYA GAON, & JEHUDA HALEVI: Three Jewish Philosophers. Ed. by Hans Lewey, Alexander Altmann, & Isaak Heinemann   TB/813

HERMAN L. STRACK: Introduction to the Talmud and Midrash   TB/808

JOSHUA TRACHTENBERG: The Devil and the Jews: The Medieval Conception of the Jew and its Relation to Modern Anti-Semitism   TB/822

Christianity: General

ROLAND H. BAINTON: Christendom: A Short History of Christianity and its Impact on Western Civilization. Illus.   Vol. I, TB/131; Vol. II, TB/132

Christianity: Origins & Early Development

AUGUSTINE: An Augustine Synthesis. Edited by Erich Przywara   TB/335

ADOLF DEISSMANN: Paul: A Study in Social and Religious History   TB/15

EDWARD GIBBON: The Triumph of Christendom in the Roman Empire (Chaps. XV-XX of "Decline and Fall," J. B. Bury edition). § Illus.   TB/46

MAURICE GOGUEL: Jesus and the Origins of Christianity. º Introduction by C. Leslie Mitton
Volume I: Prolegomena to the Life of Jesus   TB/65
Volume II: The Life of Jesus   TB/66

EDGAR J. GOODSPEED: A Life of Jesus   TB/1

ADOLF HARNACK: The Mission and Expansion of Christianity in the First Three Centuries. Introduction by Jaroslav Pelikan   TB/92

R. K. HARRISON: The Dead Sea Scrolls: An Introduction º   TB/84

EDWIN HATCH: The Influence of Greek Ideas on Christianity. § Introduction and Bibliography by Frederick C. Grant   TB/18

ARTHUR DARBY NOCK: Early Gentile Christianity and Its Hellenistic Background   TB/111

ARTHUR DARBY NOCK: St. Paul º   TB/104

JAMES PARKES: The Conflict of the Church and the Synagogue: The Jews and Early Christianity   TB/821

SULPICIUS SEVERUS et al.: The Western Fathers: Being the Lives of Martin of Tours, Ambrose, Augustine of Hippo, Honoratus of Arles and Germanus of Auxerre. Edited and translated by F. R. Hoare   TB/309

F. VAN DER MEER: Augustine the Bishop: Church and Society at the Dawn of the Middle Ages   TB/304

JOHANNES WEISS: Earliest Christianity: A History of the Period A.D. 30-150. Introduction and Bibliography by Frederick C. Grant   Volume I   TB/53
Volume II   TB/54

Christianity: The Middle Ages and The Reformation

JOHANNES ECKHART: Meister Eckhart: A Modern Translation by R. B. Blakney   TB/8

DESIDERIUS ERASMUS: Christian Humanism and the Reformation: Selected Writings. Edited and translated by John C. Olin   TB/1166

ÉTIENNE GILSON: Dante and Philosophy   TB/1089

WILLIAM HALLER: The Rise of Puritanism   TB/22

JOHAN HUIZINGA: Erasmus and the Age of Reformation. Illus.   TB/19

A. C. MCGIFFERT: Protestant Thought Before Kant. Preface by Jaroslav Pelikan   TB/93

JOHN T. MCNEILL: Makers of the Christian Tradition: From Alfred the Great to Schleiermacher   TB/121

G. MOLLAT: The Popes at Avignon, 1305-1378   TB/308

GORDON RUPP: Luther's Progress to the Diet of Worms º   TB/120

Christianity: The Protestant Tradition

KARL BARTH: Church Dogmatics: A Selection   TB/95

KARL BARTH: Dogmatics in Outline   TB/56

KARL BARTH: The Word of God and the Word of Man   TB/13

RUDOLF BULTMANN et al.: Translating Theology into the Modern Age: Historical, Systematic and Pastoral Reflections on Theology and the Church in the Contemporary Situation. Volume 2 of Journal for Theology and the Church, edited by Robert W. Funk in association with Gerhard Ebeling   TB/252

WINTHROP HUDSON: The Great Tradition of the American Churches   TB/98

SOREN KIERKEGAARD: Edifying Discourses. Edited with an Introduction by Paul Holmer   TB/32

SOREN KIERKEGAARD: The Journals of Kierkegaard. º Edited with an Introduction by Alexander Dru   TB/52

SOREN KIERKEGAARD: The Point of View for My Work as an Author: A Report to History. § Preface by Benjamin Nelson   TB/88

SOREN KIERKEGAARD: The Present Age. § Translated and edited by Alexander Dru. Introduction by Walter Kaufmann   TB/94

SOREN KIERKEGAARD: Purity of Heart   TB/4

SOREN KIERKEGAARD: Repetition: An Essay in Experimental Psychology. Translated with Introduction & Notes by Walter Lowrie   TB/117

SOREN KIERKEGAARD: Works of Love: Some Christian Reflections in the Form of Discourses   TB/122

WALTER LOWRIE: Kierkegaard: A Life   Vol. I   TB/89
Vol. II   TB/90

PERRY MILLER & T. H. JOHNSON, Editors: The Puritans: A Sourcebook of Their Writings   Vol. I   TB/1093
Vol. II   TB/1094

JAMES M. ROBINSON et al.: The Bultmann School of Biblical Interpretation: New Directions? Volume 1 of Journal of Theology and the Church, edited by Robert W. Funk in association with Gerhard Ebeling   TB/251

F. SCHLEIERMACHER: The Christian Faith. Introduction by Richard R. Niebuhr   Vol. I   TB/108
Vol. II   TB/109

F. SCHLEIERMACHER: On Religion: *Speeches to Its Cultured Despisers. Intro. by Rudolf Otto* TB/36

PAUL TILLICH: Dynamics of Faith TB/42

EVELYN UNDERHILL: Worship TB/10

G. VAN DER LEEUW: Religion in Essence and Manifestation: *A Study in Phenomenology. Appendices by Hans H. Penner* Vol. I TB/100; Vol. II TB/101

Christianity: The Roman and Eastern Traditions

A. ROBERT CAPONIGRI, Ed.: Modern Catholic Thinkers I: *God and Man* TB/306

A. ROBERT CAPONIGRI, Ed.: Modern Catholic Thinkers II: *The Church and the Political Order* TB/307

THOMAS CORBISHLEY, S. J.: Roman Catholicism TB/112

CHRISTOPHER DAWSON: The Historic Reality of Christian Culture TB/305

G. P. FEDOTOV: The Russian Religious Mind: *Kievan Christianity, the 10th to the 13th centuries* TB/70

G. P. FEDOTOV, Ed.: A Treasury of Russian Spirituality TB/303

DAVID KNOWLES: The English Mystical Tradition TB/302

GABRIEL MARCEL: Being and Having: *An Existential Diary. Introduction by James Collins* TB/310

GABRIEL MARCEL: Homo Viator: *Introduction to a Metaphysic of Hope* TB/397

GUSTAVE WEIGEL, S. J.: Catholic Theology in Dialogue TB/301

Oriental Religions: Far Eastern, Near Eastern

TOR ANDRAE: Mohammed: *The Man and His Faith* TB/62

EDWARD CONZE: Buddhism: *Its Essence and Development.* ° *Foreword by Arthur Waley* TB/58

EDWARD CONZE et al., Editors: Buddhist Texts Through the Ages TB/113

ANANDA COOMARASWAMY: Buddha and the Gospel of Buddhism. *Illus.* TB/119

H. G. CREEL: Confucius and the Chinese Way TB/63

FRANKLIN EDGERTON, Trans. & Ed.: The Bhagavad Gita TB/115

SWAMI NIKHILANANDA, Trans. & Ed.: The Upanishads: *A One-Volume Abridgment* TB/114

HELLMUT WILHELM: Change: *Eight Lectures on the I Ching* TB/2019

Philosophy of Religion

NICOLAS BERDYAEV: The Beginning and the End § TB/14

NICOLAS BERDYAEV: Christian Existentialism: *A Berdyaev Synthesis. Ed. by Donald A. Lowrie* TB/130

NICOLAS BERDYAEV: The Destiny of Man TB/61

RUDOLF BULTMANN: History and Eschatology: *The Presence of Eternity* ° TB/91

RUDOLF BULTMANN AND FIVE CRITICS: Kerygma and Myth: *A Theological Debate* TB/80

RUDOLF BULTMANN and KARL KUNDSIN: Form Criticism: *Two Essays on New Testament Research. Translated by Frederick C. Grant* TB/96

MIRCEA ELIADE: The Sacred and the Profane TB/81

LUDWIG FEUERBACH: The Essence of Christianity. § *Introduction by Karl Barth. Foreword by H. Richard Niebuhr* TB/11

ADOLF HARNACK: What is Christianity? § *Introduction by Rudolf Bultmann* TB/17

FRIEDRICH HEGEL: On Christianity: *Early Theological Writings. Ed. by R. Kroner & T. M. Knox* TB/79

KARL HEIM: Christian Faith and Natural Science TB/16

IMMANUEL KANT: Religion Within the Limits of Reason Alone. § *Intro. by T. M. Greene & J. Silber* TB/67

JOHN MACQUARRIE: An Existentialist Theology: *A Comparison of Heidegger and Bultmann.* ° *Preface by Rudolf Bultmann* TB/125

PAUL RAMSEY, Ed.: Faith and Ethics: *The Theology of H. Richard Niebuhr* TB/129

PIERRE TEILHARD DE CHARDIN: The Phenomenon of Man ° TB/83

Religion, Culture & Society

JOSEPH L. BLAU, Ed.: Cornerstones of Religious Freedom in America: *Selected Basic Documents, Court Decisions and Public Statements. Revised and Enlarged Edition* TB/118

C. C. GILLISPIE: Genesis and Geology: *The Decades before Darwin* § TB/51

KYLE HASELDEN: The Racial Problem in Christian Perspective TB/116

WALTER KAUFMANN, Ed.: Religion from Tolstoy to Camus: *Basic Writings on Religious Truth and Morals. Enlarged Edition* TB/123

JOHN T. MCNEILL: A History of the Cure of Souls TB/126

KENNETH B. MURDOCK: Literature and Theology in Colonial New England TB/99

H. RICHARD NIEBUHR: Christ and Culture TB/3

H. RICHARD NIEBUHR: The Kingdom of God in America TB/49

RALPH BARTON PERRY: Puritanism and Democracy TB/1138

PAUL PFUETZE: Self, Society, Existence: *Human Nature and Dialogue in the Thought of George Herbert Mead and Martin Buber* TB/1059

WALTER RAUSCHENBUSCH: Christianity and the Social Crisis. ‡ *Edited by Robert D. Cross* TB/3059

KURT SAMUELSSON: Religion and Economic Action: *A Critique of Max Weber's The Protestant Ethic and the Spirit of Capitalism.* ‖ ° *Trans. by E. G. French; Ed. with Intro. by D. C. Coleman* TB/1131

ERNST TROELTSCH: The Social Teaching of the Christian Churches ° Vol. I TB/71; Vol. II TB/72

NATURAL SCIENCES AND MATHEMATICS

Biological Sciences

CHARLOTTE AUERBACH: The Science of Genetics Σ TB/568

MARSTON BATES: The Natural History of Mosquitoes. *Illus.* TB/578

A. BELLAIRS: Reptiles: *Life History, Evolution, and Structure. Illus.* TB/520

LUDWIG VON BERTALANFFY: Modern Theories of Development: *An Introduction to Theoretical Biology* TB/554

LUDWIG VON BERTALANFFY: Problems of Life: *An Evaluation of Modern Biological and Scientific Thought* TB/521

HAROLD F. BLUM: Time's Arrow and Evolution TB/555

JOHN TYLER BONNER: The Ideas of Biology. Σ *Illus.* TB/570

A. J. CAIN: Animal Species and their Evolution. *Illus.* TB/519

WALTER B. CANNON: Bodily Changes in Pain, Hunger, Fear and Rage. *Illus.* TB/562

W. E. LE GROS CLARK: The Antecedents of Man: *Intro. to Evolution of the Primates.* ⁰ *Illus.*   TB/559

W. H. DOWDESWELL: Animal Ecology. *Illus.*   TB/543

W. H. DOWDESWELL: The Mechanism of Evolution. *Illus.*   TB/527

R. W. GERARD: Unresting Cells. *Illus.*   TB/541

DAVID LACK: Darwin's Finches. *Illus.*   TB/544

J. E. MORTON: Molluscs: *An Introduction to their Form and Functions. Illus.*   TB/529

ADOLF PORTMANN: Animals as Social Beings. ⁰ *Illus.*   TB/572

O. W. RICHARDS: The Social Insects. *Illus.*   TB/542

P. M. SHEPPARD: Natural Selection and Heredity. *Illus.*   TB/528

EDMUND W. SINNOTT: Cell and Psyche: *The Biology of Purpose*   TB/546

C. H. WADDINGTON: How Animals Develop. *Illus.*   TB/553

Chemistry

J. R. PARTINGTON: A Short History of Chemistry. *Illus.*   TB/522

J. READ: A Direct Entry to Organic Chemistry. *Illus.*   TB/523

J. READ: Through Alchemy to Chemistry. *Illus.*   TB/561

Communication Theory

J. R. PIERCE: Symbols, Signals and Noise: *The Nature and Process of Communication*   TB/574

Geography

R. E. COKER: This Great and Wide Sea: *An Introduction to Oceanography and Marine Biology. Illus.*   TB/551

F. K. HARE: The Restless Atmosphere   TB/560

History of Science

W. DAMPIER, Ed.: Readings in the Literature of Science. *Illus.*   TB/512

A. HUNTER DUPREE: Science in the Federal Government: *A History of Policies and Activities to 1940*   TB/573

ALEXANDRE KOYRÉ: From the Closed World to the Infinite Universe: *Copernicus, Kepler, Galileo, Newton, etc.*   TB/31

A. G. VAN MELSEN: From Atomos to Atom: *A History of the Concept Atom*   TB/517

O. NEUGEBAUER: The Exact Sciences in Antiquity   TB/552

H. T. PLEDGE: Science Since 1500: *A Short History of Mathematics, Physics, Chemistry and Biology. Illus.*   TB/506

HANS THIRRING: Energy for Man: *From Windmills to Nuclear Power*   TB/556

LANCELOT LAW WHYTE: Essay on Atomism: *From Democritus to 1960*   TB/565

A. WOLF: A History of Science, Technology and Philosophy in the 16th and 17th Centuries. ⁰ *Illus.*   Vol. I TB/508; Vol. II TB/509

A. WOLF: A History of Science, Technology, and Philosophy in the Eighteenth Century. ⁰ *Illus.*   Vol. I TB/539; Vol. II TB/540

Mathematics

H. DAVENPORT: The Higher Arithmetic: *An Introduction to the Theory of Numbers*   TB/526

H. G. FORDER: Geometry: *An Introduction*   TB/548

GOTTLOB FREGE: The Foundations of Arithmetic: *A Logico-Mathematical Enquiry*   TB/534

S. KÖRNER: The Philosophy of Mathematics: *An Introduction*   TB/547

D. E. LITTLEWOOD: Skeleton Key of Mathematics: *A Simple Account of Complex Algebraic Problems*   TB/525

GEORGE E. OWEN: Fundamentals of Scientific Mathematics   TB/569

WILLARD VAN ORMAN QUINE: Mathematical Logic   TB/558

O. G. SUTTON: Mathematics in Action. ⁰ *Foreword by James R. Newman. Illus.*   TB/518

FREDERICK WAISMANN: Introduction to Mathematical Thinking. *Foreword by Karl Menger*   TB/511

Philosophy of Science

R. B. BRAITHWAITE: Scientific Explanation   TB/515

J. BRONOWSKI: Science and Human Values. *Revised and Enlarged Edition*   TB/505

ALBERT EINSTEIN et al.: Albert Einstein: Philosopher-Scientist. *Edited by Paul A. Schilpp*   Vol. I TB/502   Vol. II TB/503

WERNER HEISENBERG: Physics and Philosophy: *The Revolution in Modern Science*   TB/549

JOHN MAYNARD KEYNES: A Treatise on Probability. ⁰ *Introduction by N. R. Hanson*   TB/557

SIR KARL POPPER: The Logic of Scientific Discovery   TB/576

STEPHEN TOULMIN: Foresight and Understanding: *An Enquiry into the Aims of Science. Foreword by Jacques Barzun*   TB/564

STEPHEN TOULMIN: The Philosophy of Science: *An Introduction*   TB/513

G. J. WHITROW: The Natural Philosophy of Time ⁰   TB/563

Physics and Cosmology

STEPHEN TOULMIN & JUNE GOODFIELD: The Fabric of the Heavens: *The Development of Astronomy and Dynamics. Illus.*   TB/579

DAVID BOHM: Causality and Chance in Modern Physics. *Foreword by Louis de Broglie*   TB/536

P. W. BRIDGMAN: The Nature of Thermodynamics   TB/537

P. W. BRIDGMAN: A Sophisticate's Primer of Relativity   TB/575

A. C. CROMBIE, Ed.: Turning Point in Physics   TB/535

C. V. DURELL: Readable Relativity. *Foreword by Freeman J. Dyson*   TB/530

ARTHUR EDDINGTON: Space, Time and Gravitation: *An outline of the General Relativity Theory*   TB/510

GEORGE GAMOW: Biography of Physics Σ   TB/567

MAX JAMMER: Concepts of Force: *A Study in the Foundation of Dynamics*   TB/550

MAX JAMMER: Concepts of Mass *in Classical and Modern Physics*   TB/571

MAX JAMMER: Concepts of Space: *The History of Theories of Space in Physics. Foreword by Albert Einstein*   TB/533

EDMUND WHITTAKER: History of the Theories of Aether and Electricity   Volume I: *The Classical Theories* TB/531   Volume II: *The Modern Theories* TB/532

G. J. WHITROW: The Structure and Evolution of the Universe: *An Introduction to Cosmology. Illus.*   TB/504